JONES, D.V.

The royal town of
Sutton Coldfield: a
commemorative history

89-321343   Pbk.

942.496

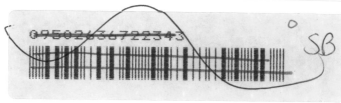

View of Holy Trinity Church and Church Hill. The old cottages were demolished in 1937.

Photograph: Sir Benjamin Stone

THE ROYAL TOWN OF SUTTON COLDFIELD
A COMMEMORATIVE HISTORY

BY DOUGLAS V. JONES

PUBLISHED BY

PRINT SHOP, 44 BOLDMERE ROAD, SUTTON COLDFIELD
WEST MIDLANDS   TELEPHONE 021-354 5913

Royal Proclamation on Accession of King George V
King Edward Square (1910)

First Edition 1973   Published by Sutton Coldfield Corporation
Second Edition November 1979   Published by Westwood Press
Reprinted 1981
Third Edition January 1984
Reprinted Autumn 1985

Printed and Published by The Westwood Press, Print Shop, 44 Boldmere Road, Sutton Coldfield, West Midlands. Produced by offset litho.

INTRODUCTION TO THE FIRST EDITION

A local history should be something more than a mere listing of facts. In ' the retrieving of forgotten things from oblivion ',
I have sought to cull those events most evocative of an era,
not forgetting that sometimes mere trivia can help in capturing
the mood of the hour.

I apologise for any errors which may, unwittingly, have
found their way into the text, and to those people who think
that something—or someone—vital to the story has been
omitted from it. In a book of this size and scope, it is difficult
to see how some omissions could have been avoided when
writing of a place with so long and colourful a past as that of
Sutton Coldfield.

Douglas V. Jones.

December, 1973

PREFACE TO THIRD EDITION

The Royal Town of Sutton Coldfield: A Commemorative History
was first published ten years ago, and after being out of print for
some time, was republished by the Westwood Press in 1979.

This, the third edition, has almost three times the number of
illustrations, many of which are of both historic interest and
nostalgic content.

Douglas V. Jones

January, 1984

SEAL OF THE CORPORATION, 1619
(From the Visitation of Warwickshire)

The Horse and Jockey, Maney (1892)
Photograph: Sir Benjamin Stone

ACKNOWLEDGMENTS

I wish to express my gratitude to those many people, too numerous to mention, who have helped me in a variety of ways in the task of writing this book. In particular I want to thank Mr. J. P. Holden, LL.B., Town Clerk of Sutton Coldfield, for sponsoring it; Mr. Norman Granville Evans, L.D.S., whose help in research and proof checking has been invaluable; Mr. Brian Cahalin, F.L.A., the Borough Librarian, and his Deputy Mr. R. M. Lea, A.L.A.; past and present Editors and Staff of the "Sutton Coldfield News"; The Birmingham and Warwickshire Archaeological Society; Brigadier E. A. James, O.B.E., T.D., D.L., J.P.; Col. J. H. C. Horsfall, D.S.O., M.C.; Alderman F. Brassington; Mr. Rowland Saxton our Printer; Mr. H. A. Hawkes, M.Sc., M.I.Biol., F.Inst. W.P.C. and Students of the Applied Hydrobiology Section of the University of Aston; Mr. J. T. Gould, B.A.; Mr. Peter L. Hardy; Miss H. M. Moss, B.A.; Miss M. Henry, M.B.E.; and Mrs. W. L. David.

I would also like to pay tribute to the late Mr. Dennis Rudder of Sutton Coldfield Central Library, whose wealth of knowledge was, until so recently, a ready source of information for all of us who are interested in the town's history.

I am grateful to my Wife and Daughter, Linda, for their great assistance in preparing the book for the press, and to David, my Son, for his companionship on innumerable local history jaunts.

December, 1973   Douglas V. Jones

CONTENTS

ILLUSTRATIONS

Unless otherwise stated all photographs are reproduced by permission of Birmingham Central Library, Local Studies Department, including Benjamin Stone collection.

Page

High Street — Mill Street junction showing The Pepper Pot (c. 1890)
Photograph: Sir Benjamin Stone

IX

Lower Parade (1889)

Penns Lane (c. 1890)

Royal Hotel, High Street (c. 1915)

X

CHAPTER I

Sutton Park—the source of our earliest history—The Roman road—
Mercia and the hunting-lodge at Maney, which became ' Southun '—
Alfred the Great and the Danes—The coming of the Normans.

SUTTON Park, now encroached upon from all sides by the
entwining fingers of suburban development, remains one of
the biggest areas of natural parkland in England. Its beauty
endures the whole year through, but it is not only for the reflec-
tion of nature's many moods that we turn to the Park. We do
so, also, for the delineation of our earliest history, recorded—
not in ancient yellowing documents—but on the broad face of
the Park itself.

Prehistoric remains, too, can be found if we accept the
possibility that a number of small mounds on the Streetly side
of Sutton Park are, in fact, part of a prehistoric cooking site.
The first of these mounds—usually called " pot-boilers "—was
discovered after a Park fire at the turn of the present century.
It is situated on the right hand side of the path leading in a
south easterly direction from the Milking Gate, and about 400
yards inside the Park. This mound, less than two feet high,
is topped by a mature but stunted oak, beneath which broken
and burnt stones have been found.

Following upon another, more severe, Park fire in 1921,
which destroyed all the vegetation over large areas, more mounds
and broken stones were revealed. Excavations were carried out
by the Birmingham Archaeological Society in October, 1926, and
the findings published in the Society Transactions, Volume LII,
Part II, 1927.

The method of cooking used was thought to have been carried
out by lining a hole in the ground with the skin of an animal
to form a water-tight vessel, or " pot ". Both water and meat
were placed inside, and the " pot " was then boiled by dropping
in stones which had previously been heated in a fire. This process would serve to explain the presence of the cracked and
broken stones.

According to the 1927 report, similar mounds of broken
stones were found in Ireland, before they were noticed in
England. These—referred to in Ulster as " Giants' cinders "—
sometimes contained flint flakes or artifacts. None, however,
were found at Streetly, and although the " pot-boilers " are
generally thought to be Neolithic, the absence of tools makes
it very difficult to date them with any accuracy. Speculation
as to the contents of the " pots " leads to a comment on cannibalism in the report:

> " There is no doubt that human flesh was cooked and
> eaten in this country at one time. St. Augustine mentions
> the fact in his writings, with some detail, and as occurring
> in his own time. Possibly this was a bit of missionary pro-

1

paganda on his part, but it is certain that cannibalism took place in Neolithic times."

In the Midlands, it is claimed, a dozen or so of these prehistoric hearths have been discovered, one or two at Rugeley, and one close to Middleton Hall, where, in 1913, a farmer removed some of the stones for road-making, but found that the fire had rendered them useless for that purpose. In Sutton Park, however, after the fire of 1921, hundreds of cartloads of what the report calls " potential pot-boilers ", were collected by the unemployed and used for mending the Sutton roads. In addition to the Sutton Park " pot-boilers ", James T. Gould in " Men of Aldridge ", mentions one near Pelsall Station, on the east bank of Ford Brook, which he describes as a grass-grown mound of stones, all broken and cracked by heat.

As the 1927 report points out, the absence of implements in the vicinity of these mounds is hardly surprising. Any flints found buried with the dead were only placed with the bodies at great sacrifice to the living, since it was believed that the departed must not be left weaponless in the other world. It is unlikely that weapons would be left at cooking sites, but flint arrow-heads were dug up some years ago by a gardener in Thornhill Road. According to the late Mr. Alfred Warren, a park forester, flint arrow-heads were also found during the last war in peat-beds near Rowton's Well by German prisoners-of-war, who were allowed to take them back to Germany.

Near Blackroot Pool, there is another site, the antiquity of which obscures its true purpose, although it is probably of much more recent origin than the " pot-boilers ". On the hill beside the railway—shown on maps as the " ancient encampment "—there are signs of an early settlement, sometimes claimed to be British, but possibly much older. Here, on the crest of the hill, thick with birch, rowan and holly, and topped by gnarled, stag-headed oaks, can be seen old earthworks and entrenchments, whose historical obscurity has fascinated successive generations of Sutton people. Midgley, in " A Short History of the Town and Chase of Sutton Coldfield ", written in 1904, reflects that:—

> " Warring Celtic tribes on this wild upland scooped out, with their rude bronze mattocks, earthworks from behind which they could shoot their arrows. And here they remain to this day, untouched by the plough, overgrown with oaks, but clearly to be seen."

The spot has not greatly changed since those words were written, and the indentations formed by the earthworks are still " untouched by the plough."

Sutton Park provides a fine and little disturbed example of a Roman road, where the Icknield Street, once marking the boundary between Warwickshire and Staffordshire, runs for $1\frac{1}{2}$ miles across its western fringe from a point near the Royal Oak Gate to Streetly ('the field on the street'). The Icknield Street was 112 miles long, stretching from Bourton-on-the-Water— where it left the Fosse Way—to Templeborough in South Yorkshire, where it joined another Roman road from Doncaster to Buxton. Its approach to Birmingham was through Alcester, to Metchley, where there was a Roman camp near the present Queen Elizabeth Hospital. Its course through modern Birmingham has, understandably, been largely lost to us, but it was probably by way of Hockley Brook, Handsworth and Perry Barr, where the name of Holford suggests a corruption of 'old ford'. This ford across the River Tame would probably have been close to Perry Barr's old packhorse-bridge, near the site of which it is claimed that Roman coins have been found.

From Perry Barr, the road approached Sutton Park by way of Kingstanding, passing on the way what that lively and entertaining chronicler of the 18th century scene, William Hutton, calls "that little artificial mount, on which Charles the First is said to have stood when he harangued the troops he brought out of Shropshire at the opening of the civil war in 1642".* Once within the Park, where nature has conspired to halt the passage of time, the ancient Roman road takes on a new dimension. Apart from a distant view of the television mast at Hill Village, and the steady hum of traffic from the Chester Road, there are few reminders of the twentieth century. Despite scars and irregularities upon its surface, and a profusion of undergrowth, the broad cambering of the Icknield Street is still plainly visible, particularly near the Royal Oak Gate. Indeed, it is possible to follow its course on foot right across the Park from there to Streetly. Dugdale, in "The Antiquities of Warwickshire" (1656), says of Icknield Street's route through Sutton Park:—

" . . . going over low ground, it appeareth to be firm and high ridged up with Gravell."

Hutton, taking a more aesthetic view-point, maintains that the true beauty of the road in Sutton Park is only to be discovered on a clear winter evening, before sunset. He tells us how he first saw it under these conditions in November, 1762. "Struck with astonishment," he declares, "I thought it the grandest sight I had ever beheld, and was amazed so noble a monument of antiquity should be so little regarded."*

The name 'Icknield' may have been derived from 'Iceni', the name of an ancient British tribe. and it is possible that a road of sorts existed along the route before the coming of the

---

* "History of Birmingham."

3

Romans. The name sometimes appears as 'Ricknield', and, according to Miss Bracken ("History of the Forest and Chase of Sutton Coldfield"), the 'R' would only signify the further, or Northern, Iceni. The name suggests that possibly the road passed through a part of the country frequented by these tribesmen, although one writer had different ideas. He was Christopher Chattock, the Castle Bromwich antiquarian. A recurring theme of his book, "Antiquities", published in 1884, is the importance of seeking and finding the derivation of place-names. Chattock believed that all the names of Roman roads were derived from those given to them by the Saxons, and for this reason, he claimed that the first syllable in 'Icknield' stemmed from 'ack', meaning oak. 'Street', he maintained, was from the old Saxon word 'Strete', meaning a straight way, since—to quote his own words—"Every schoolboy knows that the Romans nowhere used any other term but 'via', either in Britain or elsewhere as to roads."

Icknield Street is thus, according to Chattock, 'the street or straight way through the felled oaks', and its course was, as he pointed out, almost entirely through forests. Ancient writers are quoted by him as having said that the Romans lost 50,000 men in a few years in clearing and cutting passages through the woods and moors of Britain for their network of roads. Whether or not Chattock was right, we do know that there was once a peat-bed near Rowton's Well, composed of thousands of rotted trees, where sometimes the peat gatherers came across whole trees, with the marks of the axe upon them. What more likely than that these had been left behind by the Roman road-makers, as they hacked their way through the forests of North Warwickshire?

In Roman times, Sutton Coldfield probably did not exist even as a hamlet, and, according to Miss Bracken, "neither village nor house was raised on it (the Icknield Street) between Perry Bridge and the village of Chesterfield" (a hamlet just south of Wall). It is more than likely, however, that troops on their way north encamped on Rowton's Hill, since the name itself denotes 'the camp on the hill.' The spring at Rowton's too, was probably used by the Romans for a water supply, and at a later period, it acquired a great reputation for its curative properties. In medieval times the water was claimed to have miraculous powers, particularly in the cure of eye diseases. This was possibly due to its being impregnated with iron.

There has been surprisingly little archaeological research upon the Roman road in Sutton Park. In February, 1936, however, under the direction of the Park Forester, a short trench four feet deep was dug across the road between the railway line and Streetly Lane. In May of the same year, a trench, 41 feet long was dug across it, 174 feet south of the path known as Lord Donegal's Ride, leading from the Royal Oak Gate to Rowton's Hill. These sections revealed a cambered road with a surface of pitching of coarse gravel and pebbles in which the district abounds, and showed that the ground below it had been previously undisturbed.

A number of Roman coins have been found in the district. Riland Bedford speaks of a small bronze coin of Constantine's reign as being found in the Park in 1883, and in 1909, two coins of Diocletian were found at Streetly. Coins found at Kingstanding, quite close to the course of the Roman road, include those of the reigns of Domitian, Trajan, Hadrian, Antonius Pius and Marcus Aurelius.

Nearby, at Wall (Letocetum)—one of the 28 cities of Roman Britain—archaeological finds include coins, pottery and the skulls and bones of domestic animals. Some of these are on view in the well-stocked little museum on the site, where there is also a Roman bath-house, claimed to be one of the most complete examples to have been found in Britain. The site, strategically situated at the crossing-place between two Roman roads (The Icknield Street and the Watling Street), is now in the hands of the National Trust.

It was during the Roman era that Christianity first reached Britain. Miss Bracken tells us that " the Gospel, spreading from Jerusalem, through the territories of Rome, made its way to Britain and won to itself disciples equally amongst the conquerors and the conquered." " Christianity," she adds " reached this land in the purity of apostolic teaching." Persecution was to follow, since the Emperor Diocletian considered the early Christian Church to be a threat to his authority. During his reign, Miss Bracken says, " a large number of Christians were slaughtered on the spot called Christian Field, near Lichfield."

In a vain attempt to protect their homeland from the barbarians, the Romans left Britain in the fifth century. After their departure, England was divided into about 30 different states " under kings perpetually at war with each other—the most unscrupulous gaining the pre-eminence—so that this island was called the land of tyrants " (Miss Bracken). The country was quickly subjected to attack from beyond its boundaries by savage tribes—the Picts and Scots, the Jutes, the Angles and the Saxons. After innumerable conflicts, the country eventually crystallised into the so-called seven kingdoms of the Heptarchy. These were Northumbria, Mercia, East Anglia, Essex, Sussex, Wessex and Kent, the three most powerful of which—at various times—were Northumbria, Mercia and Wessex. It seems unlikely, however, that in this troubled era a settled period of fixed boundaries ever really existed. There would have been far too much jostling for power on the part of the rival kings for this to be possible.

When Mercia rose to pre-eminence, Offa (757-796), was one of its more enterprising kings. He is remembered for having added London to his domains and for having built a dyke from Chepstow to Chester to restrain the Welsh. This is still known as Offa's dyke. Tamworth became the capital, and courts were held by the Mercian kings at both Tamworth and Kingsbury. Tamworth had a Royal Mint where, it has been said, coins of such beauty were minted that they became known and admired throughout Europe.

The Mercian kings reserved great tracts of territory as hunting grounds, including Sherwood Forest and Cannock Chase. Closer to hand, the dense forest lying a few miles to the south of Tamworth was also popular. A hunting lodge was built—possibly on Maney Hill—which became ' SOUTHUN ' or SUTTON—the 'ton' or townstead to the south of Tamworth—with ' MIDDLE-TON ' situated half-way between the two. Dugdale, however, claims that Sutton's southern situation was relative, not to Tamworth, but to Lichfield. Sutton lay on the edge of ' COL-FIELD '—a name suggesting both a field on a hillside, and a place where charcoal-burning was carried out. The name of Maney comes from an old British word, ' MEINI ', meaning ' the stones '. There were, apparently, early stone-quarries on Maney Hill, and in 1853, a large, Druidical-type stone was found there, which Miss Bracken in the " History of the Forest and Chase of Sutton Coldfield ", tells us was " turned out of a hedgerow on the hill; it measured about five feet in length and two feet in width and thickness, and was of a fine grained, hard, dark substance, but it was unfortunately broken up for the roads before its nature could be ascertained. It was much worn, and retained no marks of a tool." This find helped to confirm the already established belief that the Druids held rites on Maney Hill, and possibly at Barr Beacon.

Barr Beacon was only referred to as a ' beacon ' after the region had become less heavily wooded from the fourteenth century onwards, due to the inroads made by the charcoal burners. Charcoal was increasingly in demand with the growth of metal industries in the West Midlands. Despite its consequent suitability as a beacon, there is no evidence of its being used to alert local people to the threat from the Spanish Armada in 1588. During the Napoleonic Wars, however, its crest was equipped in readiness to give warning of the landing of enemy troops, but the invasion never came.

When the whole region was forested, it would be safe to assume that the oak—a native tree which is common in the district—grew in profusion on the slopes of Barr Beacon. Oak groves were often the scene of sacred rites performed by the Druids, who were steeped in natural lore, studied the stars and believed in the transmigration of souls. For this reason, perhaps, Barr Beacon was thought to have been a Druid shrine, and Robert Plott, the Staffordshire topographer, supposed that the arch-Druid himself lived there.

In 827, Mercia submitted to Egbert, King of Wessex, who became the first monarch to take the title of King of the English—not King of England, for that term was not used until the following century. Mercia dwindled to the status of a mere earldom, and it was only thanks to Alfred, King of Wessex (871-901), that it was saved from annihilation. Teacher, scholar, translator of the classics into the common tongue, wise legislator and fearless defender of his home-land, as well as being a man of great magnanimity, Alfred the Great achieved this end by installing his daughter, Elfrida, and her patriot-husband, Ethelred, in Tamworth Castle. In a long fight against the Danish invaders, hordes of whom were then plundering and ravaging much of England, Elfrida built a line of forts from Tamworth to Stafford, and succeeded in clearing the enemy from much of the territory.

At a later period of history, however, the Danes achieved military supremacy in the region, and during the winter of 1016, the Danish king, Knut—better known to the English as Canute—reached Warwickshire, where—according to the Anglo-Saxon Chronicle—his forces: " . . . plundered therein and burnt and slew all that they met." Canute eventually became king of all England—as well as of Denmark. He had been born a heathen, but was later baptized, and after he had conquered England, he appeared to have changed his ferocious, ruthless ways for those of a wise and moderate ruler of the country.

At the time of the Norman Conquest, Mercia was in the hands of Edwin, grandson of Lady Godiva, who is best remembered for having ridden naked through the streets of Coventry in 1040 as a protest against a grievous tax, imposed there by her husband, Leofric, Earl of Chester. Edwin, Earl of Mercia, also had his own brand of courage, which led him to resist the Norman usurpers. As a consequence he was put to death in 1071, when Sutton Coldfield, in common with the rest of Mercia, passed to the Crown, and Sutton Chase became a Royal Forest.

CHAPTER II
The growth of Sutton Coldfield under the Norman and Plantagenet monarchs, and its decline after the Wars of the Roses.

IN the eleventh century, Warwickshire, like much of England, was still largely covered in great forests. The cultivated regions in the north-west of the county were probably smaller than elsewhere and the Normans, being much given to hunting, no doubt derived great pleasure from the acquisition of the largely unspoilt tract of thick forest land, where wolf, bear, wild boar and deer, abounded.

7

Naturally, Sutton Coldfield, which lay in the centre of this wild region, and was already established as a hunting seat, became a place of some importance. By the time the Domesday Book was compiled in 1086, it was rated, like Aston, at 8 hides. A hide was a variable amount of land, but was, on average, around 120 acres, and at 8 hides, Sutton Coldfield had a bigger area of cultivated land than that of any of the neighbouring villages.

The Forest—for such it was when it belonged to the king, and was only called a Chase when it belonged to a subject—was bounded by the course of the River Tame from Perry Barr in the south-west to Drayton Bassett or, possibly, Tamworth in the north-east. To the west, were the heights of Barr Beacon. The region was well watered by innumerable springs and streams, with the little Ebrook, more recently called Plants Brook, flowing through Sutton itself.

The history of the Earls of Warwick prior to the Norman conquest, is lost in a legendary past. The first earl, Arth or Arthgal—said to have been a knight of the Round Table—adopted the bear as his emblem, since his name signified a bear in the British language. According to the legend, Morvid, the second earl, met, in single combat, an immensely powerful giant, who attacked him with a tree, plucked from the ground by its roots and stripped of its branches. Having overcome the giant, it was natural that he should add the plucked tree or ' ragged staff ' to the already established emblem of the bear.

After the Conquest, Turchill, the native-born Earl of Warwick, made his peace with William and, as a consequence, was allowed to keep his title and possessions. When he died, however, the Conqueror conferred the title on Henry de Newburgh, whose name was derived from that of the castle of Neuburg in Normandy, where he was born. In 1126, Henry's son, Roger, acquired the manor of Sutton Coldfield from Henry I in exchange for the manors of Hockham and Langham in Rutlandshire. In "The History of the Forest and Chase of Sutton Coldfield ", Miss Bracken quotes the written deed which solemnized the transaction:—

> " To have and to hold the said manor of Sutton to the said Earl Roger and his heirs, with all the liberty and royalty, without suits at the hundred court, without payment of scutage, or any foreign service, with a free chase between the Tame and the Bourne, which divide the liberty of the said manor from others: And the said Roger and his heirs may have one park and one hay fenced: And they may have a free court at their own pleasure in all free customs, with view of frankpledge: Also they may have an outwood (boscum forinsecum) common to the freeholders, without a fence keeper: Also they may have in demesne two carucates of land and one water-mill,

with suits (i.e., the customs belonging to it): Also they may have eighteen fallow deer."

Earl Roger is remembered as an open supporter of Matilda, in her quarrel with Stephen over the succession to the English throne, and as a crusader who made more than one visit to the Holy Land. Miss Bracken informs us that he gave " three yardland, lying in Hill " to the Benedictine priory of Canwell, whose monks came under the protection of Pope Eugenius III in 1148. The name " Canwell " meaning " the well of power or efficiacy ", referred to a spring, within the monastic walls, known as St. Modeven's Well, and reputed to bring about " unaccountable cures of diverse ailes and weeknesses ". Earl Roger died in 1153, and it is interesting to note that in a bull of Pope Alexander in 1162, there is a reference to " three hides of land in Sutton (Warwickshire), which the Countess Gundred (widow of the Earl), with the consent of her son, William, Earl of Warwick, gave to the Priory of Trentham ".

On its north-western boundary, Sutton Chase was probably separated from Cannock Forest only by enclosures at Aldridge. The dividing line was obviously very tenuous, since Edward I granted the Earl of Warwick a special patent enabling him " to have liberty to pursue deer that fled from his Chase at Sutton into the King's Forest at Kanc " (Cannock). Because the deer of Sutton Chase were not so strictly protected as in the Royal Forest of Cannock, people who lived beyond the bounds of Sutton Chase and within the jurisdiction of Cannock, sometimes came over the border, poaching. Aldridge men were reputed to have a taste for venison obtained in this way.

Some time after the building of the hunting lodge—possibly not until Norman times—a manor-house had been erected on what consequently came to be known as Manor Hill. To the north, a village had already come into being around the reed-fringed pools which filled the valley between Manor Hill and the hill upon which, considerably later, the parish church was to be built.

A causeway or enbankment ran between the pools, forming a dam, beside which stood the lord's mill. Under the prevailing feudal laws, tenants had to grind their corn either at the lord's water-mill, or at his windmill on Maney Hill. They were also obliged to repair the banks of the mill-pool, and whenever the lord of the manor was hunting they had to ' beat up ' the game for him. At harvest time they had to help in the lord's fields, for which service they were paid " one fat sheep, four pennyworth of white bread and twelve casks of beer."* There were some rights, too, including those of house-bote, hay-bote and freedom to buy and sell in and out of the

* See document, page 16.

lordship of Sutton without challenge. House-bote was an allowance of timber from the lord's woodland for repairing tenements, while hay-bote was the wood given for the repair of fences and posts. Tenants also enjoyed free pasturage for their cattle and were allowed to collect dead wood for making fires.

Dugdale's pleasant picture of medieval Sutton, with its reference to " . . . the very goodly Mannour House with fair pools near unto it ", was bound to undergo changes. The manor house was knocked down shortly after the Wars of the Roses, whilst nowadays, Wyndley Pool and the little pond by the Youth Centre in Clifton Road may well be the only remains of those ' fair pools ' included in Dugdale's description.

All the pools of the Park and Parish are artificial, having been made by damming the streams which rise in the district, and so filling valleys with water. Wyndley Pool is known to be of considerable antiquity, being possibly the oldest pool in the district, whilst Keeper's Pool was probably made by John Holte, who was a member of King Henry VI's household. The name of the pool presumably derives from his position as ranger (or keeper) of Sutton Chase. Holland Pool, near where the Holland Road 'bus garage now stands, still appeared on late 19th century maps and was about the size of Keeper's Pool—reed beds existed in the area up to about 40 years ago. There were also two smaller pools—Skinner's Pool and Jerome's Pool—quite near to the site where, until recently, the Empress Cinema stood. The Ebrook, itself, which fed the pools, then made its way through the ' stone bed moor ' and the ' Blabbs ', or low-lying land near the foot of Reddicap Hill, once described as being " the haunt of frogs and eels."

When each county was divided into ' hundreds ' for administrative and judicial purposes, Sutton had originally been in " Coleshelle Hundred ", with its meeting-place at Coleshill. During the reign of Henry II, the administration was moved to Hemlingford, which Dugdale describes as:—

" . . . A Ford or Passage over Tame, somewhat more than a Flight shoot southwards from Kingsbury Church, of which likewise the mill near unto it is still called Hemlingford Mill."

Hemlingford Hundred had its own Court too, which sat in full session every six months in the ancient building known as Kingsbury Hall, which still stands on a promontory near Kingsbury Church.

This Court dealt with both criminal and civil matters, and its civil role is illustrated by a law-suit concerning Elias le Collier, a prosperous charcoal merchant, who was robbed of £300—a large sum of money at that time—on the Chester Road, near New Oscott, in 1324. Because his assailant was never traced, and as the Chester Road at that time was bounded on one side by Warwickshire, and on the other, by Staffordshire, he brought an action under the Statute of Winchester against the inhabitants of Hemlingford Hundred in the one county, and the inhabitants of Offlow Hundred in the other. Despite judgment being in Elias le Collier's favour, he only succeeded in recovering a small portion of the money due to him, and eventually dropped the suit.

The case of Elias le Collier is also interesting because it shows the measure of prosperity which accrued from charcoal burning in this district, where it was widely practised from the fourteenth century. The charcoal was used in the already growing metal industry of the West Midlands, and the inroads into the thickly forested area around Sutton was such that, by the sixteenth century, much of the land had been cleared of trees and supplanted by gorse and heather.

At the time of Domesday, Warwickshire's population was only about 30,000, with agriculture and smithing as its main occupations. Warwick was its largest community, with Brailes in the extreme south of the county second in importance. To the north of the county, many of the settlements consisted of isolated—often moated—homesteads. In villages such as Sutton, by early Norman times, the ordinary homes, from being made of wattle and daub, were now more solid, timber buildings, with thatched roofs. They were sometimes communal homes, in which whole families—masters and servants alike—were housed together. They must have been very draughty, as smoke from their fires had to escape through holes in the roofs, and windows were mere 'wind holes' in the walls.

It is not surprising that communications too should have been extremely primitive. Sutton had no navigable waterway, and it was only linked with other villages by rough tracks. Wyndley Lane, probably the oldest existing road in the parish, was originally a bridle-path. Making its way between steep, sandstone banks—some of which remain to this day—the lane provided a link between the Chase, where animals were pastured, and the Driffold or "drive-fold" (situated near the Manor) where the animals were counted and marked. From there, the track descended sharply before linking up with Coles Lane which led down towards the pastures along the valley of the Ebrook. Coles Lane, as its name suggests (being a corruption of Coleshill Lane), was the direct route to Coleshill in mediaeval times.

No important road passed through Sutton itself, since the Chester Road—once known as the Ridgeway—to the west of the parish, and the Coleshill—Lichfield road to the east both missed the town by several miles. These roads were so infested with vagabonds and robbers that only the most intrepid travellers used them. Some idea of the hazards of travel can be gathered from the fact that the Earl of Warwick employed two bow-bearers or officers of the Chase to conduct travellers from Pype Hayes—where there was a lodge called ' Bow-bearers' Croft '—across the Chase to Sutton Coldfield. It was no wonder that travellers on the Chester Road sometimes turned aside into the Chapel of Our Lady of Berwood to pray for or give thanks for their safe passage.

Such dangers emphasised the need for some kind of legal restraint. Man had discovered early on his capacity to sit in judgment on his fellows. By Norman times a clear picture emerges of the sort of rough justice meted out to our ancestors under the harsh continental code of laws thrust upon them. Trial by Ordeal, for instance was a frightening experience for even the bravest of men. The accused might be asked to take hold of a red-hot iron or to plunge his arm into boiling water and if, after a lapse of some days, the ill-effects of the ordeal were abating, he was declared innocent. Otherwise, if hand or arm had taken bad ways, his guilt was considered to have been proved. Trial by Battle was another method, popular with the Norman Barons, but detested by the native English. This form of trial gave the accused person the right to prove his innocence by doing battle with his accuser. Only after the murder of Mary Ashford at Penns in 1817 (See Chapter VI), when the accused man, Thornton, sought the ancient ' privilege ' of Trial by Battle, was the right removed from the Statute Books.

Dugdale speaks of a ' Court Leet ' at Sutton " with Assize of Bread and Beer ". This ' Court Leet ' was a Royal Court, convened to deal with both criminal and civil matters. The feudal lord also held a ' Court Baron ', whose authority, whilst limited to manorial rights only, was enforced by the gallows, the tumbrel, the stocks and the whipping-post. Although there are no precise records, traditionally, the stocks—used as a penalty for any number of minor offences—along with the person undergoing punishment, were drawn by asses through the Sutton streets. Sutton's stocks are still to be seen in King Edward's Square. * They formerly stood in Mill Street in the yard of the old Council House, built in 1859.

In feudal times, there was much oppression, particularly of the poor, and the land was often in the grip of famine. For centuries, inhabitants of Sutton were only allowed to keep dogs if they had been ringed and maimed in the left paw—to prevent them worrying the deer. They were unable to keep sheep,

* Since removed to Blakesley Hall, Yardley.

because their feeding habits were similar to those of the deer. Before their cattle could feed on the acorns and beech-mast of the forest, they were compelled to get permission from the forest official—the agistor—to whom they had to pay a fee.

Not surprisingly under such conditions, the deer upon Sutton Chase were sometimes poached, and in the reign of Edward I, the Earl of Warwick complained bitterly of "the misdemeanors committed by certain lewd persons in killing deer within the chase". The king sent a special commission to investigate the matter, but it seems that the culprits were never traced.

During the same period, it is recorded that Thomas de Arden, who lived at Peddimore with his wife, Rose, did:—

> " . . . exercise freedom there, not considering that it was in the compasse of Sutton Chase, where the Earls of Warwick had so much privilege relating both to Vert and Venison, so that the Earl, having begun suit against him, he was glad to seek his favour, and condescended to grant him liberty to fish in that little stream called Ebroke (the Ebrook, now called Plants Brook), as also that they might have liberty to agist Hoggs within their woods at Curdworth and Peddimore and beat down acorns for their swine, and likewise gather such Nutts as should be there growing."*

This revealing document, apart from throwing light on the social conditions created by the feudal system, shows a measure of sturdy yeoman independence on the part of one local man.

Despite the hardships, Sutton Coldfield prospered and was in the process of becoming the centre of a group of manors, which included Erdington, Middleton, Wishaw, Curdworth, Water Orton, Drayton Bassett, Aldridge, Aston and Shenstone. In 1300, Guy, Earl of Warwick, obtained a charter for a market on each Tuesday, and an annual fair, beginning on the eve of the Holy Trinity, which continued for three days. Under a subsequent charter of 1353, a second fair was inaugurated, which was held on St. Martin's Eve and Day. These fairs and markets were great 'clearing houses' for the produce and merchandise of the country-side, and Sutton became the 'market town' for the whole area.

Under the Merchant Law, courts were set up to deal, on the spot, with the disputes inevitably arising out of such diverse activities. They were known as Pieds Poudres Courts, a term referring to the dusty feet of the pedlars, minstrels, tumblers and others who had recourse to them. The English, however, in their contempt for all things Norman French, soon corrupted the name to "Pie Powder Courts."

In the third year of Edward II's reign, at a Court Leet and Court Baron for the Manor of Sutton Coldfield, a document setting out the ancient customs of the Manor was certified upon

* See page 240 of Volume 4 of "Victoria County History—Hemlingford Hundred" (1947).

Children gathering sticks in Blackroot Glade at the turn of the century
Photograph:
    W. Midgley

oath by a jury. A translation of this document from the original Latin, as given by Dugdale, appears in Miss Bracken's " History of the Forest and Chase of Sutton Coldfield " as follows:—

" The inquisition of twelve jurymen taken at this view, before Galfrid de Okenham, seneschal, by oath of Anselm de Clifton and others, jurymen, charged (to enquire) concerning the ancient customs of that lordship, as well with regard to freemen as bond-servants, what sort of customs they used to make and to have before the coronation of our lord king Henry (III), grandfather of the present king, from the days of Athelstan, some time king of England, by whom aforetime the ancient usages and customs of the lordship were made and settled.

" Who say upon their oath, that every freeman of Sutton was accustomed to hold his lands and tenements by virtue and effect of his original charter; and if there should be any plea about land between any freeman of that lordship, they used to be pleaded and concluded by writ of our lord the king, according to the law of England, before the justiciaries. And those men of bondage-tenure who held a whole yardland or more used to be officers of the king, or lord, during the lord's pleasure, whoever might have been elected to that office.

" Also, those who held half a yardland, or a nook of land, or a cottage of bondage tenure, used to be bedell of the manor and decenary. And also all those who held in bondage tenure, used to be called customary tenants. And whenever the lord came to hunt, those customary tenants used to drive the wanlass to a stand in driving the wild

14

beasts, according to the quantity of their tenure; as those who held a whole yardland, for two days, and so of others. And they used to have among them half of the fee of a woodward of the venison taken.

" Also they used to be keepers of the Coldfield heath, whenever they were chosen by their neighbours at the court; and they used to buy and sell freely, both in and out of the lordship of Sutton, without challenge. And also they used to do suit at the court of Sutton from three weeks to three weeks, and to pay the rent of assize, with tallage, according to the quantity of customary tenants of this sort, at the four usual terms of the year, &c. And they used to have house-bote and hay-bote, by view of the foresters and woodwards, in the time of Lent, enough to repair their hedges and houses in bondage tenure.

" And at the death of customary tenants of this kind, the Lord used to have, in the name of the heriot, the best animal, and no more; neither goods nor chattels, neither in the life nor after the death of a customary tenant of this kind, unless for this reason, that the lord's eldest son or daughter were going to be married. And the lord used to have, at his pleasure, of those who were dead, before the administration of the executors, the third part of all the goods of a customary tenant of this kind who was dead. And of customary tenants of this kind while living, the lord used to have in like manner the half of all his goods, saving oxen enough for ploughing, and heifers for milking, when his (the lord's) eldest son or daughter was going to be married. And if any of these customary tenants alienated his bondage tenure to any one, they used to give up that tenure in court before the seneschal (i.e., the steward), and raise and pay a fine at the lord's pleasure.

" And also, if any of these customary tenants went out of the lordship, and would not abide there any longer, they used to come into court, and give up into the hands of the lord their tenure of bondage, with all their horses and colts, and cart bound with iron, with their hogs, their whole pieces of cloth, their wool not spun, and their best brass pot; and go out and abide wherever he would, without challenge of the lord, and himself, with all his posterity, to be free for ever. And also all tenants, as well free as customary, used to have common pasturage with all their cattle, within the lordship of Sutton, in all the out-woods and other common places, at all times of the year; and also in all separate places from the feast of St. Michael the Archangel to the feast of the Purification of the Blessed Mary, excepting the lord's land and the lord's park, and excepting also the gardens of the neighbours.

" And none of these customary tenants used to grind his corn but at the lord's water-mill, so long as the mill was in repair for grinding, unless they first paid (for) the whole of the corn to the lord's miller, upon pain of forfeiture of the whole of the corn; excepting the tenants of Maney, Windley, and Wigula(?), who ground at the lord's windmill at Maney.

"And they also say, that they have heard their ancestors say, that at the time the manor of Sutton aforesaid was in the hands of the king of England all the chase was afforested, and that all the dogs within the forest used to be ringed and maimed on the left paw; and that, after they came into the hands of the Earl of Warwick, they had leave to have and to hold dogs of all kind whole and not ringed.

"And also all tenants, as well customary as free, used to have the dead wood in all the woods, wherever it might be found, for firing. And also all freeholders used to be summoned to appear for three days before the court, and the customary tenants likewise. And if there was a plea of debt or offence, or any plea between neighbours, and the defendants denied it, and waged law against the plaintiff, they used to make law with the third hand, and they used to essoin themselves of the common suit of court twice, and the third time appear and warrant the essoin; and likewise of the plea, as well of the plaintiff as the defendant, to be essoined twice of the plea, and twice of the law, and the third time to come, or have the judgment of the court. And the customary tenants used to be twice fined in court for houses found on bondage tenure; and the third time, if it was not repaired, they used to incur a punishment at the lord's pleasure.

"And the aforesaid customary tenants used to repair the bank round the mill-pool of the lord of Sutton with earth-work as often as was necessary, being warned with reasonable warning, and if they did not come they used to be fined at the court next ensuing: and they used to be fined in like manner if they did not come to the wanlass, whenever the lord came to hunt.

"And all customary tenants, who held a whole yardland in bondage, used to work for the lord for two days in autumn: and in like manner all other customary tenants according to the quantity of their tenure, at reasonable warning given by the overseer; for which they used to have one fat sheep and four pennyworth of white bread, and twelve casks of beer; and if they did not come then they used to be fined at the court next ensuing.

"And they say that all the aforesaid customs used to be kept, both from the time of King Athelstan and the time of King John, and before the coronation of King Henry III and the predecessors of the aforesaid jurymen . . . And they say that Waleran, formerly Earl of Warwick, for himself and his heirs, granted that all the customs aforesaid, and all other ancient customs, should last for ever."

In an age of faith, when men everywhere were building great cathedrals and churches to the glory of God, Sutton Coldfield had neither church nor priest. When the Norman Earls of Warwick and their retainers came to visit this remote manor house on the hill to indulge in the pleasures of the hunt they were probably well aware of the deficiency. To offset the lack of a church, they built within the precincts of the manor house, " the free chapel of St. Blaize ", which served the religious needs of the community for 200 years. The history of this little chapel, which survived until Tudor times, has not been entirely lost to us.

The saint whose name is commemorated was Bishop Blaize of Sebaste in Armenia, a physician turned religious zealot who, following his martyrdom, became the patron saint of wild animals, wool-combers, wax-chandlers and all sufferers from throat diseases. At a time when Christians were being widely persecuted, bishops were often more at risk than their followers. For this reason, Bishop Blaize fled and sought refuge in a cave when the Armenian Christians were being persecuted by Agricola, Governor of Cappadocia, under the Emperor Licinius. According to legend, the cave was inhabited by wild beasts which he cared for when they were sick or injured.

He was eventually caught and imprisoned, but on his way into captivity, he is said to have saved a small boy from dying, because of a fish-bone lodged in his throat. By touching the boy's throat, he succeeded in dislodging the obstruction—an act which some might attribute to a miracle, others to the skilful touch of a physician's hand. Before being put to death by his tormentors, Blaize's flesh was torn with sharp metal combs, as used in the preparation of wool-fibres, and so—by association —he became the patron saint of wool-combers. So it was, that St. Blaize's Day (3rd February), long continued to be a holiday in English wool-producing towns. By tradition, it was also a holiday for women, who on that day were forbidden to spin at the risk of having their distaffs burned.

On St. Blaize's Night, the punning relationship between the Saint's name and the verb " to blaze " was heralded by the lighting of hill-top bonfires in his honour. In Germany, where the verb " blasen " means " to blow ", St. Blaize became a storm saint, whose name was invoked by sailors to protect them from the fury of gales at sea. After making due allowance for the hallowing accretions of the passing centuries, the character of St. Blaize remains warmly deliniated as having a kindly benevolence extending to all living creatures. By the time of the Crusades he had become a widely acclaimed figure throughout Europe, which would account for his being known and honoured in a place as small and remote as Sutton Coldfield then was.

Several centuries after the removal of both the manor house and the Chapel of St. Blaize, Miss Bracken, writing in 1860, tells us that the site of the manor was "perfectly traceable" and that "... the summit of the hill has an escarpment which has scarcely been disturbed since Bishop Vesey removed its supporting stone wall." Today, on this still beautifully wooded plateau, so near to the centre of Sutton, yet so aloofly remote from it in atmosphere, stands a house which, though of no great antiquity, is still called, not surprisingly, the manor, and adjoining it is another building which, although used only for secular purposes, is known, not irreverently, as the Chapel of St. Blaize.

When the anomaly of Sutton's lack of a church became too great, a site was chosen on a hill crest, 400 feet above sea level. Here, on what has since become known as Trinity Hill, the parish church was built, and its first named incumbent was ordained in 1305. In "The History of Sutton Coldfield", written "by an impartial hand" (1762), we are told that it "... doth not stand due east and west, as churches are commonly supposed to do, but varies some degrees from the true points; the East end declining to the North, and the West end to the South; whether this proceeds from the ignorance of our ancestors in those easy parts of the mathematicks, which every builder understands now-a-days, or whether it arises from the continual change in the variation of the compass, I leave others to determine." According to the legend, the church was to have been built on Maney Hill, but at night spirits always carried away the stones to the present site. This legend was probably associated with a superstitious belief that Maney Hill was a place of ill omen, due to the Druidical rites said to have been practised there.

The church has been much altered over the years. It has, at various times, been enlarged, 'restored', and had its nave rebuilt. Apart from the base of the tower, probably little of the original edifice still stands. Bishop Vesey provided it with an organ and two aisles, which Riland Bedford tells us are "interesting to students of architectural change, although not possessing much intrinsic beauty of their own. Externally they accord with the battlemented parapets and depressed arches of the Tudor period." He also mentions that the peculiar mouldings of the arches which separate the chancel from the side chapels, were imitated from a church in Paris—though he could not remember which one. He adds: "As Vesey was in France with King Henry, and was frequently employed in diplomatic work abroad, it seems quite natural that he should avail himself of Parisian taste, especially if he was (as I suspect he was) his own architect." The statement concerning Vesey's being in France with the King refers to the meeting at Guisnes in 1520 between Henry VIII and Francois I. Vesey's retinue there was composed of 4 chaplains, 6 gentlemen, 23 servants and 20 horses. Because of the splendour and lavishness of the occasion, the meeting place is usually referred to as " The Field of the Cloth of Gold ". Much of the ceremony however, was marred by rain and wind.

By the fourteenth century, Sutton had acquired—in addition to a manor-house and a church—a number of other fine buildings. New Hall, moated and made of sandstone, was built around 1200, and later rebuilt. It was enlarged in 1590, and given a tower in 1796. Parts of the original house are still standing, and its name, *New* Hall, has been used for at least 600 years! Among the various families who have possessed the property were those of Thomas Gibbons, the Sacheverells and the Chadwicks.

Peddimore Hall, although it only dates back to 1659, stands on the site of a much earlier double-moated homestead. Traces of the double moat can still be seen, although now much overgrown. Langley Hall—another moated house—is thought to have been built in the thirteenth century. It belonged, in earlier times, to the Beresfords of Wishaw, one of whom—William Beresford—was appointed Chief Justice of the Court of Common Pleas in 1289. Another member of the family was reputed to be a close friend of the Black Prince—victor of Crecy and Poitiers. In 1327, Edmund Beresford was granted a licence to crenellate the house. This suggests that it was a substantial and imposing building. It was demolished early in the nineteenth century, but Langley Hall Farm and a part of the moat still survive.

Reputedly the oldest house in the Sutton district is The Grove, near Wishaw, a cruck-framed building of considerable size, whose history and origins have been lost to us despite the fact that it must have been the home of someone of substance.

Great human tragedies of the past—war and pestilence included—reduced to mere statistics, fail to evoke any strong emotions. The events in question, peopled by nameless victims in their hundreds or thousands, are too big for the mind to encompass. Such was the terrible Black Death, which swept westwards across Europe from China and India in the fourteenth century. When it reached Bristol, almost the whole strength of that town perished, and throughout England scarcely one in ten of the population survived. The Scots, hearing of the plague in England, and believing that a terrible vengeance of God had overtaken the English, came together in Selkirk Forest, intending to invade England. But the plague overtook them too, killing 5,000, and as the survivors were making ready to return north, they were subjected to a surprise attack by the English, which further greatly reduced their numbers.

There is little evidence as to what happened in Sutton Coldfield during this period, but Erdington provides us with sufficient proof of the Black Death's prevalence in the district. Within the precincts of Erdington was the separate Manor of Pipe (or Pype), which was owned by Henry de Pipe, who had many children by his first wife, Ingrith. It is recorded by Dugdale that all except one girl child, died with their mother of the pestilence. Poor Henry de Pipe's misfortunes did not end with this affliction for, as Dugdale goes on to relate, he took a second wife, Maud —daughter of George de Castello, of Castle Bromwich—and not long after the marriage he found she was with child by one, John Boote, his father's servant. This caused him such grief that he died before the child was born, " on the feast day of St. Laurence in the 36th year of the reign of Edward III."

G. M. Trevelyan, the social historian, has said that the Black Death remained in the soil of England and became known later as " the Plague ". Although it never again swept the whole country at one time, it was perpetually reappearing in different places. The Plague of London of 1665 was the last serious recurrence of the disease which had continued, on and off, for three centuries. Despite its name, it was not confined to London, and is said to have reached Birmingham from the Metropolis in a box of clothes. In Birmingham, the disease caused a high rate of mortality, but there is no evidence that it reached either Sutton Coldfield or Erdington.

Our greatest source of knowledge of Sutton Coldfield's early history is Dugdale's " The Antiquities of Warwickshire ". The place itself he says is " . . . a large parish, but (with) a barren soil and containeth divers Hamlets and Places of Note, viz. Wigginshill, Maney, Hill, Little Sutton, Warmley (sic), Langley, New Hall and Pedimore ". He quotes Domesday Book: " . . . it is rated at 8 hides; the woods extending two miles in length and one in breadth and all valued at four pounds."

Early in the reign of King John, Lord Basset of Drayton made a park at Drayton Basset which, according to Dugdale, " . . . being within the Precincts of this Chase (Sutton Coldfield), and questioned by Waleran, then Earl of Warwick, necessitated the said Lord Basset, rather than he would pull down his Pales again, to come to an agreement with the Earl." This agreement was that Lord Basset's forester should make oath to the Earl and his heirs " for the faithful custody of the venison ", and that the Earl's ranger should oversee the keepership of the deer and be recompensed for trespasses done to them. Lord Basset also undertook to provide the Earl—and his heirs—with " . . . two good bucks from the aforesaid park, taken between the Assumption and the Nativity of the Blessed Virgin Mary."

During the reign of King John, the Manor of Kingsbury was acquired, through marriage, by the Bracebridge family, who came, originally, from Bracebridge in Lincolnshire. According to Burke's "Landed Gentry", in the seventh year of the reign of Henry V, Sir Ralph Bracebridge was summoned "the first amongst other persons of note to attend the King in person for the defence of the Realm."

In 1419, Sir Ralph obtained, from the Earl of Warwick, a lease for his lifetime on the Manor and Chase of Sutton Coldfield, in return for which he undertook to serve Warwick with 9 lances and 17 bowmen in the Calais garrison. This was during an era of great strife between the English and the French, in which Henry V had staked a somewhat nebulous claim to the throne of France. Calais had fallen to the English following the Battle of Crecy in 1346, and at Agincourt in 1415, the "grey goose feather" arrows of the English bowmen had rained down death on 11,000 Frenchmen.

Riland Bedford* becomes eloquent in speaking of the English bowmen: ". . . that hardy body of men, the yeomen-archers, the mainstay of an English army in the middle ages, who took the name of yeomen, it is surmised, from the yew bows with which they did such good service." An English nobleman, according to Riland Bedford, found it advantageous to be lenient to a sportsman who was a good archer, since he prided himself more on the marksmen he could bring into the field, than upon the magnitude of his herds of deer and flocks of wild fowl. Poaching it seems, had come to be regarded as less of a crime. The loss of game was, presumably, a small price to pay for the services of a yeoman-archer who, it was boasted, carried twelve lives under his belt in his sheaf of a dozen arrows.

Bowmen were under a legal obligation to practise their skill, and, at Sutton, butts were erected in medieval times for archery purposes. Old maps of the district show Hammond's Budds and Basset's Budds (i.e., butts) in close proximity to Sutton Coldfield. From these, Riland Bedford comments, "we may recognize the spot where turf butts were erected for the practice of bowmanry". In the soft sandstone of the side wall of No. 3 Coleshill Street, marks can still be seen, said to have been caused by archers sharpening their arrows. Evidence for this may be deduced from the fact that, many years ago, at a spot called the butts just outside Coventry's ancient walls, similar marks were found in the sandstone walling. No. 3 Coleshill Street, despite its Georgian frontage, is probably of medieval origin.

It can be assumed that the 17 bowmen-defenders of Calais, recruited in the parish, did their training at the butts in Sutton. Local men, drafted to the Calais garrison, probably felt no sense of grievance, for at a time when labourers in England were paid only 4d. a day, archers in Henry V's army received 6d. a day

* " History of Sutton Coldfield."

21

on foot and 8d. a day on horseback. The strategic importance of Calais is reflected in the fact that Sir Ralph Bracebridge, by making a modest contribution to its defence, was able to acquire a life-lease on so desirable a Manor and Chase as that of Sutton Coldfield.

Today, Ralph Bracebridge is remembered less as a defender of Calais than for having had the Ebrook dammed, so creating the pool still bearing his name. His motive however, was practical rather than aesthetic. Bracebridge, like the other early pools of Sutton Manor, was used largely for the provision of fish—chiefly bream—which was so essential a part of the observation of fast days in the pre-Reformation calendar. In increasing the supply of bream by making a new pool, it is unlikely that Sir Ralph Bracebridge had the parishioners in mind, for—as Riland Bedford points out—bream was a costly luxury. When baked in flour, with spice, pepper, saffron, cloves and cinnamon (as was customary), the cost to most local people would have been prohibitive.

Sir Ralph Bracebridge's grand-daughter, Alice, married John Arden of Peddimore and Park Hall (which was in the parish of Castle Bromwich). Before the marriage there had, apparently, been some objection to the match on the Arden's side, whereupon Richard Bracebridge, Alice's father, took a number of his supporters to Peddimore early one morning and carried off John Arden, a not unwilling prisoner, to Kingsbury. The story is told anonymously in verse in a little book, published in 1904, called "Tales of Sutton Town and Chase with other Tales and Some Sketches, collected by ' T.A.U. ' and now Imprinted for the first time." It starts:—

> At Peddimore John Arden lived,
> A love-sick swain was he,
> Fair Alice was the maid he loved,
> She lived in Kingsburie.

The story has a happy ending, for the Ardens, seemingly under pressure from the Court, relented and agreed to the marriage, and Bracebridge placated the injured Arden pride by parting with his best horse:—

> To Arden père for trespass done
> And to requite his loss,
> From out the park at Kingsburie
> To choose the fleetest horse.

John Arden's younger brother, Robert, was the grandfather of William Shakespeare.

At a later period Bracebridge Pool passed into the hands of the owners of the Four Oaks Estate, and Miss Bracken—writing in 1860—said that it was at that time possessed by Sir W. E. C. Hartopp. In 1869, it was offered for sale, when the Warden and Society, under some pressure from the inhabitants, bought it for £1,520. This payment, Mr. T. Porter, the former Borough

Engineer ana Surveyor tells us, was made from money received from the London and North Western Railway Company for land at Green Lanes—presumably when the railway was built in 1862.

The Wars of the Roses were waged for the crown of England between the Royal Houses of York and Lancaster. This conflict resulted in the decline of Sutton Coldfield from a prosperous little town to a place of poverty, decay and depression. It was only indirectly, however, that this came about: the Earls of Warwick, to whom Sutton belonged for almost four centuries, wielded great power, sometimes extending far beyond the bounds of their own earldom. Such was the case to an exaggerated degree with Richard Nevil— Earl of Warwick, who—because of his influential position and his deep involvement in the Lancastrian cause—earned for himself the title of " Kingmaker ". But in 1471, during the Battle of Barnet, Warwick was killed, and in due course Sutton Coldfield, along with the other manors of the earldom, reverted to the Crown. Thus, according to Miss Bracken (" Forest and Chase of Sutton Coldfield "), " . . . fell the noble house whose titles and honours of four centuries' growth he had unworthily borne in a political career purely selfish. His high talents had been lost to his country. His inordinate pride had in it nothing of patriotism, but was rather the spring of contentions which saturated the land with the best blood of England."

Sutton Coldfield, having lost its patron, declined in importance. The town became depopulated and poor, the markets and fairs were abandoned, and the manor-house was eventually pulled down. This, Miss Bracken tells us, was undertaken by a man named Wingston, an officer of the King who made profit out of selling timber from the hall to the Marquess of Dorset, who used it in building a mansion at Bradgate in Leicestershire.

CHAPTER III
Bishop Vesey—John Leland, the King's Antiquary—Shakespeare and Robert Burton.

DURING Sutton's era of depression, in the late 15th century, a local boy named John Harman was spending his impressionable years around his birthplace, the old stone farmhouse at Moor Hall. He was the son of William Harman—described as ' a substantial yeoman ' and Joan, daughter of Henry Squire, whose family had, for some centuries resided at Ley Hall, Handsworth. As a young man, John Harman entered Magdalen College, Oxford, where, after graduating, he obtained a fellowship, and was made Professor of Civil Law. He formed a close friendship with Thomas Wolsey—later Cardinal Wolsey—and himself entered the Church. His clerical career began with his appointment as chaplain of the free chapel of St. Blaize at Sutton Coldfield, which, it might be surmised, was a lowly position, for the chapel lay within the precincts of the manor, which was in decline at the time. He won favour at Court and by a succession of appointments made advancement in the Church.

In 1515, on the birth of Princess Mary—heir to the throne —John Harman was nominated as her tutor. Her brief reign from 1553 to 1558 is remembered for religious oppression, when almost 300 people were burnt alive for their beliefs. In 1519, Harman was appointed Bishop of Exeter, a see which, Riland Bedford comments, was " at one time, the richest in the kingdom, but which had already began to feel the exactions of those who had learned the easy lesson of rapine ". By this time, he had, for some unaccountable reason, taken the name of ' Vesey ', possibly due to his having been sponsored by someone of that name in early life, for he had lost his father when young.

Bishop Vesey was to become famous in Sutton Coldfield, not for his advancement in the Church, but as benefactor of his native town. His attempts to restore Sutton to its former prosperity included the revival of ancient fairs and markets and the paving of the town. He also built bridges at Water Orton and Curdworth with stone from the old Manor House. In his role as social reformer, he endowed and built a grammar school, provided for poor widows to receive pensions and built 51 substantial stone houses, mainly for the poor.

In the remoter parts of the parish, these houses (usually referred to as ' Vesey Cottages '), were used as guard-houses. In these, Vesey installed members of his own police-force, who are said to have helped the bishop to coerce some of the numerous vagabonds and beggars into collecting and piling stones from the very bad roads of the district. Up to the year 1765, maps of the period showed the 113th mile from London on the Coleshill— Lichfield road as " the Bishop's heap of stones ". In a curious tract, mentioned by Riland Beford, and entitled " The Recantation and Conversion of Mr. Stanley, sometime an Inns of Court gentleman, and afterwards, by lewd company, become a highway robber in Queen Elizabeth's reign ", the author speaks of:—

" a godly and charitable gentleman, one Mr. Harman, a Warwickshire gentleman, dwelling about Sutton Coleill, who, seeing his Parish to be pestered extremely with sturdy Beggars and wandering Rogues, did take order that they should all be sent to his house, and presently he set them to work to gather stones forth of his grounds, and gave them some small reliefe in meat and drink, and a penny a day, and held them hard to work (having lustie stout servants to see to them), and when he had made an end of gathering his own grounds, he set them to work in his neighbour's grounds, and paid them their wages, which thing when all the rest of the wand'ring Beggars and Rogues understood, they durst not one of them come a begging in that parish, for feare they should be made to work."

It is said that this tract was not printed until the year 1646.

Vesey built the bridge at Water Orton with what remained of the stone from Sutton's manor-house. Dugdale tells us also that he " built it in Henry VIII's time at his own charges." On the north side of the bridge, built into the parapet wall are what Riland Bedford refers to as:—

" . . . sundry carved stones; one, a figure, which was evidently a corbel in some structure ornamented with carving of a much earlier date than that of the construction of the bridge."

From " Gleanings from Water Orton ", written by A. Morris in 1935, we gain more specific information about the presence of such stones:—

"When the ' bog ' was about to be filled with rubbish, the Rector of Curdworth (the Rev. L. M. Mitchell, M.A.) entreated the authorities and rescued the Panel of St. Gabriel (together with another stone), once in the Chapel of St. Blaize at the Manor House of Sutton Coldfield, and built into the bridge at Water Orton, C.1550. In 1926, they were removed to the Parish Church of Curdworth."

It is common knowledge that Vesey tried, unsuccessfully, to introduce to Sutton Coldfield the weaving of coarse woollen cloth known as Kersey.* This was part of his overall plan to increase the prosperity of the town, since he would undoubtedly have had his eye on the expanding market. During Tudor times, kerseys, together with lead and tin, were a staple export from England to the Levant states. Fynes Morison, writing at the end of the sixteenth century, recorded that " The English bring to the Turks kersies wrought and dyed, of divers kinds and colours, but they bring little broadcloth, wherewith they are abundantly furnished from Venice." The export of kersies seems to have declined sharply at the beginning of the seventeenth century.

Riland Bedford, in " The Vesey Papers " claims that in those cottages in which weaving was to be carried out, Vesey's foresight went as far as providing one large window to ensure the necessary light for the work. It has also been said that, early in the 19th Century, the remains of a loom were found in one of the Vesey houses, which caused Riland Bedford to add that there was thus:—

* Derived from Kersey in Suffolk.

" at least a prima facie case for supposing that a number of these stone houses were the residences prepared for
the Devonian emigrants, whom Vesey's bounty attracted
from their southern homes to the bleak slopes of Sutton
with the expectation of utilising their skill."

Presumably—since Vesey was always looking after the interests
of his own town-people—the " Devonian emigrants " would
have been there, primarily, to teach Sutton people the trade of
weaving.

Less well known is the claim that Vesey brought the fiddle
and the fiddle-stick from Devon to his home town. Thomas
Fuller in " The Worthies of England ", having retailed this
quaint piece of intelligence, goes on to say that Vesey:—

" . . . brought not the resin therewith to make good
music; and every country is innated with a peculiar genius,
and is left-handed to those trades which are against their
inclination."

The inference to be drawn is, surely, that Sutton's would-be
fiddlers lacked a sense of vocation.

The dissolution of the monasteries during the reign of Henry
VIII led to much pauperism, for the great religious houses, in
addition to keeping many people in employment, also helped
to succour the poor and deprived. Vesey was always alert to
the opportunity of helping his under-privileged fellow-townsmen, and in addition to his other charitable activities, his efforts
during these difficult times also included the protection of
grazing rights for poor tenants' cattle, and ensuring that the
population had a liberal supply of fuel from the woods.

Dr. A. L. Rowse in " Tudor Cornwall " tells us quite a lot
about Vesey, both before and after he became Bishop of Exeter.
Belonging as he did to the official class, he was a good clerical
courtier and a man of accomplished manners and business
talents. He accumulated a mass of preferments by the favour
of Bishop Arundell, Wolsey and the King. In 1503, he became
Canon of Exeter, and Dean from 1509. He also became Dean
of the Chapel Royal and of Windsor, and was necessarily much
about the Court. Of Vesey's later life, Dr. Rowse tells us that:—

" . . . he lived in retirement at his native Sutton Coldfield in great profusion and hospitality, where he lavished
the revenues of the see upon the little town . . . constructing market-place and moot-hall, procuring a charter, granting it his manor, park and chase, rebuilding the aisles of
the church and making himself a magnificent tomb in which
he now lies."

The reason for Vesey featuring in a book about Tudor
Cornwall is that, from the early Middle Ages to 1876, Corn-

wall was part of the diocese of Exeter. Dr. Rowse makes the point that, partly on account of Vesey's liberal spending at Sutton, but still more due to pressure put upon him to grant away the possessions of his see, Exeter, from being one of the wealthiest became one of the poorest of English sees. Fuller, in his " Church History " is more forceful in condemning Vesey on this account:—

> " He robbed his own Cathedral to pay a Parish Church —Sutton, in this county where he was born, whereon he bestowed many benefactions . . . "

Riland Bedford in " Vesey Papers " suggests that Fuller's verdict in this matter might have been reached on the authority of some " irritable Devonian ". In the " Lives of the Bishops of Exeter ", George Oliver asserts that:—

> " It cannot be denied that our obsequious prelate went all the lengths of King Henry VIII in the affair of the divorce of Queen Katharine, of the supremacy and the dissolution of the monasteries. In truth, he was a perfect courtier—a character unsuitable to that of a Christian bishop."

Even so, Dr. Rowse informs us, Vesey is remembered in Cornwall for having enforced the monastic vow of purity in one priory where the brothers were notorious for their incontinency. " No brother," Vesey said, " was to leave the precincts without leave, and then only with a companion; all windows and places by which women might enter or brothers go out were to be closed."

Miss Bracken tells us that neither episcopal duties nor episcopal palaces held Vesey in Devonshire, and in 1527, determining to have a residence at Sutton, he obtained from the King certain parcels of enclosure, called Moor Crofts and Heath Yards. " Here," she says " he built from the ground near the ancient Moat House of his ancestors (Moor Hall Farm), the mansion of Moor Hall." Following Vesey's death the Hall was inherited by his nephew, John Harman. It passed into the hands of the Addyes family in the 17th century, and was later bequeathed to the Hackets who, according to Riland Bedford, were descendants of Bishop Vesey. During the 19th century the Hall was let to a series of tenants, and was demolished in 1903; the present Hall was completed two years later, as the home of the late Colonel Ansell.

In the woods near Moor Hall, there is a lot of old dry walling in the local sandstone—seemingly made with material from the old Hall. There is also a large bear-pit with walls of old sandstone. This was later made into an ornamental water-garden, with various embellishments in a different kind of stone. Apart from Moor Hall Farm, there is at least one other surviving building of historical interest on the estate—Tudor

Cottage, Moor Hall Park, formerly known as Moor Old Lodge. Its principle feature is an octagonal lodge, made of part sandstone footing and part narrow brick, but with a facade of stucco and mock-Tudor facing, effectively disguising its true Tudor origins. Traces of carved sandstone have been found within the grounds of Tudor Cottage, similar to pieces found in the woods at Moor Hall, and there is little doubt that this lodge-house was built contemporaneously with Moor Hall.

The original Hall reflected Vesey's rich and influential position, since he is reputed to have lived there in great opulence, with 150 serving men in scarlet caps and gowns. Dr. Rowse's verdict on Vesey is that he was " . . . generous to a fault, cultured, affable, easy going, in fact a spendthrift, a regular Renaissance prelate ". Riland Bedford (" Vesey Papers ") saw Vesey as being " a man in advance in many respects of the age he lived in, a sound political economist, a liberal-minded generous promoter of education, and an unselfish benefactor to his poorer neighbours." He adds: " At Sutton, I think Vesey ought to have a champion, and I venture to ask for him a better verdict than that which posterity has for the most part bestowed."

It is hardly surprising that Vesey should, at times, have fallen into disrepute through his close association with Henry VIII—an association which may have arisen through the all-powerful position of his friend, Wolsey. One little-known chronicler—Sir Simon Degge—claims that Vesey was responsible for the dissolution of Canwell Monastery, which, he says was " Purchased or otherwise obtained by John Harman, alias Vesey, Bishop of Exon." In view of Vesey's cordial relationship with the King, it is natural that such speculation should arise. Vesey may have been acting as agent for the King, for Dugdale tells us that, following the dissolution of Canwell—in the 17th year of the King's reign (1525)—the Manors of Hill and Little Sutton together with the site of the religious house and other possessions were granted by the King's Letters Patent—dated 20th January, 1526—to Cardinal Wolsey. Soon afterwards, Dugdale tells us, Wolsey conferred them on the Dean and Canons of his College, then called Cardinal College, Oxford.

At a later date the property was bought by Francis Lawley and the stables of the house at Canwell were said to have been built out of the ruins of the monastery. Plott, the Staffordshire topographer, speaks of the house " about which are lovely plantations of trees and walks."

Vesey's most reprehensible public act took place at Exeter, when a young man named Thomas Bennet, M.A., of the University of Cambridge, publicly avowed his religious beliefs. He was charged with heresy, brought before Bishop Vesey in open consistory, and, on being found guilty, was condemned to be burnt at the stake. Miss Bracken tells us that " The sheriff ordered a stake to be erected at Southerhay, but the chamber of Exeter did not allow it, and the terrible scene was enacted at a place called Livery Dole." So it was, she continues that " we see the polished courtier, the amiable philanthropist, the large-minded patriot, compelled by his church, to be the perpetrator of the cruellest of deaths . . . "

In 1528, Vesey was able to perform his best remembered act on behalf of his fellow-townsmen. He obtained a Charter from Henry VIII, placing the Chase and Manor of Sutton Coldfield in the hands of a local body, known as 'the Warden and Society', for the benefit of the inhabitants in perpetuity. Riland Bedford (Vesey Papers) says:—

> " In 1528, he developed his machinery for the aggrandisement of his native place by procuring from the crown a charter of incorporation for it, as a Royal Town, manor and lordship; and obtaining a grant of the remains of the Chase and the park, once the demesne of the Earls of Warwick, and now by their forfeiture of the king."

According to tradition, the association of Vesey with Henry VIII was also instrumental in giving to Sutton Coldfield the Tudor Rose as its emblem. Henry VIII's father, Henry Tudor, Earl of Richmond, and grandson of Owen Tudor, a Welsh knight, had become the first sovereign of the House of Tudor. Not caring greatly for the complicated heraldic devices of mediaeval times, he took for his own emblem a simple rose, whose petals of both red and white, symbolised the reconciliation which took place between the Houses of York and Lancaster at the end of the Wars of the Roses.

While hunting one day in Sutton Park, Henry VIII, accompanied by Bishop Vesey, was subjected to a sudden and quite unexpected charge by a wild boar. Before the animal could harm the king, however, it fell dead with an arrow through its heart. The cry went out for the king's unknown saviour to be brought forward, so that royal gratitude could be shown in some tangible way. Much to the King's surprise the unseen marksman was found to be a young and beautiful woman, and when Henry was told that her family had been dispossessed of their property, he ordered that restitution should be made to them. To the young woman herself he presented the Tudor Rose, his family emblem, which he said should henceforth also be the emblem of Sutton Coldfield—the girl's native town.

This legend accounts for the old armorial device of Sutton Coldfield bearing the Tudor Rose upon one of its two angled shields. It was not until 1935, however, that the town received a coat of arms which was authenticated by the College of Heralds.

As a direct consequence of Vesey's charter, we, in Sutton Coldfield still enjoy all the advantages of 2,400 acres of parkland at our own doorsteps. The Charter also saw the end of feudal tenure in Sutton, since fixed rents took the place of the old systems of service to the lord of the manor.

Vesey nominated his brother-in-law, William Gybons, or Gibbons, of New Hall as first Warden and, in accordance with the Charter, the inhabitants were provided with a moot hall, or house of assembly, for the holding of courts-leet, elections and other meetings. Provision was also made for the Warden to arrange an election to choose 24 inhabitants who, with the Warden, were to form the Society for the government of the town.

Bishop Vesey died at Moor Hall in 1555, at a very advanced age. Riland Bedford tells us:—

> " The monument erected to his memory in Sutton Church is in many ways a very interesting one, even passing by the claims it has on the reverential gratitude of sucessive generations of his townsmen. For it is the only monumental effigy of a Bishop in Warwickshire. The figure represents him vested in the Alb, Dalmatic, and Chesible, with the Mitre on his head, and holding the Crozier, the crook of which is of late date. He is represented in the meridian of life . . . "

In 1875, Sutton Coldfield Corporation decided to restore the Vesey monument. The work so stimulated the curiosity of the people responsible that they decided to see if the Bishop's remains were really interred beneath the monumental stone. The tomb was opened—we are told—with ' the most reverential respect ', in the presence of, amongst others, the Warden, the Rector, the Corporation Surveyor and an Architectural Sculptor. Inside they found the upper part of the skull of what had been a very full, round head, an under jaw-bone, with only two teeth in it, showing evidence of extreme age, a piece of a thigh-bone, part of an arm bone and other bone fragments. No episcopal vestments or personal adornments, which in Vesey's day were usually buried with the bodies of distinguished persons, were found. It was evident that the tomb had been opened before, and in " Aris's Birmingham Gazette " for 28th April, 1875, an interesting theory was propounded:—

> " It is thought by some that the recumbent effigy of the bishop over the tomb is not of the date of the prelate's death, but in all probability had been placed there at a time when it is surmised the tomb had been previously opened, probably a little over a century ago. There is, we may state, a rumour, which competent authorities regard as being well founded, to the effect that when the tomb was opened on the former occasion the form of the deceased prelate was distinctly traceable, but that when exposed to the air the remains crumbled to dust, and the recumbent

figure now in the chancel was made to imitate as nearly as possible the form as it then appeared."

The bishop's bones were reinterred, and a parchment recording the occasion, signed by those present, was enclosed within the tomb.

The verdict of history must be that Vesey, by "swimming with the tide" and accepting Henry VIII's claim to being head of the Church, was able to gain wealth and favour, both of which he turned to the advantage of his home town. In the words of Midgley ("Sutton Coldfield Town and Chase "):—

"Vesey found Sutton a decayed village, he left it a prosperous little country town."

or, in a phrase attributed to an unknown Devonian:—

"He robbed his see to enrich a beggarly village."

The town's status and administration was certainly greatly enhanced by the provisions of the Charter, and its ideas on local government were far ahead of its time. The Warden was appointed as clerk to the Markets and Fairs, Coroner, Weights and Measures Officer and Treasurer. He was empowered to buy land, to appoint a person learned in the law to be Steward of the Corporation, to hold Courts and to administer profits from the land for the benefit of the poor. Any person willing to build and inhabit a house was allowed to enclose 60 acres of contiguous waste-land. This administrative system ensured Sutton's continued progress and growth for almost three and a half centuries.

During the course of its quite considerable recorded history, Sutton Coldfield has been written about and commented upon by various writers. Among the historians, antiquarians and travellers who have passed this way, Sir William Dugdale, author of "Antiquities of Warwickshire", is often thought to be our earliest source of knowledge. In fact, he was preceded, a century earlier, by John Leland who, after being appointed chaplain to Henry VIII, was given the title of "King's Antiquary". This post, which was apparently created especially for Leland, enabled him to follow his own bent and to travel all over England in pursuit of antiquarian lore. His energy was directed towards preserving the ancient church manuscripts, which were then at risk of being lost due to the dissolution of the monasteries, and we are told "he wandered from place to place, wherever he thought to meet with the footsteps of Roman, Saxon or Dane."

For six years Leland roamed the countryside, collecting "a whole world of things, very memorable", and he then spent the rest of his life trying to classify this mass of material. Much of his life's work is contained in his "Itinerary", and in it we

The old Cup Inn was an attractive one-storied wayside inn where, in season, they had dancing on the green.

Photograph: W. Wort

learn how his wide-ranging travels brought him into Birmingham from the south, by way of Deritend. The journey to Sutton took him to Salford Bridge and up Gravelly Hill, which he described as being: " . . by sandy grownde, betar woodyd then fertile of whete . . . there is some rye, barley and ots . . . the soyle is sandy and dry, and good for conyes " (rabbits). Of Sutton Coldfield itself, John Leland recalled that in the Earl of Warwick's time it had a " market privelegyd ", but after the Earl's death " . . . the towne of Southton standynge in a baren soyle fell dayly to decay and the market was clene forsaken." After speaking of Vesey's various acts to assist his fellow-townsmen, Leland, as if to emphasise the barrenness of the soil makes passing references to " . . . good frewte trees, set there by the byshope, grown with some difficultie."

When one of the Peddimore Ardens died without issue, all his rights accrued to his brother, Sir Henry Arden, the founder of Park Hall in Castle Bromwich. From this time, Peddimore declined in importance, and it is recorded by Camden (1551-1623), the antiquary, who was a contemporary of Shakespeare, that " All is level with the ground, and the site not discernible." The fact that the house was in a state of decline at that time is consistent with the present house at Peddimore having being built in 1659. That the site was "not discernible", however, is hard to accept, particularly in view of the presence of a double-moat to mark the spot. It is also evident that the present house has been built on to the foundations of an earlier building.

Shakespeare, who was no stranger to travel and who was known to be proud of his mother's well-born relatives, would hardly have failed to visit Park Hall. It is also likely that he would have continued the short distance to Peddimore, to see the scene of his family's former glory. Shakespeare, too, was reputed to be a friend of Edward Pudsey, who lived at Langley, the next house to the north of Peddimore, which would be another reason for visiting the district.

From either Peddimore or Langley, it would have been no great distance for Shakespeare, afoot or on horse-back, to continue on to Sutton. When he put into the mouth of Falstaff the words:

> Bardolph, get thee before to Coventry. Fill me a bottle of sack: our soldiers shall march through; we'll to Sutton Cofil tonight. (Henry IV, Part I, Act IV, Scene 2.)

we can safely assume that the name had not been picked at random, but that he was quite familiar with the place and the way to it from the London—Shrewsbury road, through Coles-hill. From Walmley he would have descended the hill in Wylde Green Lane, crossed the ford at the ford-keeper's cottage, built by Vesey, and—by way of Old Coles Lane—reached the little town of half-timbered houses, clustering around the church on the hill.

Falstaff's visit to Sutton Coldfield is commemorated in verse in "Tales of Sutton Town and Chase, with other Tales, and some sketches, Collected by T.A.U. and now imprinted for the first time" (1904). Under the title "Mine Host's Story", it begins:

> A portly knight, long years ago
> To Sutton Coldfield came,
> A valiant soldier he I trow,
> John Falstaff was his name.

The tale—claimed by the author to be based on the 'best local tradition' and on conversations with 'the oldest inhabitant'—tells how the fat warrior, Falstaff, with his men, all knaves intent upon not paying the landlord for their ale and board, arrived at a Sutton inn. The alewife had her suspicions about Falstaff:

> A drunken oaf, she said he was,
> A slither-pudding too
> Only soldiering because
> He nothing else could do.

The next morning, Falstaff—impecunious after claiming to have been robbed by his missing Corporal, Bardolph, was offered the loan of a horse by the credulous landlord to enable him to go in pursuit. This generous offer was accepted by Falstaff, who promised to return the horse and pay for his accommodation.

> But I've not seen my horse again
> Nor yet my portly knight.

lamented the inn-keeper and—worst of all—every time he afterwards bickered with his wife, she would remind him of his folly with an appropriate " I told you so." According to tradition, the inn was on the site of the present " Three Tuns."

Shakespeare's slender associations with the district are hardly the basis of a literary reputation for Sutton Coldfield. A more positive connection is with Shakespeare's near-contemporary, Robert Burton, author of " The Anatomy of Melancholy ", one of the most curious books in the English language. Though born in Leicestershire, Burton spent a part of his boyhood in Sutton Coldfield, and in his famous book he quotes Camden as having described Sutton as being " in a bad and barren situation." However, he defends the town of his adoption by adding that it is " in an excellent air, and full of all manner of pleasures." He does not enumerate the pleasures of being a resident of Sutton Coldfield in the late 16th century, but since it was once said of him that he lived " a silent, sedentary, solitary life ", it is doubtful whether his early pleasures would have been other than of an intellectual kind, appropriate to the future author of a book renowned for its quaint scholarship.

The school which Burton attended was the grammar-school founded by Bishop Vesey in 1541, and situated near the top of Trinity Hill, or Blind Lane, as it was then called. It was not until 1728 that this building was replaced by a new school in Lichfield Road.

Despite his early connection with Sutton, Robert Burton spent much of his mature life at Oxford, where he became a student of Christ Church. There, it is said, in busying himself incessantly with the subject of melancholy in all its aspects, he attempted with varying degrees of success to rid his own mind of melancholy thoughts. " The Anatomy of Melancholy " was first printed in 1621, and was so successful that it made a fortune—for its publisher—and passed rapidly through several large editions.

Robert Burton died in 1639, but through the pages of his famous book he lived on to influence later writers. Even the great Doctor Johnson came under its spell, for he declared that it was the only book " . . . that ever took me out of bed two hours sooner than I wished to rise."

In " A Short History of English Literature ", Ifor Evans (now Lord Evans) describes how Burton " explored the human mind with the aid of all the learning of the classical world. He was a marauding scholar, who found his prizes all equally worthwhile, and all equally relevant to the great purpose which he had in hand. He examined the disease of melancholy, Hamlet's disease, which was to that period what neuroses have been to the twentieth century. Few volumes in English are so full of curiosities, and this eccentric writer has given pleasure to discerning minds in all the centuries since his death."

CHAPTER IV

The parish registers—Sir Wm. Dugdale—the Civil War—the Commonwealth and Restoration—Travel and the importance of the Chester Road—Dr. Sacheverell—John Wyatt—The eighteenth century scene.

IN 1538, Thomas Cromwell, minister to Henry VIII, ordered every parish to acquire a 'sure coffer' for the safe keeping of the recently instituted parish registers. These were to contain the records of all baptisms, marriages and burials within each parish. Sutton Coldfield seems to have been tardy in starting its parish register, for the first known one was commenced in 1603, and in the following 20 years there were 645 baptisms and 501 burials.

From the pages of the parish registers we glean many curious items. In 1668, for instance:

"Buryed Elionor Clibery, widdy; alsoe William Clibery, sonn of the sd Elionor; was buryed the same 4th day of June. Both brought to their graves together (who were both of ym drowned in a pytt in goeinge into a pytt to ffetch out a gosling, as it was credibiely reported)."

In 1677:

"Buried the wife of John Norris, of Four Oaks, being the sixth wife."

and in 1678:

"Married John Norris unto ffelis Dibble, she being the seventh wife which he hath hadd."

1728:

"Buried Thomas Eastham, a stranger, found murdered at the upper end of Holly Lane, by Edward Powers, who was gibbeted on Little Sutton Common."

Baptisms, marriages and burials were the essential substance of the parish registers, but sometimes something quite unprecedented would occur, which would prompt the clerk to record it for posterity. In 1668, for instance, Sutton experienced the worst flooding in its history when, following a great storm, Wyndley Pool broke its banks, causing considerable damage and loss in the town. The event is recorded in the parish register:

"There was a great fflood of water, so great here at Sutton pools, that it ffloed over the stone wall at the further end of the dam, by reason of a suden Rayne, which did breake downe Wynly-poole Dam, and alsoe Brass bridg pool dam. July 24."

Following upon this flooding, Riland Bedford tells us, the town pools were drained and turned into pasture, but the stone dam remained as the highway between Sutton and Birmingham.

The ever-present spectre of poverty in past centuries is reflected throughout the annals of Sutton Coldfield's parish registers, which are strewn with such references as the burial of " a poor man, a stranger ", " a widow pauper ", " a poor traveller's child ", " a poor travelling man ", " a poor travelling woman ", " a poor child from the workhouse ", " a spinster pauper " and many entries with the one descriptive word " pauper ".

The original parish registers for Sutton Coldfield from 1603 to 1924 are held by the Warwick County Record Office at the Shire Hall, Warwick (Telephone No. 0926-43431). Photostat copies of the registers from 1603 to 1747 are available at the Birmingham Reference Library.

Despite the cataclysmic disturbances of the twentieth century, civil war—in England, at any rate—has not been one of them. It is therefore difficult to project the mind back to the time of the great struggle between King and Parliament, over 300 years ago. Turbulent times often produce a strange duality of personality, and men of quiet pursuits find themselves caught in a vortex of activity. Such was William Dugdale, county historian and author of " The Antiquities of Warwickshire ", who was born at Shustoke, near Coleshill, in 1605. He received his early education from the curate of Nether Whitacre before going to school in Coventry. He returned home to study law and history under his father, a man of some academic distinction, and by the time he was 17, he was married. Early in life he established his reputation as · an antiquarian and, following the death of his father, he bought Blythe Hall, Coleshill, which suggests that he must have inherited considerable wealth. It was, perhaps, during his early sojourn there that his monumental work on Warwickshire first began to formulate in his mind, although it was not published until 1656. His intimate knowledge of the county must have been the consequence of many a fact-finding trip into scattered parishes, and we know from his writing that he was on terms of familiarity, not only with places the size of Sutton Coldfield, but also with the tiniest hamlets.

When the civil war came, Dugdale, who had been made pursuivant of arms, was commanded by King Charles I to fulfil the duties arising out of that appointment. In August, 1642, he was sent by the King to demand the surrender of Warwick Castle, held by the Parliamentarians under Sir Edward Peto. Sir Edward, breathing defiance, hung his banner over the battlements, with a winding sheet suspended from one corner and a bible from the other, to demonstrate that he did not fear death, and placed his trust in God. Dugdale was forced to retire without having taken Warwick Castle.

The following month he was present at an event which, apart from being the first occasion on which blood was shed in the Civil War, was also the only action of the war to take place in the neighbourhood of Sutton Coldfield. Dugdale had been appointed as guide to Sir Richard Willys, who took two troops of horse and one of dragoons to Kenilworth to arrange the evacuation of the castle there. The mission having been accomplished, they were on their way to Nottingham when intercepted by a force from the disaffected City of Coventry. On the little hillock beside Curdworth Church, to quote Dugdale's words:

> " They chardged these Rebells (tho' five to one in number) so stoutly that they put them to the rout and tooke some of them prisoners, whom they brought that night to Tamworth."

Sutton, it seems, had Puritanical leanings. The High Steward of the Corporation was the Earl of Essex, commander-in-chief of the Parliamentarians at the beginning of the war: the Pudseys of Langley played an active part in the cause of the Roundheads, and the Rector of Sutton, Anthony Burges, was said to be " a Puritan divine of considerable repute " (Midgley). Despite these facts, however, the town successfully avoided any direct participation in the struggle, and the inhabitants made no great display of their sympathies which were, in the main, of a luke-warm and half-hearted nature. Anthony Burges, on the near approach of the Royalist army in 1642, found it necessary to leave the district. He went, first, to Coventry, then, later, to London, but as the Civil War progressed to the advantage of the parliamentary party, he soon returned to Sutton and resumed his ministry until 1662.

King Charles' presence in the district in 1642 is well-authenticated. He was not without support in the area, and one of his most loyal subjects was Sir Thomas Holte of Aston Hall. It was, in fact, after staying at Aston Hall that the king came to Barr Common (as it then was), to address a gathering of his supporters. The hillock upon which he stood was, according to tradition, thrown up by soldiers with spades, so that he could stand above the people he was addressing. This fits in with the theory that the king was a short man, possibly no more than 5′ 2″. The hillock which gave Kingstanding its name can still be seen at the top of the hill in Kingstanding Road, on the left-hand side when travelling towards the Parson and Clerk.

There is a story, dating back to the enclosure of the common in the early 19th century that the tenant of a nearby farm sent his men to level the site. Lord Calthorpe of Perry Hall, when he heard of this intention, came galloping up on horseback, just in time to prevent its happening. To ensure that there should be no future risk to the site, he planted it with trees and fenced it round. The fencing has only very recently been removed.

In 1643, Prince Rupert, nephew of the king, and known as "the mad cavalier" because of his fearlessness in battle, came to punish Birmingham for supplying arms to the King's enemies. After defeating its defenders at Camp Hill and pillaging and burning the town, Prince Rupert and his troops passed, without incident, through Sutton Coldfield. The governors of King Edward VI's School in Birmingham had, seemingly, anticipated the events of 1643, for it is recorded that they sent the marble bust of that monarch to Sutton Coldfield during the Civil War, to be kept in safety by the Warden, from whom they later received it back for reinstatement at the school.

Later in 1643 it is claimed that Cromwell stayed at the "Three Tuns" in Sutton, but this is not well authenticated. Following the defeat by Cromwell of the Royalist army under the Duke of Hamilton at Preston in 1648, many Scots prisoners were driven on a terrible journey south to London, the first stage of their transportation to slavery in the American colonies. They suffered great hardship and privation, and we are told that those who passed through Sutton Coldfield were reduced by hunger to devouring cabbage stalks and carrot tops.

On 30th January, 1649, King Charles I died on the scaffold in Whitehall, an event which G. M. Trevelyan in "England under the Stuarts" said: "outraged beyond hope of reconciliation the two parties in the State who were strong in numbers and in conservative tradition, the Presbyterians and the Cavaliers; and it alienated the great mass of men who had no party at all."

During the Commonwealth and Restoration periods, according to Midgley, Sutton became a Nonconformist stronghold, and he mentions, among other Puritans, John Ray, F.R.S., the origial proposer of the Linnaean system of classification for naturalists. Ray, sometimes called "the father of English natural history", was a blacksmith's son from Essex, and a Fellow of Trinity College, Cambridge. He worked in collaboration with Francis Willoughby, the naturalist son of Sir Francis and Lady Cassandra Willoughby of Middleton Hall.

Ray and Willoughby travelled widely during the years 1662-1666, studying botany and zoology. They intended making a new system of classification of the animal and vegetable kingdoms, but Willoughby's death at the age of 36 in 1672 prevented his full participation in the project. However, the two men did write a paper on the motion of sap in trees, based on experiments made in the grounds of Middleton Hall. The enquiry seems to have been made with a view to establishing whether the circulation of the blood in human beings—newly discovered by William Harvey—had a parallel in the world of trees.

Ray was elected a Fellow of the Royal Society in 1667, and following upon his friend's death, he stayed on at Middleton for a while helping with the education of Willoughby's children and preparing for the press what was virtually the first illustrated bird-book ever to appear—Willoughby's " Ornithology."

The Commonwealth period was followed by the Restoration, which brought a general lessening of restrictions throughout the country, and Charles II's easy good humour made him —for a time at least—a great favourite with a population wearied by the demands of Puritanism. The ale flowed, playhouses reopened, maypoles reappeared on village greens up and down the land, and a miller at Charlton in Kent set fire to his windmill as a bonfire to celebrate the King's return. According to Riland Bedford (" Vesey Papers "), the Cromwell regime had interferred considerably with local rights and privileges. This may have been a factor in Sutton's veering away from the Puritan cause at the time of the Restoration.

King Charles had expensive tastes and many mistresses, and he was constantly on the look-out for ways of raising money. At this time, Sutton Coldfield—although it had only 300 houses —was increasing in prosperity—a fact that did not go unnoticed by the King. He had devised a scheme for extracting money from towns with Royal Charters by graciously renewing them—at a price—and Sutton Coldfield received a new Charter from him in 1662.

Not only did this Charter authorise the Warden to carry a white staff, which, as Riland Bedford tells us, signified that he exercised within his own jurisdiction the full authority of a sheriff, but it also provided for the appointment by and from the Corporation of " two honest and discreet men of the Society ", to be called " Capital Burgesses ". These men were to assist the Warden in the administration of justice in all cases except those of life and limb. George Pudsey and his son, Henry, were the first to be nominated to hold this office.

The person thought to be responsible for this administrative change was Sir Richard Newdigate, Member of Parliament for Tamworth, Chief Justice under the Commonwealth, and a Sergeant-at-Law at the Restoration. Riland Bedford says:

> " We may, I think, safely surmise that Sir Richard Newdigate held the appointment of Steward of the Manor, to preside at the Court-leets and View of Frank-pledge, and the Court of Record to sit every Monday to determine all suits, complaints, trespasses, debts, covenants, etc., as prescribed by the first Charter."

Judge Newdigate, who died in 1678, is reputed to have given much valuable advice to Sutton people, who—Riland Bedford tells us—had some impracticable ideas, including " the singular claim to restrain the town of Birmingham from holding a market on Monday, lest it should interfere injuriously with the chartered market at Sutton."

Another of Charles II's fund-raising activities was that of dispensing knighthoods to those who were willing to pay for the privilege. One recipient was William Wilson of Sutton Cold-field, an architect and stonemason, believed to have studied under Sir Christopher Wren. He built both Peddimore Hall and the old Rectory (demolished in 1936).

The new house built by Wilson at Peddimore in 1659 was occupied by William Wood, a prominent Royalist and Warden of the Corporation in 1662 and 1676. With memories of the Civil War still fresh, a site surrounded by a double moat may well have appealed to him, especially as his neighbours, the Pudseys of Langley Hall, had played an active part for Parlia-ment. Over the door of Peddimore Hall, inscribed in stone, are the words: " DEVS NOSTER REFVGIVM " (God is our Refuge)—a sentiment which, as Chattock comments, sounds rather like " Fear God and keep your powder dry!".

William Wilson, as a young, handsome, but impecunious stonemason, married Jane, the rich widow of the last of the Pudseys, and it was she, apparently, who—despite her first husband's opposition to the Royalist cause—induced Charles II to bestow a knighthood on her second, talented husband. When the King asked what estate Wilson had, he replied that his lady had £800 per annum, but he himself only had £3.

In marrying the Pudsey widow, Wilson was moving ' outside his station ', and Jane's relatives were quick to deplore her taste in leaving moated Langley Hall to marry a ' mere stonemason '. His answer was to build his own ' Moat House '—in Lichfield Road—to prove that such grandeur was not beyond his means. This house, which still survives, retained its moat until 1860, prior to which time the front door was approached over a stone bridge. Riland Bedford comments that Moat House was: " built in the style compounded of Inigo Jones and the Dutch taste of King William's day, which suits so well the red brick material of the Midland counties." (" Three Hundred Years of a Family Living.")

The Langley Hall estate passed to Anne, the younger of Jane Pudsey's two daughters, who married William Jesson, son of Sir William Jesson of Coventry. Her elder daughter married an Irish peer, Lord Ffolliot, who was responsible for the build-ing of Four Oaks Hall, which was designed by Wilson himself.

When his wife died, Sir William Wilson, in contempt of his title, returned to work with his mason's tools, and—being well regarded in the district—found himself fully employed. It was

Wilson who built Nottingham Castle, and he was also appointed by the Crown Commissioners to reconstruct St. Mary's Church, Warwick, which was destroyed by fire in 1694. Other examples of his work are the Pudsey monument in Sutton Coldfield Church and the large sandstone figure of Charles II at Lichfield Cathedral, which Riland Bedford refers to as a "tasteless image."

Although Lord and Lady Ffolliot thought it no disgrace to have a mason for a father-in-law, the Jessons were snobs, and when, in old age, Wilson made it known that he wished to be buried with his wife in the Pudsey vault inside the church, they raised objections. He therefore bought a plot of land outside the church, but adjoining the Pudsey vault. "There will only be a single stone wall betwixt us, and as I am a stonemason, there will be no kind of labour or difficulty in cutting my road through the wall to my old bedfellow," was Sir William's comment on a very human situation. Posterity has done something to redress the balance, for, in 1874, the clergy vestry was built over Sir William Wilson's grave, so that his remains are now *inside* the church, and his restored monument has been fitted to the vestry wall, immediately behind the Pudsey monument in the north wall of the church.

The connection of the Sacheverell family with New Hall, Sutton Coldfield, is well known. Doctor Henry Sacheverell, D.D.,

Four Oaks Hall, built around the end of the 17th century, was designed by Sir William Wilson for Lord Ffolliot, an Irish peer. The picture shows the Hall after alterations by Simon Luttrell. It was demolished in 1898.

namesake, associate but not a relative, is still remembered, less as an eminent divine, than as a cleric who used the pulpit as a means of stirring up religious intolerance and political unrest. In 1709, while he was rector of St. Saviour's, Southwark, he preached a sermon in St. Paul's, in the presence of the lord mayor and aldermen of London. Combined in his oration, was a call for the punishment of dissenters—urging all good citizens to rally round the church, which he declared to be " in danger " —and a personal attack on Lord Godolphin, the Whig Prime Minister. Apparently, the lord mayor of London was in sympathy with Sacheverell's views, and urged him to have the sermon committed to print. This Sacheverell did, which prompted the government to charge him with sedition.

The trial of Dr. Sacheverell lasted for three weeks, and was attended daily by Queen Anne, who was brought in her sedan-chair to lend support to the Doctor. By-standers shouted: " God Bless the Queen and Doctor Sacheverell!" Alarm, confusion and a state of near-riot prevailed in the capital, and several dissenting chapels were burned down by the mob to show support for orthodoxy and zeal.

Sacheverell was found guilty of " a malicious, scandalous and seditious libel ", and as punishment, he was forbidden to preach for three years. The offending sermon was ordered to be burned by the public hangman. The lightness of the punishment was regarded as a political triumph for the Tories, and a moral victory for Henry Sacheverell who, soon after the trial, took up residence at New Hall. On 20th October, 1714—the Sunday before the Coronation of George I—Sacheverell preached at Sutton Coldfield Parish Church when, according to Riland Bedford, his congregation was augmented by some 200 Birmingham Jacobites.

In " Tales of Sutton Town and Chase ", there is a long poem beginning:

> Thou hast summoned me Sacheverell,
> Perforce I must obey,
> And render thee the service due,
> For which thy soul shalt pay.

The one summoned is the Devil, and the ensuing dialogue reveals Sacheverell's motives:

> I've called thee from thy haunts below
> To help me in my quest,
> To find of all the gunpowders
> The deadliest and best.

The poem, is must be assumed, was written by one of Dr. Sacheverell's many enemies, and its significance may lie in the fact that the offending and inflammatory sermon in St. Paul's had been delivered on 5th November.

A number of consequences have been attributed to the trial of Dr. Sacheverell—dissenters suffered; support for the Church of England strengthened; the Whig ministry fell; Marlborough was eclipsed; and the Tories enjoyed a brief return to power.

During the early part of the eighteenth century, the water of Sutton Park's streams was harnessed for industrial purposes. Although James Watt's static steam-engine had not yet revolutionised manufacturing methods, Sutton still made considerable industrial progress. Water, not steam, was to provide the key to its production of blades and gun-barrels, button-polishing, the grinding of knives, bayonets, and axes and the manufacture of spades and spade-handles.

One man, closely associated with this era of the town's development, was John Wyatt who was born at Weeford in 1700. Nothing is known of his technical education, or the development of his engineering skill, but the increase of local industrialisation may have made him aware of the scope for his developing talent. At 30 he invented a machine for cutting files, which was taken up by a gunsmith named Richard Heeley. This project necessitated Wyatt being constantly in Birmingham. But despite the difficulty of travel at that time, it seems he continued to live at Sutton Coldfield.

He became interested in the problems of the weavers, who were then experiencing difficulties in obtaining for their looms an adequate supply of thread from the spinners. He determined to dispense with the hand-wheel by employing a pair of rollers for delivering, at any required speed, a sliver of cotton to the bobbin and fly-spindle. This idea, in a more developed form, was to bring success and fame to Richard Arkwright, but for Wyatt, the concept was a source of many trials and tribulations.

His spinning machine was designed with some help from a man named Lewis Paul. In 1733 he made a working-model of this device at Sutton Coldfield which, in his own words, he tried out: "in a pleasing but trembling suspense." According to contemporary records, this experiment was carried out in 'a small building' in the town, but Mr. T. Porter, the former Borough Engineer and Surveyor, suggests that it took place at Powells Pool Mill which, he claims, was erected by Wyatt for the purpose of spinning cotton.

Already, Wyatt was dogged by shortage of money, and as a consequence, all the expenses of developing the cotton-spinning project were borne by Lewis Paul who, in 1737, moved into a fashionable house in the Old Square, Birmingham. The following year, Paul took out a patent for the invention in his own name, and poor Wyatt, now a mere employee of Paul, witnessed the specification. In spite of Wyatt's loss of the patent rights of the machine, his interest in its improvement remained unabated.

During his long and arduous efforts in this direction, he underwent great privation, even having to pawn his clothes.

In 1741, having probably left Sutton, Wyatt installed 50 spindles in a warehouse at the Upper Priory, Birmingham, where two asses were employed as " prime movers " for the machinery. His efforts were all in vain, and being weighed down by debt, he was finally declared bankrupt. His spindles were sold to help pay off his creditors, and he was committed to prison in the Fleet—the notorious debtors' gaol, which stood in Farringdon Street, London. Even here, Wyatt's inventive spirit was unquelled, and during his imprisonment, he was working on plans for a weighing machine, which was later to prove successful, and which brought him employment at Matthew Boulton's world famous Soho Foundry.

In the Weights and Measures Office, Birmingham, there are two working models of this weighing machine with compound levers, which was invented and made by Wyatt. The original was erected in Snow Hill for the Overseers of the Poor, and was removed in 1851 because it had by then become an obstruction to passing traffic. John Wyatt's declining years were spent at No. 7, Snow Hill, Birmingham. He died in 1766, and both Matthew Boulton and John Baskerville, the printer, attended his funeral, when it is recorded that Baskerville wore a gold-laced coat " as a protest against superstitious custom." The grave of John Wyatt and of his wife, Marabella, was, until recently, to be seen in St. Philip's Churchyard, Birmingham, but in Sutton, no commemorative stone has been raised in honour of his frustrated genius.

The presence of mills in Sutton was no innovation, for in medieval times there was a windmill on Maney Hill and the site of a watermill is commemorated by the name of Mill Street. It seems that spades and other agricultural implements had for long been made in and around Sutton, and consequently a number of mills were built for this and other trades during the eighteenth century. The mill built at Powells Pool, possibly used initially by John Wyatt for spinning cotton, was soon given over to spade making, and the presence of many mature ash trees in the Boldmere and New Oscott districts may be due to the fact that they were cultivated for their hard wood, which was used for making spade-handles. It has also been claimed that the very first all-steel garden-fork was made here. Although Powell's Mill was always known as ' the old Spade Mill ', it was, during its later working life, used to roll steel for pen-making. It eventually fell into disuse, and by the early nineteen 'thirties was in such a bad state of repair that a part of the roof gave way. It was demolished in 1936.

During the seventeenth century some of Sutton's manor pools had been drained and converted into rich meadow land, but a century later, with the onset of the Industrial Revolution,

Longmoor Pool was made in 1735. The mill was once used for producing buttons and, later, for milling flour.

mill-pools became a pressing necessity for manufacturing purposes. Both Blackroot and Longmoor Pools were made in the eighteenth century, the waters of Blackroot being used to operate a leather-mill, while Longmoor was the site of a button-mill. The name Blackroot derives from a black root or stump of an oak tree, used for tethering boats, which once stood on a mound in the middle of the pool; it was also known as Perkin's Pool, from the name of a man who rented it. There was another mill at Park House, Sutton Park, which was once called Blade Mill and, later, Brown's Mill, from the name of an occupant; at Holland Pool there was, from the middle of the eighteenth century, a mill for grinding gun-barrels. Longmoor Pool was made in 1735 by John Riland, John Gibbons and William Rawlins, when an agreement between Gibbons and Rawlins stated that Rawlins should "make a good and substantial dam of turf and gravel for a pool at Longmoor Brook in Sutton Park, to be completed for the sum of seven pounds."

When Miss Bracken wrote her "History of the Forest and Chase of Sutton Coldfield" in 1860, she was able to record that there were still six mills operating in the area without the assistance of steam-power: Longmoor; Powell's; Wyndley; Holland; New Hall and Hill Hook. She adds that others formerly existed "of which the most important has only recently been removed." This is probably a reference to Penns Mill which, from about the middle of the eighteenth century, was operated by the Webster family for drawing wire. Walmley, at this time, was an obscure hamlet on the southern edge of the parish of Sutton Coldfield—a place where several roads met, with a few houses near their intersection. Despite the sparse population, the Websters were able to recruit sufficient labour to create a flourishing business at Penns, in addition to which they also acquired Plants Mill and forge at Minworth; a wire-mill at Perry Barr and another forge at Hints, Sutton Coldfield.

Probably the most pressing industrial problem in the eighteenth century was that of transportation. The Websters' pig-iron was brought from the Forest of Dean and had to be handled three times in transit. It was bought at Chepstow and conveyed by barrow, by river and by wagon to its destination. The Birmingham—Fazeley Canal, built by John Smeaton in 1783, was a boon, for it actually passed beside the forge at Minworth and, no doubt, did much to ameliorate the firm's transport problems. To sustain the output of Penns Mill, a lake, or mill pond, was made to increase the power supply of the stream. This was done over a period of several years with spade and barrow by the mill employees themselves.

In the nineteenth century, Joseph Webster joined forces with James Horsfall, who had achieved success at the Crystal Palace Exhibition in 1851 with a high-tensile piano-wire which he had developed. Webster had an established business with world-wide connections, while Horsfall had patents for his inventions and personal qualities to lead him to success. The merger between the two men was a logical and mutually satisfactory outcome of the situation, and Webster & Horsfall, Wire Drawers—now of Hay Mills, Birmingham—has survived to this day. The story of the firm is told at some length in " The Iron Masters of Penns " by John Horsfall (1972).

In 1859, production at Penns was discontinued and on 21st November of that year the water-wheel of the mill turned for the last time. Considerable hardship must have been caused by the closure and during 1860 the population of Walmley dropped by 100. Presumably, however, some of those employees thrown out of work at Penns were absorbed at Hay Mills.

Not everyone favoured eighteenth century ' progress '. The anonymous author of " The History of Sutton Coldfield " (1762), signing himself " an impartial hand ", complained that:

> " Vast quantities of timber have been sold and disposed of and many of the valleys which are by far the most valuable part of the waste land have been granted away by the body corporate to several of their own Aldermen and members for the making of pools and other purposes."

This seems to have been a legitimate complaint, for although a Court injunction had been made in 1675, ruling that the enclosure of the park and commons and the felling of timber without the consent of the freeholders was contrary to the letters patent of Henry VIII, this had been conveniently forgotten. Further proceedings were brought in the Court of Chancery towards the end of the eighteenth century, when the Corporation was again restrained from cutting down timber without the Court's sanction.

We are indebted to this " impartial hand " for many snippets of information about Sutton two centuries ago. Provisions in the town, he asserts, were at least ten-per-cent dearer than at neighbouring market towns. Townspeople here were enjoying the taste of sea-fish for the first time, made possible by the improved state of the roads, following the introduction of the stage-coach. Deliveries were three times weekly, and with the fish came what must then have been a dietary novelty, the lobster: price a shilling a pound.

We learn from the same authority that " No place formerly was more noted for hard drinking than Sutton: scarce a night happen'd but most of the better sort of people assembled together, either at the public, or some of their own private houses, to spend the evening, which was generally done in a very jovial manner . . . the only ambition was, who had the best tap of ale, and too often who could drink of it longest . . . " We know that there was a certain amount of tippling in high places. In 1697, for instance, the Corporation granted to William Jesson of Langley Hall the right to add to Lindridge Pool and to make a dam there, the rent for which was three shillings and six bottles of wine to the Warden.

It is recorded that in the mid-eighteenth century a Deputy Steward and Clerk to the Corporation, so mixed business with pleasure that:

> " Certain parchments and other archives of the Corporation were lost by the corrosion of droppings of port wine from bottles which he kept for his refreshment in the same coffer with these ancient documents."

According to a paper by Riland Bedford on " The Municipal Manor ", an article appeared in " The Times ", referring to this " sad blight to the antiquarian hopes of the present generation " caused by the Oporto stains. The article was written by Robert Lowe—later Lord Sherbrooke—who held office both as Chancellor of the Exchequer and Home Secretary. Lowe was a friend of Joseph Webster of Penns, from whom he heard the tale when on a visit to Sutton, " and hence the selection of our borough by the future Chancellor of the Exchequer " says Riland Bedford " as a frightful example of how not to do it." He adds: " The grievous truth that very few documents are in existence must be admitted, however and whenever the destruction of the missing ones was effected."

The curiosities of the Park, " an impartial hand " tells us, included black game and wild horses. Rowton's Well, though largely disregarded by local people, attracted strangers, who came to drink and bathe there. The salts in the water, it was claimed, had been known to cure some inveterate cutaneous and chronic diseases which had long baffled the best efforts of medicine. The treatment was observed to succeed best in children and " in thin and lean subjects." An added attraction in one of the woods was a kind of white sand which was found to contain a considerable portion of silver, " . . . even sufficient to defray the expense of collecting and working it."

Doctor Samuel Johnson's observation that " the paucity of human pleasures is illustrated by the fact that hunting should be reckoned as one of them " was, obviously, not appreciated by his contemporaries at Sutton. Both hunting and shooting were the constant preoccupations of the well-to-do in these parts, and from the august pages of the " Gentleman's Magazine " we learn that there were a great many foxes, hares and partridge in the area, with many wild duck on the pools. Six packs of hounds were kept in the neighbourhood and it was, no doubt, a cause of regret that deer were no longer available as quarry.

In all probability the majority of Sutton people were hardly aware of Dr. Johnson's existence for, to return again to the trenchant pen of " an impartial hand ": " . . . the polite arts are as little admired and cultivated in this place, as perhaps in any of His Majesty's corporate towns in England . . . " The inhabitants would probably not have been particularly interested to know that Johnson, as well as Shakespeare—possibly the two most revered and quoted writers in the English language— had sentimental maternal links with the parish of Curdworth. Johnson's mother once lived at Dunton Hall—there is a memorial in the floor of the nave of Curdworth Church, commemorating the fact—while Shakespeare's mother, Mary Arden, was a descendant of Thomas de Arden who, in the thirteenth century, built the original Peddimore Hall, just a stone's throw away.

The Birmingham based Lunar Society, consisting of some dozen or so eminent local men, had a great influence on eighteeth century life and thought. It was so called because its members met once a month on the Sunday nearest the time of the full moon, so as to have its light by which to return home. The meetings were held at members' houses, and dinner was always followed by a discussion of the varied interests and scientific problems of its members. Among the distinguished men belonging to the Lunar Society were Matthew Boulton; James Watt; Erasmus Darwin, the Lichfield doctor, who was grandfather of Charles Darwin; Josiah Wedgwood, the potter;

James Keir, described as "an able chemist and distinguished for much originality and independence of mind"; Dr. William Withering, who discovered the medical uses of the foxglove (digitalis); and Dr. Joseph Priestley, discoverer of oxygen.

The occasions were informal, and, unfortunately for posterity, no records were kept of their deliberations. In "Tales of Sutton Town and Chase", there is a long poem about an imaginary meeting of the Lunar Society at Sutton, but there is no evidence to prove that such a meeting ever took place. There were, however, meetings at Great Barr Hall, the ancestral home of the Scotts of Great Barr. Sir Joseph Scott, a prodigious spendthrift—after squandering three inherited fortunes—found it necessary to lease the hall to Samuel Galton, Junior, who was a member of the Lunar Society.

Galton, like his father, was a Quaker, and both men were accused by the Society of Friends for their association with the arms industry, from which they had gained great wealth. Galton, Senior, retired from the trade, but not so his son, who was expelled by the Quakers. This fact, however, did not deter him from continuing to attend their Meeting House in Bull Street, Birmingham.

In 1724, the Society of Friends built a Meeting House at Wigginshill, Sutton Coldfield. The Quakers—by which name the Society of Friends became better known—had had a hard time prior to the passing of the Toleration Act in 1689, and were frequently prosecuted by the authorities for their unorthodox views. After 1689, when freedom of worship was granted to nonconformists, things had improved for a time, although the Quakers were still precluded from holding office of any kind. Frequently they were imprisoned for refusing to pay tithes, and their opposition to taking the oath in courts and elsewhere, which they believed produced dual standards of truthfulness, often landed them in trouble.

The Quakers were implacably opposed to war, on the grounds that it was fundamentally contrary to the teachings of Christianity. In 1759 a riot broke out in Birmingham over the Quakers refusing to celebrate a Thanksgiving Day to commemorate the taking of Canada from the French. As a consequence a number of Quakers had their homes and property destroyed or damaged.

The Quakers place of worship at Wigginshill has been described as a homely little Meeting House, with an adjoining cottage. It seems to have provided a much-felt need, for as early as 1670 there is a record of a meeting of Quakers at Wishaw, and shortly afterwards, of another at Coleshill. The building of the meeting house at Wigginshill meant that all the Quakers from miles around, most of whom were agricultural workers, could assemble there. The cost of the building was a little over £100, £40 of which was raised by collections within the county, and the balance was supplied by Quakers in the immediate neighbourhood, some of whom also gave timber and lime for the building work. Strange to relate, however, despite this zeal and dedication, within a few years the Wigginshill Quaker congregation began to dwindle in numbers, and the meeting house finally closed after serving its purpose for a little over a century.

Today, Wigginshill, a diminutive place between Wishaw and Minworth, has three main buildings dating from the seventeenth century. These are a black and white half-timbered cottage with a large barn to match—both of a style rarely seen in the district —and a farmhouse with an interesting curved " Dutch gable."

The inhabitants of Sutton were still largely cottage dwellers, and as late as 1774 there were still twice as many cottages as there were freehold houses in the town. Enterprising cottagers sometimes supplemented their meagre earnings by working in their own homes. One ' cottage industry ' peculiar to Sutton was the making of besoms and kids (bundles of heath and furze), and cottagers collected the material for these from the Park in winter. At Hill Village there were cottages with especially large open chimneys for drying the ling used in making the besoms. " Brushing the road " did not mean sweeping it, but filling the worst holes with kids. Judging by the reputed state of the roads in the district, kids must have been in great demand.

One of the most interesting of Sutton's remaining cottages is at High Heath. This is the smallest and least altered of the Vesey Cottages and stands beside a quiet farm-track in the green belt area. Like the other Vesey cottages, it has three storeys and a spiral staircase, with a fireplace in the top bedroom, which must have been an innovation in Tudor times in so small a building. There is a tale about a former occupant of this cottage, who was found to have stolen some sheep—a very serious offence at this time. He barricaded himself in his home with the stolen sheep and threw missiles at those people who tried to apprehend him. This resulted in the cottage becoming known as " Mutton Castle ", but no-one seems to know if the thief was ever brought to justice.

The native heath gave way to cultivation about 150 years ago, but the crest of High Heath is still a quiet spot, where natural sounds prevail. Here the plaintive call of the peewits rise above the ploughed fields of Wheatmoor Farm and spring mornings are alive with the songs of larks and yellowhammers.

Vesey, in choosing to build one of his cottages at High Heath, had security in mind. It was, in his day, a remote spot surrounded by heathland, on the outskirts of Sutton, and being 500 feet above sea-level, was intended to house a member of his private police force. Riland Bedford, in a paper on " The Vesey Buildings at Sutton Coldfield " conjures up a picture of a traveller from Coleshill to Lichfield, benighted on these wild heights. His view of Basset's Pole is obscured by the gathering twilight and scudding flakes of snow. Suddenly he sights the twinkling light from the cottage on High Heath and he remembers that " a stout keeper and his trusty mastiff are located there." The traveller's fears are dispelled, for not only is he spared the misery of being lost under such circumstances, but he is assured of guidance through a region of great lawlessness. The duty of the " stout keeper "—Riland Bedford points out— is to pilot the traveller across Collet's Brook, and to defend him should " the banditti from Roughley or ' The Den ' " be lurking in the vicinity. ' The Den ' refers to Muffin's Den, or Ruffian's Den at Roughley—a name which suggests " Ruffian's field ". The place, Dugdale remarks, " was deservedly styled the den and haunt of thieves."

It has been claimed that the most notorious of all highwaymen, Dick Turpin, had his ' hide-out ' at Muffin's Den, where he is reputed to have stayed before setting out to waylay travellers on the London road. Tom King, a friend and fellow highwayman of Dick Turpin, was born at a farm near Stonnall. The gallows brought an end to the career of many a highwayman, Turpin himself having met his fate at the end of a hangman's noose. Names like Gibbet Hill (at New Oscott) and Gallow's Brook (at Middleton), tell their own grim stories. The house now known as Vesey Grange at Roughley was built by Vesey on a piece of waste called Cotty's Moor, containing nine acres. It was probably built in recognition of the lawlessness of the region for the purpose of housing another of Vesey's ' law enforcement officers.'

Highway robbery had reached its peak during the first half of the eighteenth century. Up till then, many Englishmen had rarely left their own parishes because it was too difficult to travel along the rutted cart-tracks which served as roads. Many towns and villages, however, had markets and fairs, which encouraged more active people to move around the countryside, either on foot or on horse-back. During the middle ages, roads had been maintained by the manorial courts and town guilds, but by the mid-sixteenth century, this system had fallen into disuse and the roads had then become the responsibility of the parishes through which they passed.

In Elizabethan times, heavy goods had first been carried by road in waggons, and the rich had started to travel by coach. Stage coaches, when they first appeared had no springs, and left much to be desired in the way of comfort. In 1670, however, the steel spring had first been introduced in England and this had led, in time, to the " C " spring and leather-strap suspension. These innovations had made the travellers' lot easier, and, as a consequence, more people had taken to the road.

The Chester Road had become increasingly important, for it was the main road from London to Chester—the port of embarkation for Ireland, since Holyhead was almost inaccessible. In the summer of 1690, the troops and waggons of an army under King William of Orange had probably passed along the Chester Road on their way to Ireland, where the deposed James II had been defeated by William's forces at the Battle of the Boyne.

The Chester Road was wild, lonely and ill-kept, running through extensive uninhabited common land, with Sutton Chase to the east of it and Barr Common to the west. It had, early on, acquired a bad reputation for its highway robbers—so much so that Sutton people avoided it as much as possible. In 1729, a man was hanged near the present site of Oscott College for robbing and murdering a London silk-merchant. In 1742, Sansbury, a notorious highwayman, was caught, with an accomplice, when drunk and asleep in a corn-field, and hanged. And in 1750, Henry Hunt of Birmingham was waylaid by two highwaymen on the Chester Road, and robbed of his watch and money. The victim appealed to his assailants to give him back some silver, which they did, but they promptly rode off and robbed another traveller within sight of their first victim.

Riland Bedford (" Vesey Papers ") refers to a novel published at the end of the eighteenth century, called " Spiritual Quixote ", in which two belated travellers from Lichfield to Sutton are represented as being startled by finding what they took to be a direction post between Shenstone and Four Oaks, but proved to be a gibbet, with a body swinging from it. The body, Riland Bedford suggests, might have been that of a highwayman, one of two mentioned in a letter from Simon Luttrell to the Rector of Sutton Coldfield, in which he referred to all his servants having gone off in pursuit of two highwaymen on Four Oaks Common.

Older than the Vesey cottage at High Heath, is the Smithy at Maney, parts of which probably date back to the fourteenth century. Its name seems to date from the beginning of the present century, when it was the home of a local blacksmith. At a time when there were as many as 13 mills in the parish, it was occupied by a millwright. The real antiquity of the Smithy can only be seen by going to the back of the building. The huge timbers of its cruck frame, twenty feet or so in height, are pitted with age, and have probably supported the cottage since the time of the Black Death.

The only other cruck-framed house in the district is the much bigger building near Wishaw, called The Grove. According to P. B. Chatwin and E. G. Harcourt (" The Bishop Vesey Houses and Other Old Buildings in Sutton Coldfield "):

"The oldest part of this building is on the south side, the two main gables with the entrance in the centre of the front of the house, and consists of four 'bays' of roof carried on crucks placed about 15 ft. apart and forming a hall about 60 ft. long and 19 ft. 6 in. wide; the ridge being about 20 ft. above the floor. It has, of course, been considerably modernized, but its ancient construction is quite obvious. The main beams forming the crucks are made of oak purposely chosen because of their being somewhat curved, but a great deal of work with the adze was necessary to make them the correct shape. They are very roughly finished and variable in size."

In 1745, the claim of the "Young Pretender" to the English throne led to some concern in England. The Highland rising in his support—known as the "Forty-five"—did not improve the situation, and when "Bonnie Prince Charlie" (by which name the Pretender was popularly known), marched south, tension increased. On 4th December, 1745—a day known in London as Black Friday—the Prince's forces reached Derby. The capital was panic-stricken, and there was a run on the Bank of England. It was rumoured that the Highlanders were nearer than they actually were, and when they were said to be at Lichfield, serious misgivings were felt at Sutton Coldfield rectory for the safety of the family plate. It was all, including a silver tea-kettle, relegated to the depths of a fish-pond in the rectory garden. This must have been an earlier pool than that said to have been made there by the rector in 1761 where, it was claimed, there were carp—"great big creatures like sucking pigs."

On reaching Derby the Pretender called a council of officers. They decided, in view of the superior forces lying ahead, to abandon the march south. So it was that the Highlanders set out on the long route back to Scotland. In the meantime, however, the Duke of Cumberland was sent with an army in pursuit, and some of his troops passed through Warwickshire on their way north. When they reached Tyburn, the advance force asked the way of a man who had no roof to his mouth, and he being unable to make himself understood, was presumed to be a spy. On the order of the commanding officer, he was summarily executed, and his body thrown into a ditch at Eachelhurst. His head was carried on a halbert to New Shipton, where it was tossed into an oak, said to have been one of the biggest trees in the parish. The troops in question had stayed the previous night at Castle Bromwich. The officers spent the evening there at the "Bradford Arms", with much revelry and by the following morning, according to Riland Bedford, the officer in command was still not sufficiently sober to know that he was without his sword, and only discovered his loss on reaching Basset's Pole.

In 1827, both the body and the head of the unfortunate victim were recovered within weeks of each other. The body was exhumed when Eachelhurst meadows were drained: the skull was a grisly trophy for the men who felled the old oak tree at New Shipton Farm.

The farm at New Shipton can still be seen standing four square on the top of the hill as one travels along Wylde Green Road towards Walmley. It is situated just beyond the Vesey Cottage and the bridge over the brook, while on the lower slopes of the hill is a black and white timber-framed house called " Wincelle ". This building originally stood at Wigginshill, from whence it was brought in 1910 and rebuilt in its present position.

From the high fields of New Shipton Farm, shelving steeply towards the valley of the Ebrook, there is a wide view. Almost a mile to the west is Maney Hill, now largely built up, and in the direction of Birmingham there are more distant prospects of suburban growth. Below, almost hidden by trees, lies New Hall. The age of New Shipton is uncertain. It has been claimed that in the great days of the Earls of Warwick, it was built as a fold for their flocks. The name appears in old deeds as " New Shippen ", which suggests the joining of a house and a barn under one roof. Stalling for cows would be contained in the shippen, and there would be an internal door, leading from it into the house. This would have enabled the cattle to be fed in bad weather without going outside. The idea is an old one, probably brought to this country by the Norsemen, whose home-steads were sometimes built on this principle. The present farm building is said to be late seventeenth century, but a large timber framed barn is probably considerably older.

A quarter-mile to the north-east of New Shipton Farm, stands Warren House Farm. The rough-cast walls of this build-ing, with its western wing inscribed 1671, are deceptive. It is, in fact, yet another stone-built Vesey Cottage, the main part of which is probably at least a century older than its eastern wing. The peeling rough cast reveals a solid, stone structure beneath. which is in keeping with the massive southern buttress. Both farms, covering 220 acres, form part of the New Hall estate. From Warren House Farm to Wylde Green Road, there is a footpath which, in Tudor times must have been a link between two Vesey houses—the Ford-keeper's Cottage and Warren House Farm.

CHAPTER V
More about the eighteenth century—The Four Oaks widow who was instrumental in the passing of the Royal Marriages Act— The enclosure movement—The Birmingham Riots, which brought William Hutton to Sutton Coldfield, as a refugee.

IN the eighteenth century, stage-coaches operating along the Chester Road took six days to reach London from Chester, and were often drawn by six or even eight horses. These coaches, which travelled from dawn to dusk, stopped for passengers to sleep at inns at Whitchurch, Stonnall, Coventry, Northampton and Dunstable. Following the Post Office Act of 1711, a regular mail service was commenced in England. The benefits of a daily postal service, however, were not enjoyed by people in the Birmingham area until 1748. The first stage coach to carry mail as well as passengers commenced in 1784, and operated, at first, between London and Bristol.

The idea was a success, due largely to the fact that such coaches had armed guards as protection against highway robbers and were exempt from turnpike tolls. They also had a reputation for high speeds, and the " Irish Mail " no doubt rattled along the Chester Road and across the Coldfield at a rate which would not have compared too unfavourably with that of peak-hour traffic on the same route today.

In 1759 an act was passed for turnpiking the whole of the road between Castle Bromwich and Chester, and at the " Welsh Harp " there was a toll-gate where, not only the well-to-do coach traveller had to pay, but even the humble pack-horse or mule was charged 1d. and a horse and cart 3d. Near the junction of Chester Road and Sutton Road stood an old posting house called the " Bell and Cuckoo ". In 1750 the landlord of this house wrote a hand-bill:

> " To all Gentlemen, Tradesmen, etc. Give me leave to inform you that the House known by the sign of the Bell, on the Chester Road, near Cuckoo's Corner* has lately been put in very neat repair, where you may depend on being accommodated in the most obliging manner by your humble Servant, William Haynes."

The landlord followed this up with a eulogy of his house and its surroundings:

In these green lanes the cuckoo sings,
    Here talks the mimic jay;
Here the pale primrose early springs;
    And here the blackbird sweetly sings to usher in the May.

'Tis here the flying coaches speed their way,
    And equipages grand, with pompous show,
All Colours display, so brilliant they,
    When noble Lords to Senate go . . .

The turnpike roads were not universally popular. One opponent wrote a pamphlet called: " Indisputable Reasons against the proposed scheme for a Turnpike Road, between Sutton and Birmingham ", in which he said:

> " Turnpike Acts are always undesirable, except where necessity compels their establishment. A large Proportion of the Tolls is ever sunk upon what does not a whit Benefit the Travellers. Gates, Houses, Salaries for Keepers, Clerks,

* Shown on old maps as " Cuckold's Corner ".

endless Advertisements, and the enormous Exactions attending the procuring of the Act. Besides, an opening is continually afforded for clandestine Jobs, which the Vulgar Phrase of "You scratch me, and I'll scratch you", will in a shorter manner, at least, explain, than the Recital of Particulars . . .

" . . . There will also remain this singular Injury to the Town and Inhabitants of Sutton Coldfield, if this project is brought to bear, viz., that a weighing Engine will undoubtedly be erected at the Toll gate, and whatever general Uses the Prohibition of high Weights may have, here it will be peculiarly injurious, because the Farmers fetch their muck from Birmingham, buy it by the Load, and if they are once restrained from large weights there is an end of that Traffick, and an end of all workmanlike cultivation; for their Land will not do its best without it, and it will never answer to go thither for a small Load. Moreover it is said, that an Act now in Force requires Wheels of a particular Construction to be had for all Waggons that pass a Toll gate, which Act is suspended for a while, until the Owners of Carriages can provide them. If then every poor Farmer of Sutton, or its neighbouring Hamlets, must be forced to get these expensive Wheels, or keep from Birmingham Market, the alternative is terrible to these poor hardworking wretches, who live but from hand to mouth already; while their overgrown Neighbours whose Brows don't sweat Half so much, will with their strong backed Teams, and Parliament wheels, engross all the muck and all the market! Good gentlemen consider—a poor scrattling Rack-Rent Ploughman, should not be cut out of his Bread for the Sake of Whiskies and Phaetons . . . "

The road from Birmingham, through Sutton Coldfield, as far as Watford Gap, was only made into a turnpike following an act of 1807, in the 47th year of the reign of George III. There was a toll-gate at the bottom of Gravelly Hill and another at the northern end of Sutton. The " Bell and Cuckoo " was thus placed in a favourable position at the crossing of two turnpike roads.

The Chester Road became so busy in the eighteenth century that the " Welsh Harp " at Stonnall could not accommodate all the travellers who wanted to put up there. A smaller house was, therefore, built on the opposite side of the road, where less prosperous travellers were boarded. The story is told of a Jewess, a pedlar of jewellery in the Midland counties, who, one November evening in the eighteenth century, set out from the " Bell and Cuckoo " to walk across the Coldfield to Stonnall, where she was seen to arrive at night, and to enter the smaller of the two inns. She was never seen again. It was only some time later that, when she was missed from her usual haunts—for she was known to a wide circle of acquaintances—enquiries were instituted. She was traced by friends to Stonnall, and the house was searched, but nothing was found. Rewards were offered, but with no results.

Years later, when the poor Jewess was almost forgotten, the people who kept the inn moved away, and fresh people took over. Business was bad and the inn gained the reputation for being haunted. One autumn evening, a party was being held there to celebrate " Harvest Home." There was dancing, singing and drinking. Suddenly, someone shrieked. All eyes were turned in one direction where, standing on a settle and wrapped in a luminous robe was a woman of melancholy countenance. In a few moments the apparition passed slowly from view, and the party broke up in disarray. No-one would live in the house after that, and after standing empty for some years, it was pulled down. When the settle was dismantled, beneath it was the skeleton of a woman which, everyone said, was that of the Jewess. The remains were buried in the churchyard, from which time the ghost of the pedlar was never seen again. People in and around Stonnall for long gave credence to this story.

The inn which used to be called the " Royal Oak " is now better known as the " Parson and Clerk ". There were once two figures on top of the building, one of a parson leaning his head in prayer, the other of a clerk with uplifted axe about to chop off the parson's head. The figures had been placed there by John Gough of Perry Hall to commemorate an earlier law-suit between himself and the Rev. T. Lane, each having annoyed the other in petty ways. Having won the case, Gough perpetuated his victory by putting up the figures, and on the end of the house he had painted:—

" These Buildings were licensed houses and were un-
lawfully witheld and undermined by the Rev. T. Lane and
Solomon Smith, his Clerk, in the year 1788, afterwards rebuilt by the lawful owner, J. Gough, Esq., Perry Hall."

This account of the feud is confusing, however, since the parson and clerk are described as being in league with one another—a fact which hardly accords with the clerk's uplifted axe.

Another interesting commemoration is still to be seen on a wall at Hill Hook, where there is a memorial to a young man named John Bickley, who—on 1st August, 1797—was struck dead by lightning there, together with the horse of which he rode. " Happily he was an amiable youth " the inscription tells us, but otherwise we know little about John Bickley, except that his family were farmers at Hill Hook, and that they were in-volved in protracted litigation with the Corporation over the ownership of Hill Hook Mill.

Human tragedy is always with us, but when it involves the young, it has a particular poignancy. In the chancel of Holy Trinity Church is another reminder of human vulnerability. It is an early 17th century brass in memory of Barbara Eliot, who is depicted in hood, ruff and farthingale, with her two tiny children beside her. She was the wife of the Rev. Roger Eliot, Rector of Sutton Coldfield from 1595 to 1617, and was only 23 when she died in 1606, so that her children were deprived of a mother's care at an early age.

In the eighteenth century, prize-fighting became very popular and was probably the first sport to which spectators travelled long distances for the pleasure of watching contests. The funds raised by the tolls having led to some improvement in the hither-to shocking state of the Chester Road, the common-land which lay on either side of it, between Sutton Park and Barr Beacon, became the chosen site of some of these illegal prize-fights.

These barbaric bouts certainly deserved to be illegal, but the law was often unenforced (and unenforceable). Among the base tricks of some of the fighters, or " bruisers " as they were called, was that of gouging out an opponent's eye when the referee was looking the other way. When two contestants met on one occasion for a prize bout, the one held the other down by his long hair while hitting him. As this was not ruled out of order by the referee, prize-fighters afterwards always took the precaution of having their hair cut short.

When a prize-fight was arranged, news of the event would spread quickly, and large numbers of spectators would descend on the chosen spot—either on foot, on horse-back or by any cart or carriage available. In " Men of Aldridge ", Mr. James T. Gould tells us of one such encounter on ' the Coldfield '—possibly within the Park itself. The contestants were named Griffiths and Bayliss, and a one-time champion of the ring, named Belcher acted as a ' second '. The scene of this bout, it can be assumed, was well chosen, for the Chester Road—as well as being the means by which participants and spectators reached the spot—was at that time also the county boundary between Warwickshire and Staffordshire. This meant that on whichever side of the road the ring was pitched, it would only have necessi-tated crossing to the other side at the appearance of a parish constable, to be outside his jurisdiction. By this stratagem it would have been possible to get the fight over before the con-stable's opposite number from the next parish could be tipped off. It is worth recalling that, before the creation of police-forces, the constable wielded considerable authority at parish level, in criminal, civil and military matters, and that the stocks, whipping-post and ducking-stool were all under his control.

Griffiths v. Bayliss, which attracted a crowd of many hundreds—some from as far off as London—ended in a draw. Despite so large a gathering, however, which one might expect would not go unnoticed by the constable, the fact that the fight ran to 213 rounds does not suggest that there was any police intervention. Perhaps more remarkable was the fact that neither participant in this long slogging match got himself killed—or died of exhaustion.

The " Gentleman's Magazine " (1762), gives us a description of eighteenth century Sutton Coldfield. " The parish ", the writer says " is nearly oval in its figure, the longest diameter 7 miles, and the breadth four; the face of it is agreeably diversified with gently rising hills, and valleys of tolerably fruitful meadows. It is bounded on the north by Shenstone, on the west by Barr, on the south by Curdworth and Aston, near Birmingham, and on the east by Middleton. It contains four hamlets, viz. Maney, Hill, Little Sutton and Walmley . . . " Speaking of the church, the writer mentions that the nave, being very old and decayed in the foundation had been lately taken down and rebuilt with a hard sandstone, " of which there is a plentiful quarry within the distance of half a mile."

The vaults of the church, the writer says, were unusual for consuming the bodies deposited in them very quickly. " In two of them lately opened " he tells us " corpses have been found to have been reduced to mere dust, together with the coffins of wood which enclosed them, the interment of which has been within the memory of man." He adds that " The height of the churchyard and the sandiness of the soil may contribute to this."

" Some rivulets that take their rise in the Park " the writer continues " feed several mills built in and near it, not only for grinding corn, but for boring musket barrels, polishing metal buttons, making saws, grinding axes, knives, bayonets, and performing various other operations for the mechanical traders in Birmingham who, having had great numbers of their workmen impressed, or voluntarily enlisted into His Majesty's service during this war, have set their inventions to work to perform by mills many operations which used to employ more hands than can be procured in the latter end of a war, when so many have been buried in Germany and Canada ". The military campaigns referred to appear to be the Seven Years' War and the Capture of Quebec.

In 1772—ten years after the article on Sutton Coldfield in the " Gentleman's Magazine "—we have another description of the parish, this time from the pen of the Rev. Richard Bisse Riland. This description was contained in a letter to his bishop. It is quoted by his descendant, the Rev. W. K. Riland Bedford, in the " History of Sutton Coldfield." " The parish ", he says " comprehends several hamlets, viz. Maney, Hill, Little Sutton, Walmley and Wiggins Hill, besides several single farmhouses and cottages dispersed at considerable distances from each other and from the church ". There were in the region of 370 houses in the parish, and the families of note were said to be those of Lord Irnham (formerly Simon Luttrell), of Four Oaks Hall; Charles Sacheverell Chadwick of New Hall; R. Lawley; John Hacket of Moor Hall; T. Duncumb; and W. Jesson.

Following this geographical run-down of the place and the list of local families, the Rev. Riland turns, not surprisingly, to the various religious denominations in the parish:

" . . . There are three Roman Catholic families . . . one family of Quakers . . . no Anabaptists, nor Moravians, nor Presbyterians who abstain from the church as such."

This was a time when some of the harsher measures which had been brought against Nonconformists in the previous century were to some extent relaxed, and meeting houses were built in many places by men of various persuasions. "There is one meeting house of Independents within the town of Sutton Coldfield " said the Rector, " which is duly licensed at the sessions, whither they who are called Methodists do also resort." On the subject of education, the Rector describes the town's grammar school and the means by which it was administered by " about a dozen of ye neighbouring gentlemen."

When Langley Hall estate passed to Anne, the younger daughter of Jane Pudsey, the elder daughter sought a comparable home in the district. She therefore prevailed on her husband Lord Ffolliott to avail himself of a clause in the Charter granted to the Corporation, enabling any person erecting a dwelling-house to enclose sixty acres of common land. The ensuing mansion was Four Oaks Hall, attributed in design to Sir William Wilson. This house survived until the autumn of 1898 and was described by Riland Bedford in its decline as " a mansion now falling into decay, not with the broken outline and soft gray tints which make a venerable ruin a thing of beauty, but in unpicturesque shabbiness, every defect exaggerated and every redeeming feature disappearing." To offset this, he adds: " It is a house which has known, assuredly, many pleasant hours in bygone times, reminiscences of books, and art, of mirth and friendship."

Lord Ffolliott died in 1716, but his widow survived until 1744, following which the estate was sold to Simon Luttrell, of Luttrellstown, in Ireland. Riland Bedford adds that " it was not until 1757 that the royal assent was given to an Act of Parliament to enable the Warden and Society of the King's town of Sutton Coldfield, in Warwickshire, to grant part of a common, called Sutton Coldfield Park, unto Simon Luttrell, Esq. Forty-eight acres were thus added to the demesne at an annual rent of £12." Luttrell's standing in society seems to have increased with the growth of his estate, for Miss Bracken tells us that " in 1768, he was created Baron Irnham, in 1780 Viscount Carhampton, and in 1785, Earl Carhampton." Lord Irnham sold Four Oaks Hall to the Rev. Thomas Gresley in 1778, and between that date and 1792, when the estate was bought by Edmund Craddock Hartopp, it changed hands several times.

One of Baron Irnham's daughters, Anne—a woman of considerable beauty—married Christopher Horton of Catton Hall, Derbyshire, but was widowed early. Her second husband was Henry, Duke of Cumberland—the younger brother of King George III—whom she married in 1771. The king, whose other brother had also married a subject, was very annoyed by the match, and rather peevishly refused to meet the new duchess. To show his annoyance in a more tangible way, he secured the passing of the Royal Marriages Act of 1772, which enacted that:

"No decendant of the body of the late Majesty, King George II, male or female (other than the issue of princesses who have married or may hereafter marry into foreign families) shall be capable of contracting matrimony without the previous consent of His Majesty, his heirs or his successors."

Riland Bedford quotes a sneering reference to the Duchess of Cumberland by Horace Walpole: "She had the most amorous eyes in the world, and eyelashes a yard long, a coquette beyond measure, artful as Cleopatra." Riland Bedford adds, however, that Walpole was untrustworthy in matters of personal predilection or family interest. His niece had married the Duke of Gloucester—the king's other brother—and she, according to Riland Bedford, did not shine by the side of her brilliant sister-in-law. We also learn from Riland Bedford of the beneficial result of marriage on the Duke of Cumberland. "The judicious influence of his wife and the affection which she bestowed upon him, caused a great alteration in his demeanor for the better, and as a patron of the musical art, and a collector of fine old instruments, he became a not entirely useless member of society."

Many local people, remembering the beautiful Four Oaks girl, Anne Luttrell, were probably interested to learn of her marriage to the king's brother. It is unlikely, however, that the majority of Sutton's 2,500 inhabitants were interested in the implications of the Royal Marriages Act. Most of them were far too busy eking out a meagre living—and avoiding the workhouse. In 1737, the Corporation had ordered that a number of almshouses in Mill Street, which had been provided under the Charter of 1528, should be knocked down, and a workhouse built on the site. The inmates of this detested institution often lost the will to live, and in Sutton's parish register many burials from the workhouse are recorded. In 1777, there were six in one week. During this era there was no hospital in the parish, no almshouses and no school for the poor. Sutton's workhouse operated until 1834, when the poor law was placed on a more centralised footing and for administrative purposes, parishes were grouped into "Unions", each of which was obliged to provide a "well-regulated workhouse". As a consequence Sutton Coldfield became a part of the "Aston Union", and the town's workhouse closed down.

From 1700, the manorial system was declining. The common land began to be enclosed and the face of the countryside was taking on its familiar patchwork appearance created by hedgerows dividing up the fields. It is claimed that Joseph Duncumb, who was Warden of the Corporation in 1760 and 1761, introduced to the Sutton district a large breed of Leicestershire sheep. This breed contrasted with the diminutive Shropshire variety of downland sheep that was reared locally. The excellence of its mutton, which compared favourably with Welsh mutton, was due to its feeding on the unenclosed heathland vegetation still existing around Sutton.

In 1778, a proposal came from Sir Joseph Scott of Great Barr that all the common land in Sutton Coldfield, including the Park, should be enclosed. He was a member of the Corporation and wished to divide the land among all the landlords of the district " . . . in proportion to their interest in the soil." The move was supported by the rector (the Rev. R. B. Riland), his curate, and 87 landlords, but was strongly opposed by the townspeople, and it was at this stage that the Corporation enjoyed its finest hour. It resolved that:—

> " The design of applying to Parliament for a bill for enclosing the Park waste and common lands within the parish of Sutton is an unjustifiable attack on the undoubted rights and privileges of the Corporation, seems calculated to wrest from them their property and estate, solemnly granted and confirmed to them by charter and will tend eventually to dissolve their existence as a body corporate, that this Corporation will oppose such application in Parliament."

The " obnoxious proposal " (as Riland Bedford calls it), was withdrawn, but although the Park remained inviolable, the same did not apply to the thousands of acres of common land beyond its bounds. Until the late eighteenth century, enclosures were few, small and scattered, whereas the common land extended over a large area and to the north of Sutton. Basset's Pole was, in fact, a pole, or mast, some 25 to 30 feet high, necessary for guiding travellers over the heath. Four Oaks had its own common, while enclosures around Sutton Rectory were divided from the town by an irregular waste, called ' the mettals '. The flat, low-lying common land along the valley of the Ebrook, frequented by frogs and eels, was known as ' the Blabbs ', while to the south of the town, ' the wild ', or ' Wildgreen ' was hardly touched by cultivation. To the west, the great Coldfield, which merged with the expansive Barr Common and Aldridge Common, was spanned by the Chester Road.

By the end of the eighteenth century, Basset's Heath had been enclosed, and two acts of parliament were passed for enclosing 2,300 acres of waste land around Aldridge and Barr, some of which came within the ancient bounds of Sutton Chase. In 1825, an enclosure act for Sutton Coldfield, excluding the Park, was passed, and a further 3,500 acres of common land, belonging to the whole community and used by cottagers since Saxon times, were conveyed to the chief landowners of the parish, and became their freehold property.

When the Rev. R. B. Riland died in 1790, he was succeeded at the rectory by his younger brother, John, who—unlike his brother—was a strong opponent of the enclosure movement on the grounds that it would be detrimental to the interests of the cottagers of the parish. This opposition is indicated in the words of an epigram, quoted by Riland Bedford (" Vesey Papers "):

> If 'tis a crime in man or woman
> To steal a goose from off a common,
> Then surely he has less excuse
> Who steals the common from the goose.

John Riland was given to walking many miles along the lanes and over the heaths to visit the scattered hamlets of the parish, " his pockets laden with comfits for the children, his mind stored with quaint sayings and simple doctrine for the edification of their elders " (Riland Bedford). His death in 1822, resulting in the cottagers being without a champion, may have been a factor in the passing of Sutton's Enclosure Act in 1825. But if John Riland's fight against enclosure was a lost cause, his advocacy of elementary education in the town was to bear fruit in 1825—three years after his death (see Chapter VI).

As a footnote to enclosure, Midgley—writing in 1904—commented:

> " Not content with this great haul the landlords have ever since been encroaching on any land that may have been left at the side of the highways. It is impossible to walk along any of the country roads round Sutton without noticing the strips of land which have been thus pilfered from the public, and the practice even in the last few years has been continued in the quiet lanes."

An interesting sidelight on eighteenth century Sutton is pro-vided by a German traveller, C. P. Moritz, in his book " Journeys of a German in England in 1782 ". He tells us that:

> " The road out of Birmingham is not of the best, being rather sandy. I got as far as the small town of Sutton by that evening. It seemed too superior a place to spend the night until, right at the far end, I came to a small inn with the sign of the Swan and underneath the landlord's name and occupation—Aulton, Brickmaker.
> " This inn looked more inviting for such as I, so I went inside. I didn't immediately ask for accommodation, however, but ordered a pot of beer, or, as they say in these parts ' a point of ale '. They addressed me as ' master ' and

sent me into the kitchen where the landlady sat at a table complaining of toothache. My sympathy for her misfortune soon put me in her good books, however, especially as I was a foreigner, and she herself asked me if I should like to stay there for the night. Of course I agreed. So again I had shelter for the night. There I met a woman chimney-sweep and her children, who at once drank my health very amiably and talked freely with me and the hostess."

Upon being told that there was a grammar school in Sutton where the headmaster's salary was worth two hundred pounds a year, plus the scholars' fees, Moritz expressed surprise that the pay in such a small place should compare so favourably with the pay of schoolmasters in Berlin.

When Moritz came to pay his bill the following morning, he tells us that he couldn't help but notice the great difference in their charges compared with Windsor, Nettlebed and Oxford:

" In Oxford I had to pay at least three shillings for supper, bed and breakfast, besides giving a shilling to the waiter. At Sutton I was charged only one shilling for supper, bed and breakfast, and when I gave the daughter of the house fourpence for doing the duties of a chambermaid, she thanked me most politely and gave me in addition a written recommendation to an innkeeper in Lichfield with whom I could get a good lodging—for in general the people in Lichfield are haughty."

The " Swan ", where Moritz stayed, became known later as the " Old Top Swan ", to distinguish it from the other " Swan ", by which name the present " Royal Hotel " was formerly known.

The Birmingham Riots of 1791 no doubt made a considerable impact on the minds of Sutton people. When a dinner was held in Birmingham by the liberals to celebrate the anniversary of the fall of the Bastille, a mob assembled outside the hotel and smashed the windows. They then marched to the New Meeting House where, after destroying the pews, cushions, books and pulpit, they set it on fire. The Old Meeting House suffered a similar fate, following which the rioters marched on Dr. Joseph Priestley's house at Sparkbrook, which was plundered and burned, and his library and scientific appartus destroyed.

Priestley, who was both a theologian and a scientist, was famous for his research into chemistry and electricity. In Birmingham, however, he was perhaps better known as a dissenting minister of unorthodox views, and his sympathy towards the aims of the French Revolution is often blamed for the Birmingham Riots. Ironically, however, he was not at the Bastille Day dinner, following which the violence started. Priestley, as a result of " that effervescence of the public mind "—the term used by Pitt for the Birmingham Riots—became a refugee, and for a short while is said to have stayed at the " Three Tuns " in Sutton, before moving further afield and eventually emigrating to America.

Among the other dissenters, radicals, intellectuals and well-to-do victims whose homes were sacked and burned was William Hutton, the Birmingham historian, a self-made man, whose main cause of offence to the rioters was apparently that he was a Presbyterian. Despite the fact that he tried to bribe the mob, they were not to be deflected from their course of plunder and destruction, and his house at Washwood Heath was completely destroyed. He fled, with his family, to Castle Bromwich from where, under pressure from his daughter, he agreed to hire a post-chaise to Sutton Coldfield.

In his autobiography, Hutton tells us that, on reaching Sutton, he and his family " took apartments for the summer ". Here he fell into company with a clergyman, a lawyer, a country squire and two other people, who all lamented the events at Birmingham, and blamed Dr. Priestley for what had happened. Hutton engaged in an argument on the subject and, by the same evening, he informs us, " the mistress of the house was seized with the fashionable apprehensions of the day, and requested us to depart, lest her house should be burnt. We were obliged to pack up, which was done in one minute, for we had only the clothes which covered us, and roll on to Tamworth."

Hutton's misfortunes were not shared by any of the inhabitants of Sutton, where no sacking and burning took place. In " The Iron Masters of Penns ", however, John Horsfall tells us that the house at Penns had been earmarked by the rioters for destruction, presumably because the Websters, who lived there, were also Presbyterians. He claims that, had it not been for the arrival of the cavalry, the house would have been set on fire. In anticipation of this event, members of the Webster family, having first had their valuables packed in chests and sunk in Penns lake, took refuge by fleeing across the fields to Pype Hayes. The feared event, however, did not take place, and they were able to return home within the week.

In 1792, Sutton's continuing prosperity was emphasised when the Corporation paved the streets with cobblestones at a cost of £350. In the same year, following upon proceedings by a number of townsmen, a Court injunction was granted, restraining the Corporation from selling Park timber, and impounding the proceeds of former sales. This was only one of a number of law-suits to be brought against the Corporation in the person of the Warden, for various alleged acts of mismanagement. Complaints were made against them over a period of several centuries of such acts as stocking the Park with strangers' cattle, spoiling the woods, employing profits belonging to the town to their own use, conveying away farms and tenements, felling timber without the consent of the major part of the freeholders (contrary to the letters patent of Henry VIII), increasing the fees for the pasturage of horses and cattle in the Park, and injuring freeholders by enclosing common land.

CHAPTER VI

The first census—Sutton Coldfield in Napoleonic times—The Mary Ashford case—Sutton Coldfield's enclosure act—elementary education—The beginning of the Victorian era—Dr. Bodington —the " Holbeche Diary ".

IN 1802, Lord Nelson—accompanied by Sir William and Lady Hamilton—visited the West Midlands. In Birmingham, where Nelson was given a tumultuous welcome, the party toured the factories and visited the theatre. At a grand banquet to which Nelson was invited by the High and Low Bailiffs of the town, it is recorded that " Lady Hamilton condescendingly gratified the company with several most appropriate charming songs." It is not certain whether Nelson visited Sutton, but according to tradition Lady Hamilton planted a clump of beech trees at Streetly, overlooking the Park, which suggests that Nelson too, may have been in the locality.

Robert Southey in " The Life of Nelson " says of Emma, Lady Hamilton, that she was " a woman whose personal accomplishments have seldom been equalled and whose powers of mind were not less fascinating than her person." She greatly influenced Nelson's life in the years before his death at the Battle of Trafalgar in 1805, and her portrait hung in his cabin on the " Victory ". Robert Southey was himself a visitor to the district in the 1830s, when he stayed at Pype Hayes Hall, the home of the Rev. Walter Bagot—a friend of William Cowper, the poet, whose biography he was writing at the time.

The first census had taken place in 1801, when Sutton Coldfield had a population of 2,847. By 1811, this had risen to 2,959. During the year 1811, Sutton's population was augmented by the arrival of troops in the parish, and a military camp was built to accommodate men of the Edinburgh and Sussex Militias, the 7th Dragoon Guards and a Brigade of Artillery. The site of the camp is commemorated in the name of Camp Road.

The 7th Dragoon Guards—now a part of the 4th/7th Royal Dragoon Guards—were known as " The Black Horse " because, as a Horse Regiment on the Irish Establishment in the mid-eighteenth century, they wore black facings to their tunics. They, together with the Brigade of Artillery, belonged to the regular army. Since 1757, however, the militia had been chosen by lot and consisted of men between 18 and 45, called to the colours for three years. They were raised on a county footing, with a quota from each of the various parishes.

Although the militia forces were non-professional soldiers and not normally on a permanent footing, they were, during the greater part of the Napoleonic Wars, permanently embodied. By 1812 there were 250 regiments of local militia, with an establishment of 240,000 men, but after the peace settlement of 1815, these forces were disbanded and the militia allowed to fall into abeyance.

The war-torn year 1812—three years before the defeat of Napoleon at Waterloo—has been described by Tolstoy in " War and Peace " as a time when:

> " Millions of men perpetrated against one another such innumerable crimes, frauds, treacheries, thefts, forgeries, issues of false money, burglaries, incendiarisms, and murders as in whole centuries are not recorded in the annals of all the law courts of the world."

In Sutton Coldfield that momentous year it is said was marked by many baptisms from its military camp and unfamiliar names in the parish register. The families of some of the local girls who married soldiers must have been shocked, for even the Duke of Wellington—victor of Waterloo—said of his troops: " They are the scum of the earth " although he did add " and it is really wonderful that we should have made of them the fine fellows they are. With such an army we can go anywhere and do anything." The lowly standing of the common soldier in society, however, was indisputable, and this was reflected in the lot of his wife which, in Napoleonic times, was extremely harsh —particularly if she shared barrack life with her husband.

In 1813, Sutton Coldfield Corporation proposed " that all such pits or springs as may be adjudged to be convenient for waterings or other public uses, and especially such springs as are adjudged to be medicinal, shall be reserved for the benefit of the public with convenient roads for access thereto." The proposal was implemented in 1815, when wells were made on the sites of springs in Pool Hollies Wood (Druid's Well), and near Keeper's Pool. Rowton's Well, it has been claimed, was made at the same time, but there was, apparently, a well on the site prior to that date, for in " The History of Sutton Coldfield " by " an impartial hand " (1762), the author refers to it as " a spring called Rounton Well, a water remarkably cold, and which is quined round with stone and discharges a prodigious current of water . . . "

The Corporation, in providing wells and making easy access to the ancient springs of the Park, was no doubt supplying a long-felt need. One of the requirements of ' easy access ' at Rowton's Well was provided by a pole marking the site—for the approach to it was, and is, over rough terrain and the well is only visible at close-range. It has been said that when it was 'ladies' day' for bathing and taking the waters at Rowton's Well, a flag was flown from this pole in intimation of the fact. This, however, is unauthenticated, as is the claim that a man once came daily to fetch a supply of water from Rowton's, with which the patients of Birmingham Eye Hospital bathed their eyes.

On the morning of Tuesday, 27th May, 1817, the body of a young woman was found, drowned in a marl-pit in Penns Lane. The victim was Mary Ashford, aged 20, a gardener's daughter, whose home was in High Street, Erdington. The previous day—Whit Monday—she had spent the evening at a dance at Tyburn House, and there was no shortage of evidence to prove that she danced almost exclusively with a young man named Abraham Thornton from Castle Bromwich. There was also evidence from several independent witnesses to show that these two had been seen together after the dance during the early hours of the morning of 27th May.

Thornton was arrested and charged with having murdered Mary Ashford and by the time he came up for trial at the Warwick Assizes, great public interest had been aroused in the case. He was charged with having " on 27th May last. in the Town, Manor and Lordship of Birmingham, in the County of Warwick, not having the fear of God before his eyes, but being moved by the instigation of the Devil, wilfully murdered Mary Ashford by throwing her into a pit of water." The evidence was inconclusive, and he was acquitted without the jury having even retired.

This, however, was not the end of the matter, for Mary Ashford's brother, William, by means of taking out a private summons, was able to ensure a fresh trial which, this time, was set down for hearing at the Court of Kings Bench in London. Being, in effect, an appeal against an earlier decision, more than one judge was to hear the case, and the Court was to be presided over by the Lord Chief Justice, Lord Ellenborough. When, on 17th November, 1817, before a crowded court, the defendant was asked whether or not he was guilty, he replied in a loud, clear voice " Not Guilty, and I am ready to defend the same with my body!" whereupon he threw a gauntlet to the floor of the court, at the same time challenging William Ashford to a duel. This was known as invoking " wager by battle ", an almost forgotten legal right which had not been exercised for centuries.

Ashford was no physical match for the burly Thornton, and the challenge was not taken up, which meant that the accused man was released. Within the shortest possible time, however,

" wager by battle " was abolished by parliament, and the case became part of English legal history, known to law students as " Ashford v. Thornton ". Thornton himself emigrated to America, where he married and lived until his death in 1860. His father, a Castle Bromwich farmer, well regarded in the local community, was said to have been broken hearted by the affair. William Ashford was for many years a fishmonger in Birmingham, and died in 1867.

It is only fair to Thornton to say that the evidence against him was of an inconclusive and circumstantial nature, and the mystery surrounding Mary Ashford's death remains. Her grave can be seen in the churchyard of Holy Trinity Church, Sutton Coldfield. The flat headstone is now so badly defaced that it has become impossible to read the inscription. It read, originally, as follows:—

As a warning to female Virtue
And a humble monument of female Chastity,
This stone marks the grave
of
Mary Ashford
Who, in the twentieth year of her age,
Having incautiously repaired
To a scene of amusement
Without proper protection
Was brutally violated and murdered
On 27th May, 1817.

    .   .   .   .

Lovely and chaste as the primrose pale
Rifled of Virgin Sweetness by the gale,
Mary! The Wretch who thee remorseless slew,
    Avenging wrath, which sleeps not, will pursue
For though the deed of blood be veiled in night,
    Will not the Judge of all the earth do right?
Fair blighted Flow'r! The Muse that weeps thy doom
    Rears o'er thy murder'd Form,
      This warning tomb.

    .   .   .   .

Mary Ashford's epitaph was written by the Rev. Luke Booker, LL.D., who also wrote a pamphlet in refutation of the case for the defence of Thornton at the first trial.

At the time of Sutton Coldfield's enclosure act in 1825, Sir Edmund Hartopp, availing himself of the facilities afforded by the act for exchanges of land, obtained legal sanction to enclose 63 acres of Ladywood, Four Oaks, until then a part of Sutton Park. The whole question of enclosure was a very ' live ' issue at that time, and Sir Edmund's action caused considerable bitterness among local people—so much so that one Sunday morning a number of parishioners attempted to set fire to Ladywood in several places simultaneously, but due to a sudden fall of rain, it seems that very little damage was caused. In return for the annexation, and possibly as an act of atonement, Sir Edmund Hartopp gave 93 acres of land to the Park. This land, situated on the side of the Park nearest to the town, included the Meadow Platt* Under the same settlement a new road—Park Road—was made to what is now the main entrance. Formerly the approach from the town had been by way of Manor Hill and Wyndley Pool dam. As a result of this transaction, Sutton Park was increased in size by 30 acres.

In "Sutton Coldfield Town and Chase", Midgley tells us that the law-suit following the injunction of 1792 dragged on for nearly 40 years, by the end of which time over £40,000 of Sutton money had accumulated in the hands of the Lord Chancellor. This, it will be recalled, was money impounded by the Court, relating to acts of alleged mismanagement by the Corporation over a period of several centuries (see Chapter V). The Rector of Sutton Coldfield, John Riland, urged that the money should be used for founding elementary schools, and in 1825 the proposal was sanctioned by the Court. Miss Bracken, writing in 1860 (" History of the Forest and Chase of Sutton Coldfield "), speaks of " the various charities " which were allowed by the Court of Chancery in 1825. These included seven free schools in which 120 boys and 120 girls were clothed and educated. Provision was also made for about 20 additional places for scholars from outlying districts. By 1860 about 600 children received instruction and some 400 had the benefit of free medical attention.

Other charities included 10 almshouses, the gift of 50 blankets, at the cost of £30 a year, to poor inhabitants, a ' lying-in ' charity of £76 per annum and the apprenticeship of 10 children annually. Financial assistance was given to 24 boys in their education at the Grammar School, or other schools in the parish at the cost of about £50 per annum. Expenses incurred also included the maintaining of a public weighing-machine and a parish hearse and the payment of municipal officers, park keepers and woodmen. It was calculated that upwards of 700 people received benefits from the various charities. and Miss Bracken adds: " The inhabitants also derive from the park the depasturing of their cattle and labour for men in the winter in making kids and besoms for sale; and also fuel picked for their own use."

One of the advocates of National Schools (according to Riland Bedford in " Vesey Papers ") was the master of the Grammar School, Charles Barker, who wanted to get rid of English teaching in his school, and was " anxious to uphold the full dignity of a classical seminary, untinctured by any obligation

* Sometimes written " Meadow Plat."

Sutton, in 1840, viewed from Maney.

From a drawing by Miss A. Bracken

to teach the three Rs ". However, during the headship of his predecessor (William Webb), we learn that the literary reputation of the school stood high, so that there is nothing to suggest any traditional neglect of the " three Rs ". Among the school's pupils of this period was H. F. Cary, who, while at the school, made frequent contributions to the poetical pages of the " Gentleman's Magazine ". He is remembered for having, in later life, translated Dante into English, made verse translations of Aristophanes and the Odes of Pindar, and for having written the " Lives of English Poets ", reputedly in continuation of Samuel Johnson's Work under a similar title.

In an unpublished History of Sutton Coldfield, written by Z. Twamley (c. 1855)* we learn that its author " received a plain yet useful education at the school, top of the town, then called the Free School, during the time while the late Mr. William Webb was the Headmaster." Both the Classics and English, Twamley tells us, were then taught free for 12 months to boys whose parents lived in the parish, and the ability to read was the qualification for admission. After 12 months the boys paid six-pence a week to the under-master for teaching arithmetic. Two months of the year, Christmas and Mid-summer, were fixed holidays.

When William Webb died, according to Twamley, the school became ' unsettled ', and under Charles Barker's headship, day pupils of the English department were turned away, except a few who continued because they were also taking Classics. Charles Barker's headship continued to 1842, when, Twamley tells us, he was found dead in the road, having fallen from his horse. At that time, Twamley adds, there was only one day pupil being taught the Classics, so that Barker's situation had " nearly become a sinecure." Riland Bedford relates that in 1840, the affairs of the Grammar School occupied the attention of the House of Commons, when the unsatisfactory teaching and management of the school was brought to the notice of the House by Sir J. E. Eardley Wilmot, a Member for North Warwickshire.

The next headmaster was James Eccleston, who held the post for 5 years, during which time he was chosen by the Corporation as a member of that body and in November, 1848, was elected to the office of Warden. Twamley tells us: " He left the schoolhouse and Sutton Coldfield altogether in a very dishonourable way, not paying one single sixpence in the pound on any of his debts in simple contract at law." On 4th June, 1849, he started to leave by the Tamworth to Birmingham horse 'bus which passed through Sutton at about 9 o'clock in the morning. However, he was:

" . . . captured at Birmingham and afterwards sent to Warwick; at which place he took the benefit of the Insolvent

* The manuscript is held at Sutton Coldfield Central Library.

72

Act. He was there tried and sentenced for some imprisonment, but by pleading his own case so ably afterwards, His
Honour, who sat as Judge in that Court, released him. He
somehow or other obtained to procure an appointment at
Hobart Town, to be made Rector of the High School there.
Then, last of all, he took his wife and family along with
him and started for Van Diemen's Land. He died there on
8th March, 1850, where he lies interred. Aged 34 years."

In 1825, the Corporation Boys' and Girls' National Town
School was founded, the educational target of which was "the
moral and religious instruction of 50 male and 50 female children
of the poor inhabitants." The history of this school is well
documented, thanks largely to the Rev. W. K. Riland Bedford,
and the interest and enthusiasm of Miss M. Henry, M.B.E., a
former Headmistress of the Town County Primary School. She
has succeeded, among other things, in saving from oblivion the
School's original log-book.

This log-book—the first entry in which was made on 23rd
January, 1826, is of great interest because it shows the occupation
of each child's father. The fathers of the 23 children recorded
on the first page of the log-book are shown as:

Labourers	12
Tailors	2
Spd. (Spade?) Maker	1
Cow Leech	1
Mason	1
Wiredrawer (Penns)	1
Sawyer	1
Barber	1
Shoemaker	1
G.B. Borer (Oughton's Mill)	1
Keeper (Sutton Park)	1

Other trades shown in the log-book are: Blacksmith,
Grinder, Carpenter, Boatman, Accountant, Basketmaker,
Moulder, Wheelwright. Miller, Saw-maker, Servant, Millwright,
Clerk and Painter.

Many pupils of the Town School were clothed from the
funds available and a "School of Industry" was set up. The
children were to be employed in making their own clothes, and
the girls were to knit stockings for the boys and to make up
linen to be lent or given to the poor married women of the
parish. This "School of Industry", however, seems to have
been unsuccessful from the start.

One of the rules of the school was punctual attendance, and
parents were not allowed to keep their children away from school
for any reason other than illness. The rules were enforceable
by fines. The term 'National' signified that the school was
founded under the auspices of the National Society, set up in
1811, the full title of which was The National Society for

Promoting the Education of the Poor in the Principles of the Established Church throughout England and Wales." Not surprisingly, therefore, the Rector of Sutton Coldfield took a keen interest in the Town School and its activities. In 1828, two galleries were built in the parish church for school children to attend services there.

The 'gothic' part of the present school was built and opened in 1870—the year in which elementary education became compulsory. Sanitary conditions at the school were bad, and there were outbreaks of scarlet fever, diphtheria and other ailments. In 1873, the Rev. W. K. Riland Bedford, accompanied by a surveyor and a sanitary inspector, examined the school drains, following an outbreak of scarlet fever. The same disease was responsible for the school being closed for three months in 1876. Up to the year 1889, it is said that there were no wash-bowls, and the only drinking-water tap was next to the toilets, which were two open earth closets. All the classes were taught in one room, which was adequate for the 84 children who attended the original school, but by 1898, with 203 pupils, the room was, understandably, overcrowded and badly ventilated. Enlargement of the school did not take place until 1902-04, when the Boys' building was opened.

In 1873, the lessons consisted chiefly of reading, writing, arithmetic, scripture, singing and needlework. There were three teachers—the headmistress and two assistants—and a monitress, who helped to teach the younger children.

In 1826, a Charity School was built at Walmley in that part of the parish called 'Beyond the Wood'. It stood in Fox Hollies Road, and was capable of housing 60 children. It had an adjoining dwelling-place, and was built at a cost of £343. A mistress was appointed at £25 per annum, plus a free supply of fuel. Before the building of Walmley Church in 1845, this school was also used as a place of worship. When a bigger school was built in the village, next to the church, in 1851, the original school was converted into two cottages, and a letting notice was affixed to the door of Sutton Parish Church:—

> NOTICE IS HEREBY GIVEN: That the two houses and premises belonging to the Warden and Society, and lately used as a School situate at Thimble End, Walmley, are to be let. Applications for the same to be forthwith made at the Office of Holbeche & Addenbrooke, Deputy Stewards, Sutton Coldfield. 9th September, 1851.

At Hill, a similar school was built to accommodate the children of Hill and Little Sutton. Its school-master was paid £40 per annum and in 1828, the sum of £30 per annum was allocated for paying a school-mistress.

Another Charity School was built in 1840 in Green Lanes, on the outskirts of the parish, which was described in the nineteenth century as being: " an out of the way sort of place, not far off the Chester Road." It was built as a boys' school, and drew pupils from a very wide area. The school-master, who was accommodated on the premises, received a salary of £50 per annum, with an additional £5 for fuel. Later, a school was built at Boldmere to accommodate the girls of the same district.

The completion of the turnpike road between Birmingham and Lichfield entailed making a raised road along the line of the present Parade. This was then called the Dam—a name which, for centuries, had described its function. At the same time the gradient of Mill Street was reduced by lowering the level of the road at the top of the hill. For this reason some of the windows and doorways of the buildings appear to be higher than normal. The necessity for this alteration was on account of the difficulty experienced by horses in pulling a laden stage-coach up so steep a hill. Under the turnpike act, toll-gates were built at the bottom of Gravelly Hill and at the northern end of Sutton. Midgley tells us: "This became the chief road from Bristol to the North of England, and before the time of the railways, twenty-four coaches a day rattled through the Sutton streets at ten miles an hour, and woke up the sleepy borough with their horns." Miss Bracken, however, refers to only six coaches.

The Coronation of Queen Victoria in 1838 was celebrated in style at Sutton Coldfield. Arrangements were made for ten musicians from Walsall " to be in attendance on the morning of the Coronation at ten o'clock, for the whole of the day, at ten shillings each man." An Ale Committee arranged that ale should be supplied by ten public-houses and four beer-houses in the town. The Warden was to provide five hundred medals at a halfpenny a-piece, for the children. £5 was allocated for ' tea drinking ', and the rector and two members of the local gentry each made a gift of a fat sheep. Various committees and officials were appointed and two ' Conservators of the Peace ' were named.

The feast provided by the local gentry for the poor was laid out in Coleshill Street on twenty trestle-tables, for which forty carvers were appointed (one of whom was the Warden). Thirteen beer stewards were on duty to see that everyone had a share of the ale, which had cost £50. The day might have passed without mishap had it not been for the fact that a special local version of the National Anthem had been composed in readiness for the Coronation. One of the verses ran:

Let then our Royal Town
True to its old renown
This day be seen
Steady to England's Throne

Parade. In the top picture, taken around 1865—when it was still known as "the Dam"—its western side lay undeveloped. In the bottom picture—at a later date—a great change has taken place in the road's appearance.

Be our devotion shewn,
While in our hearts we crown
Victoria Queen.

In their anxiety to do justice to this up-dated version, it is
recorded that: " A goodly company of ladies and gentlemen
mounted one of the tables to sing ' God Save the Queen ' when,
unhappily, down came the table, but no serious harm was sus-
tained."

The only damage was probably to the dignity of that
' goodly company ', especially since social barriers between rich
and poor formed an integral part of the social order. Viewed
through the eyes of today's affluent society, some of the aspects
of past social life—overshadowed as it was for the poor, by the
spectre of the workhouse—appear strange. The relief of poverty
and the administration of the Poor Law devolved on the parish,
through the offices of the church-wardens and overseers of the
poor. This system operated for over three-hundred years, and
due to bad administration, the workhouse often housed hosts of
children, as well as adult paupers. Parish relief was sometimes
augmented by charities of various kinds. At Sutton, for instance, there were annual awards of marriage portions of £24
each, to four " poor maidens " who were natives of or had been
long resident in the parish. These girl recipients were often
domestic servants, and the custom continued well into the present
century. It is recorded that " the highest testimonials " were
required, not only for the " poor maidens ", but for the men
they proposed to marry. One year, the ' intended ' of one of
Sutton's under-privileged girls defected before the wedding day
and married a widow with five children, thus making one ' poor
maiden ' the poorer by £24—and a husband.

Doctor George Bodington of Sutton Coldfield came of good
Warwickshire yeoman stock, and his family it is claimed, had
tilled their own land in the parish since the time of Henry VIII.
During the early part of the nineteenth century he established
himself in the village of Erdington as a successful medical practitioner, but was soon drawn back to his home town to devote
himself to the care of the mentally sick at the Driffold House
Asylum. He became proprietor there, and was later succeeded
by his son, Dr. G. F. Bodington. His busy professional life
did not prevent him from participating in other activities. He was
a magistrate, and twice Warden of Sutton Coldfield.

Doctor Bodington's real claim to fame, however, stems from
a paper he wrote in 1840 entitled ' An Essay on the Treatment
and Cure of Pulmonary Consumption.' In this paper he ex-
pounded what were then highly revolutionary ideas on the
subject. Arguing against " . . . the value of antimony, calomel

and bleeding ", he advocated " . . . nutritious food and stimulants, with plenty of exercise in pure air." He set no great value by sea air, but favoured a dry, preferably frosty atmosphere, which he claimed " . . . had a most powerful influence in healing and closing of cavities and ulcers of the lungs."

Because the theories of Dr. Bodington were in advance of the times in which he lived, he was occasionally subjected to attacks upon his reputation. When his views came to be more widely accepted, however, a German doctor named Koch claimed to have pioneered the theories which he had propounded. A correspondence arose out of the issue, and found its way into the columns of " The Times."

Many local people will still remember the White House at Maney, which was demolished in 1935 to make way for the Odeon Cinema. It was here that Doctor Bodington had his sanatorium, where he put his advanced theories into practice. No case histories of his patients are available, but it must be assumed that he met with some fair measure of success. At any rate, when he died in 1882 (in his 83rd year), the " Lancet " obituary notice described him in terms of unstinted praise. " We are glad," they said, " to claim for a general practitioner the high credit of having been the first, or among the first, to advocate the rational and scientific treatment of pulmonary consumption."

The name of George Bodington is linked through marriage with that of another local celebrity, for his wife was the granddaughter of William Fowler of Gravelly Hill, who died on 28th July, 1804, at the age of 107, having enjoyed the rare distiction of living in three centuries. William Fowler came from Pelsall as a young man to take up the post of Steward of the Aston Hall estate when it was still the home of the Holte family. In 1748 he bought several acres of land, where he built Gravelly Hill House, in which five generations of his family lived. The family vault, where old William Fowler is buried, is in front of the west door of Aston Church, but the spot was tarmaced over many years ago.

A graphic account of life in Sutton Coldfield in the mid-nineteenth century is contained in the unpublished " Holbeche Diary ". The Holbeche family once occupied the still existing No. 3, Coleshill Street, said to have been the first rectory. Thomas Holbeche was a solicitor, a county magistrate and Deputy Steward (legal adviser) to the Corporation, and Riland Bedford tells us that his ancestors had been landed proprietors in North Warwickshire for several centuries. He died in 1848.

The Holbeche Diary was written in 1892. Its authorship is not made clear, and we are not told which member of the Holbeche family wrote it. It is not, in fact, a diary, but a nostalgic evocation of past scenes, events and personalities, committed to paper after a lapse of about 40 years, in which the writer proclaims: " . . . I have thought it well to put pen to paper in order to have some record of what it was like in my boyish days, and to keep my memory green as to the old people, the like of whom no-one will see again, and some of the customs of the old-world town which have also passed away." Holbeche describes his old home, and its garden, at considerable length. Someone, he said, had compared the house to a rabbit warren, because the numerous rooms led into each other in what, to a stranger, was a most perplexing way. He tells us, too, about the out-houses—a large tithe barn, with a granary and loft, a three-stalled stable, a saddle room, a pigsty and a dairy where, when no-one was looking, the children dipped their fingers in the cream.

He remembers the trees and shrubs with loving detail—the yew which his Uncle Henry Addenbrooke had brought as a seedling from his dog's grave at Kingswinford; a pink hawthorn, a holly and a lilac; a cherry tree near the door leading from the yard; a profusion of wild clematis and an enormous oak, a beautifully stately and symetrical tree, cut down around 1860. There was a crab-tree, too, on which his brother had carved his initials; some fine walnut trees, a pear tree that bore thousands of indigestible pears; and " a dear old mulberry tree which showered bleeding fruit, and which we climbed and swung upon and sat in." There were, besides, guelder roses, and two beautiful willows and " a wee little pond, banked on one side with bottle reeds, and a little trickling stream, bridged by a rough and broad oak planking, which took us to a black wicket gate, opening on to the field."

Holbeche describes a good many of Sutton's inhabitants, including members of his own family. He tells us that it was Doctor Bodington who brought him into the world and that he (Doctor Bodington), frequently reminded him of the fact—once at a public dinner, rather inconveniently. The patients at Doctor Bodington's lunatic asylum at the Driffold interested the children very much, in particular, one " Mr. Fisher who wore a grey tail coat covered with buttons and a white beaver hat." One of his childhood memories was of wearing white drawers with starched frills round their bottoms. " I was breeched in '59 " he tells us, and adds: " This I remember to have been a comfort, for as all the seats were covered (at home) with horse-hair, and very prickly, it was necessary to sit down with some circumspection."

William Betts, Holbeche recalls, was inn-keeper at the " Old Sun " in Coleshill Street, and a very popular host, whose house in the pre-railway days was a great meeting place for Birmingham tradesmen, who on Sundays drove their wives in gay bonnets, to take the Sutton air. " They came in smart dog-carts,

drawn by fast trotting ponies." The one and only policeman—
a smart and soldier-like man—lived in a white house next to the
churchyard, and Holbeche recalls: " When we were coming out
of church one Sunday, I remember his telling my father of the
death of the Prince Consort." The policeman was named Com-
mander, and was a successor to Thomas Butler who—following
a meeting of the Warden and Society in 1836—had been
appointed first policeman at one guinea a week. He had to submit
a weekly report to the newly formed Police Committee, and his
duties supplanted those of the Parish Constable, who had been
appointed annually by the Justices of the Peace.

After describing the church and its congregation, Holbeche
adds: " The churchyard was very badly kept, and sheep grazed
it. It was unenclosed and Birmingham roughs used to sit and
make a noise about Mary Ashford's grave during service." In
Vesey House in High Street, Holbeche reminds us, lived three
sisters, the Misses Bracken:

" The eldest was Agnes, the like of whom I do not know
or have ever known. A woman first, authoress, artist, antiquarian, philanthropist, of the strongest individuality, with
the softest heart, such was Agnes Bracken, and I speak of
her with respect and affection. Her delightful book on the
place she loved so well, is a local classic, her pictures adorn
many of the drawing-rooms of what few old Suttonians
remain, and record the park at it was, the town as it was,
and many friends as they were.

" She was thorough; her mission work, her activity in
every thing that was likely to benefit others or animals,
are not likely to be forgotten till the old Sutton folk have
quite died out, which will perchance be ere long.

" She took great pains in trying to teach me water
colour drawing, and would take me for long walks in the
park, telling me of the Roman roads, barrows and crom-
lechs. She went to her rest in 1877."

Agnes Bracken was born in Erdington in November, 1800,
and came to live at Sutton with her family in 1816. She became
a school-teacher in 1820, in which profession she continued all
her life. She was an artist of considerable talent, whose scenes
of old Sutton are still widely appreciated, an archaeologist, and
authoress of " A History of the Forest and Chase of Sutton
Coldfield."

The " Holbeche Diary " finishes on a wistful note: " Many
more and great changes will happen, but the greatest of all have
already taken place; when Sutton Coldfield lost its character of
being a sleepy old-fashioned town; when the people and the
customs changed; when the freshness of country life disappeared,
and the ideas and manners of a large provincial town were substituted. ' So the old order of things giveth place to the new.' "

In 1849, Sutton Coldfield's original Charters were sent to
London to be translated into English. They were in Old Latin,

with many abbreviations and very difficult to understand. The intention was that their contents should be made readily available to the Warden and Society. At the same time measures were taken to preserve the old skins from being worn-out or becoming illegible from frequent use and handling.

CHAPTER VII

Sutton Coldfield in the mid-nineteenth century—The growth of population—The coming of the railways—The Crystal Palace.

IN the mid-nineteenth century, Sutton Coldfield was a vastly different place from the town we know today. The bed of the old mill pool beside the dam—later to become the Parade—lay undeveloped. The old workhouse still stood in Mill Street, and adjoining it was the town gaol. At the top of Mill Street stood the Moot Hall—the second one to stand on the site since Vesey's day. The first Moot Hall had had to be pulled down in 1671, following the funeral of Thomas Dawney, on which occasion the Sutton register records that " The Towne Hall floore fell downe by a presse of people there." They were there for the handing out of a funeral dole, when they fell from the upper floor to the bottom floor, which was then open as a market-place. Fortunately no-one seems to have been killed or seriously injured. The second Moot Hall became unsafe, too, and was demolished in 1854. Holbeche tells us that the old workhouse was renovated and turned into municipal offices. This may have been around 1854. In 1859, a new Town Hall (now the Masonic Building) was built on the site of the workhouse and gaol. The almshouses which stood below this building survived until 1924, when the occupants were rehoused in new almshouses at Walmley.

The site of the Vesey Gardens was occupied by a group of old buildings, including two inns— the " Old Sun " and the " Royal Oak ". Opposite, the building now used as the Post Office, was the Emmanuel College Arms. The land on which it stands is said to have been bought by the Lord Mayor of London in 1585 to provide an endowment for Emmanuel College, Cambridge. There was still a town pump in Mill Street, where the inhabitants gathered with their pails, as much for the gossip as for the water. The South Staffordshire tapped water was not brought to the town from Shenstone until 1892, but the streets were already lit by gas—supplied by the Sutton Coldfield Gas, Light and Coke Company, situated in Riland Road. One of the shareholders was the Rev. W. K. Riland Bedford, the Rector, and in the Central Library there is a Certificate of a Ten Pounds Share in his name, dated 3rd February, 1854. The town was still paved with cobblestones—large ones for the streets and smaller ones for the paths.

Vesey House in High Street—the home of the Misses Bracken—was sometimes called " up the steps down the steps ", because of the steps it once had on either side of the front door. During the Commonwealth the house was occupied by Thomas Willoughby, the magistrate administrator, appointed by Cromwell who officiated at civil marriages in the town. The "Three Tuns" —possibly the oldest inn in Sutton—also has associations with Cromwell, who is said to have had a meeting there with a number of his officers after the Battle of Worcester in 1651. William Frederick Woodington was born at the "Three Tuns", and became a successful sculptor in the nineteenth century. He was responsible for some of the bas-relief work at the base of Nelson's Column in Trafalgar Square. He exhibited a statue in the Royal Academy in 1877, called " The first sorrow—Poor Robin ", depicting a boy holding a dead bird. A model of this statue stands in the entrance to the Town County Primary School. A later visitor to the "Three Tuns" is reputed to have been Vesta Tilley, who has been described as " one of the first of the great male impersonators."

In the 1850s, the present Royal Hotel was the home of William Morris Grundy, who was engaged in his family business of currying and tanning. He was a pioneer of photography, and had a van—which he used as a mobile dark room—drawn by an old brown horse. When he died in 1859 he left an estate worth £25,000—a substantial amount in those days. Behind his house there was an attractive walk down the hill, over beautiful turf, to the Park. On the opposite side of the road, where the railway bridge is now, was the old sandstone tithe barn, built by Vesey in 1529. It had yew trees on each side of its porch, and brick steps leading to an upper storey with tall mullioned windows, which had apparently been a dwelling house at some earlier period. During its latter days the tithe barn was converted into a malt house. The gable of the building was, as Riland Bedford points out (in " The Vesey Papers "), " ornamented with some very curious fragments of figures, including the stag's head, the Harman crest." In the last century, when it was found that the malt house was in the line of the proposed railway cutting and bridge, it was sold to the Midland Railway Company for £4,000. In the deeds of this transaction, the land to the rear of the malt house is referred to as " Vesey's Croft ". The house beyond the malt house was also sold to the railway company, but continued to be used as a school by John Henry Cull, one of whose pupils is said to have been Francis Brett Young, the doctor-novelist, who wrote " My Brother Johnathan " and " The House Under the Water ". The building still survives.

Near to Moat House stood Cock Sparrow Hall, a pretty, half-timbered black and white house. Its disappearance from

The old Pie Shop, on the corner of Manor Road, was a familiar and friendly landmark for generations of local people.

Photograph:
James Speight

the scene prompted Holbeche to say in his " Diary ": " May the possessor of the property be forgiven for demolishing it, for it was wanton: a pure piece of vandalism."

In the lower part of the town, at the bottom of Mill Street, there was a blacksmith's forge, and by the " Dog in the Hole "— once known as the " Talbot "—there was a dairy and a pound for stray animals. A local conundrum posed the question:— " Where do they sell beer by the pound?" and the answer was, of course, " At the ' Dog '." Neighbouring " Ashby House " with its reputedly fine Queen Anne fire-places, was then the " Coach and Horses " inn. There was, according to Holbeche, a mill at Skinners Pool, and across the road—now Park Road— was a pretty lane with high, white thorn hedges, almost meeting overhead. The view west from the dam, before the building of the railway embankment, offered an open vista of the Park. At the southern end of the Dam—on the corner of Manor Road, stood the old Pie Shop, a familiar and friendly landmark for generations of local people. It had a low beamed kitchen and a stone flagged floor. Sides of bacon and hams hung from the roof beams, and the counter, which was scrubbed white, displayed home-made pies, tripe, chitterlings and other goodies. Hot pies and muffins each cost a penny. The Cup Inn was an attractive one-storey wayside inn where, in season, they had dancing on the green. It was replaced by the present building around the turn of the century.

Even before the coming of the railway, Sutton was a place which Birmingham people liked to visit. Miss Bracken reminds us that there were " omnibuses oscillating between Birmingham and Sutton, with multitudes imported for a few hours' respiration of Coldfield air." The " Holbeche Diary " gives a description of an omnibus from Birmingham, crowded inside and out, " toiling up the hill, with its four steaming grey horses." The journey from Birmingham to Sutton Coldfield by horse 'bus took 80 minutes. A favourite spot in the town for visitors was the Museum Hotel on the corner of Park Road (only recently demolished). This once boasted a large, free museum of birds, animals, reptiles and fishes. It was said to have been the biggest museum in the Midlands. It also had tea gardens with " summer arbors and a large green for dancing." The hotel itself provided a sandwich and a glass of ale for 3d., plain teas at 8d., or with ham and beef 1/-.

Riland Bedford tells us that there were many old families among the yeomen, freeholders, cottagers and labourers in the parish. Many of these had occupied the same dwellings and cultivated the same crofts for generations, but following upon the repeal of the Corn Laws, he claims, their numbers were much diminished. He also refers to a " fluctuating element in the population ", caused by the large number of well-to-do residents who were constantly importing servants, many of whom married and settled in the parish. This resulted in strangers coming from " the remotest parts of the three kingdoms, and even, in the last century, from other quarters of the globe." In support of this latter contention, Riland Bedford gives two instances from the parish registers:

" Baptized November 27th, 1765, a native of Jamaica, being a person of riper years, now in the service of Simon Luttrell, Esq., named Philip, to which afterwards was added the surname of Sutton."

and

" 1789—There was baptized the 23rd day of November, Bartholomew, a negro, and servant to Mr. Goward, of this town, aged 30 years."

According to Miss Bracken (writing in 1860), the owner of the manor-house and estate was also a member of an old family. He was the 16th Baron Somerville, one of whose ancestors came to England with the Conqueror. The house, built on the site of the original manor and still standing, Riland Bedford tells us, dates from about 1820, when the estate first came into the hands of the Somervilles. It had, for the previous two centuries, belonged to the Holtes, and was part of the Aston Hall property until 1817, when the last baronet, Sir Charles Holte, died. His wife was a member of the Jesson family of Langley Hall, Sutton Coldfield.

James, the 11th Lord Somerville, according to Miss Bracken, was author of the memoirs of the Somervilles, and an ancient branch of the family was represented by William Somerville of Edstone, Warwickshire, the author of "The Chase", and other poems. John, the 15th baron, introduced the merino sheep into Great Britain—a pioneering act which is not, however, recalled with any measure of gratitude, for the moistness of the climate here is not conducive to the fine growth of wool usually associated with the species.

Sutton's rising population resulted in the expansion of outlying districts. At Boldmere, a new parish was formed, which originally extended from the Erdington boundary to that of Walmley, and included the Banners Gate and Powells Pool areas. This large parish, at its inception, probably had a population of 500 to 750 people. Church services were held, originally, in Green Lanes Boys' School, and when, some years later, a school for girls and infants was built in Boldmere, services were held there. Funds were raised locally for the building of a parish church, and we learn from the "Holbeche Diary" of a great bazaar which was held on the slope close to Blackroot Pool, for which event a military band was in attendance. "It was, I believe, a great success" the "Diary" tells us "and the building fund of Boldmere Church gained considerably." The planned new church was sponsored by the Rev. W. K. Riland Bedford, Rector of Sutton Coldfield, and the Chairman of the Committee set up to deal with the issue was Dr. George Bodington, who was then Warden of Sutton Coldfield. St. Michael's Church, when built, was consecrated in 1857. There were 55 acres of glebe land attached to it, and the first vicar, the Rev. E. H. Kittoe was described as being "a dignified, scholarly, fine old English gentleman with a personality which commanded the esteem and confidence of the parish. He was kind and generous to the needy; and it was said of him that he gave away to the poor the whole of his official stipend. He knew how to be severe with evil-doers and was a wise counsellor to such as desired guidance in personal or family affairs and altogether an ideal pastor." He was responsible for the laying out of the vicarage gardens and for the planting of the avenue of limes leading to the church from Boldmere Road. Several gardeners were employed, and the vicarage grounds became well known as a local beauty spot. The spire and north aisle of the church were built in 1871.

The history of Boldmere itself is obscure, and little is to be learned from the early writers. It has been claimed that the church was built on the site of an ancient British fort, but there is no positive evidence of this. We know there was once a lake at Boldmere, but its history has not been preserved, and we do not know when, or why, it was drained and filled in. It still existed in 1857, when St. Michael's Church was consecrated, for we are told that the church was built "on the eminence above Baldmoor Lake on the Chester Road."

Boldmere, now mainly built-up, has diminished in area with the formation of neighbouring ecclesiastical parishes. The coming of the railway played no small part in Boldmere's rise in population. It enabled people who worked in Birmingham to live in a semi-rural environment, within easy walking distance of Sutton Park, yet only a short distance by train from where they worked. Like so many other parishes around Birmingham's green perimeter, Boldmere rapidly became a popular residential area. Today, with most of the available building land used up, Boldmere's leafiness has not been entirely lost. When the wooded acres of the old vicarage grounds were considerably reduced in size by 'development' some years ago, many fine trees were felled, but fortunately many more survived and the church remains at the 'green heart' of the parish.

The growing use of steam as a motivating force undoubtedly represented a considerable acceleration of the Victorian ideal of Progress. Boulton and Watt at Handsworth in the latter half of the eighteenth century had greatly improved the efficiency of the static steam engine, but it was not until 1825, that the application of the principle produced the first railway worthy of the name, operated by steam locomotives. This was the Stockton to Darlington line, brain-child of George Stephenson and a few other pioneers.

Here, indeed was Progress! Soon all the big towns and cities of England were linked by the gleaming steel tracks of the railways, and, almost overnight, the problems of time and distance were annihilated. It was an era of unbridled competition, and railway companies, each with its distinctive livery, were increasing in numbers year by year. In 1838—the year after Victoria came to the throne—Birmingham and London were linked by rail. This, however, was not Birmingham's first railway, for the town was already joined to the Liverpool and Manchester Railway by way of the 'Grand Junction' line.

Suburban lines, understandably, came some time after the main lines, and it was not until 1862 that the existing London and North Western Railway line between Birmingham and Aston was extended to Sutton Coldfield. There was much competition in this project too, for the Midland Railway offered an alternative route to that eventually chosen. This would have left the existing Midland Railway track at Saltley, crossed the line of the present Tyburn Road (which was not cut until 1912), and proceeded up the eastern side of Gravelly Hill, through Wood End, to a station in Mason Road, at the rear of Erdington Village Green. In addition, there was to have been a station near Sir Josiah Mason's Orphanage on Chester Road, another in Wylde Green

Sutton Coldfield as a railway terminal in 1865. The hotel in the background was built for the use of rail travellers. It later became the Council House. The line was extended to Lichfield in 1884.

Road, and the Sutton terminus was to have been on the marshy land below the dam, to the east of what is now the Parade.

These rival lines, which Riland Bedford tells us divided the public opinion of the district for many months, were known, respectively, as the Eastern and the Western lines. Local landowners in particular were divided as to which route should be taken, and eventually two rival Bills were considered by a committee of the House of Commons. After hearing the expert evidence, the parliamentary committee eventually approved the Western line, and the work on its construction started with the minimum of delay.

The project was completed in just over 18 months, at a cost of £60,000. A bridge of five arches was constructed over the Tame, and another of three arches over the canal (both at the foot of Gravelly Hill); a deep cutting was made through Gravelly Hill itself and a 40 feet wrought iron girder-bridge built over the Chester Road. Apart from these, the engineering difficulties were described as being ' of a very trifling character.' The line, at that time, terminated at Sutton, and there was a turntable there for turning engines round for the journey back to Birmingham. The present council-house was built in 1863—as an hotel for railway travellers—and was called the Royal Hotel.

The extension of the line from Sutton Coldfield to Lichfield was opened on 15th December, 1884. Expresses were then run

Sutton Coldfield High Street in Victorian times.
Photograph: Sir Benjamin Stone

between Birmingham and Lichfield, and a through train from New Street, Birmingham to Derby made its first stop at Sutton Coldfield. The driver of an engine called "Sister Dora" habitually did the journey to Sutton in well under the scheduled running time, and passengers were regularly alarmed by the speed at which the train negotiated the bend beyond Aston Station. "Sister Dora" belonged to the "Precedent" Class and was a 2-4-0 express engine, built at Crewe c.1870. It was still known to be running in 1924.

By rail the journey to Birmingham only took 15 minutes, and Sutton's popularity as a healthy residential area grew accordingly. The population of the town increased from 4,662 in 1861 to 7,737 in 1881, and in 1869 the "Birmingham Daily Post" proclaimed that the railway was responsible for its passing "from rural sleepiness to bustling activity." It was also responsible for the Park becoming a popular rendezvous for the working people of Birmingham and the Black Country, and the railway company was quick to exploit the Park's all-the-year round attraction. In 1870, for instance, an advertisement in the "Birmingham Daily Post" for a Christmas trip to the Park ran as follows:

LONDON AND NORTH-WESTERN RAILWAY
Skating on Windley Pool, Sutton Coldfield
A CHEAP EXCURSION TRAIN will run from New Street Station at 12 noon and 2.15 p.m. to SUTTON COLDFIELD, THIS DAY (Monday), December 26, and every day during the Frost. Fare there and back including admission to the Royal Promenade and Windley Pool, 9d. Covered Carriages.

The Park's popularity prompted Dean Hole to say of Bracebridge Pool, after comparing it favourably with Killarney, that it was:

" . . . one of the prettiest spots in England, whose tranquil loveliness is a refreshment and a blessing to thousands of our weary artisans."

Something of this tranquil loveliness, however, was soon to be lost, for it was during this period that the western vista of Bracebridge Pool was defaced by the Midland Railway Company's line through Castle Bromwich, Penns, Sutton Park and Streetly, to Walsall. Some years previously, Sutton Coldfield Corporation had indicated its opposition to a railway through the Park, and it seems to have been tacitly assumed that their continued opposition would prevent the accomplishment of this act. Such was not the case, however, and after a meeting to discuss whether the line should cross the Park by way of Bracebridge Pool or Rowton's Hill, the former course was approved, and the townspeople were awakened to the fact that they had been committed to supporting a proposal for a railway going straight through Bracebridge Wood.

Feelings in the town ran high, and there was considerable opposition to the proposal. Birmingham also registered a protest, and Joseph Chamberlain appealed for funds with a view to taking the matter to the House of Lords. This idea was popular in Sutton, too, but when the suggestion was put to the vote in he council chamber, seven were in favour of appealing to the Lords, eight against. Hopes of preserving the sanctity of the Park were, by this time, being abandoned. Many of the poorer people of the town were rallied to support the bill. Its promoters called a meeting of the cottagers, whose only knowledge of the Park, according to Midgley ("A Short History of the Town and Chase of Sutton Coldfield") was that they pastured their donkeys there. This meeting was presided over by Dr. George Bodington, who beguiled those present with the promise of cheap coal for Sutton from the Black Country as a consequence of the railway, and a resolution was passed in the bill's favour. Its enactment became a mere formality, and a strip of land almost two miles long was sold to the Midland Railway for £6,500. The railway was built and the line opened to passenger traffic in 1879. There were stations at Penns, Sutton Town (Midland Drive), Sutton Park, Streetly and Aldridge.

The fact that Streetly lacked the focal point of a village created a problem. What should they call the station there? Someone suggested 'Jervistown' after the Hon. Parker Jervis, who lived at Little Aston Hall. However, 'Streetly' was eventually agreed upon—a name commemorating the passing of the Roman legions, almost 2,000 years ago. (Streetly—'the lea or field on the street.')

Another and less publicised consequence of the building of the 'Penns Line' was the altering of the course of one of the oldest lanes of the parish. That part of Coles Lane which now runs parallel with the railway line was diverted from its original course, for it previously joined Wylde Green Road further east than at present. Prior to the building of the Bishop Walsh School, the old hedgerow trees, marking the lane's former course, could be seen a few yards to the east of the railway bridge. Coles Lane extended from the junction of Holland Road to Wylde Green Road, and the name 'East View Road' is only of recent origin.

In Victorian times it became popular amongst Black Country people to make annual, organised visits to Sutton Park. These expeditions, known as "Maying", were the occasions for considerable merriment, necessitating stopping at every inn on the way, as well as imbibing liberal quantities of beer which the

90

trippers brought with them. According to a newspaper report of one such annual visit: " Drunken yells, boisterous shouts and incoherently-rendered comic songs, interspersed with an occasional free fight formed the chief characteristic of the mob." The local police—now greatly augmented in numbers—were usually at the ready to deal with such revelry, and it was not unknown for whole brake-loads of constabulary to turn out for the purpose of restoring order among noisy visitors.

The summer of 1868, was one of great heat and drought, without rain between April and August. On August 4th of that year, a fire broke out near the Beggars Bush, which rapidly spread through the gorse and undergrowth then flourishing around Sutton Park's boundaries, and soon reached the Park itself. It seemed at one stage that the conflagration had been controlled, but a sudden breeze caused it to break out again with renewed fury. After lasting for several days, the fire destroyed between 500 and 800 acres of parkland.

The precise cause of the fire was never established, but it was suggested that it may have been due to " the careless throwing away of a lighted vesuvian ". The authorities, however, took a serious view of the occurrence, for—in addition to closing the Park to the public for a while following the fire—a reward of £100 was offered by the Warden and Society of Sutton Coldfield " in pursuance of the apprehension and conviction of parties guilty of incendiarism." The reward was unclaimed.

Another event of 1868 was the opening of the Royal Promenade Gardens on the site now occupied by the Youth Centre. The Gardens comprised a fernery, sheltered by rhododendrons and azaleas, separate beds of rhododendrons occupying nearly two acres, a large rosery, an Italian Garden, lawns and ornamental plantations, a bowling green and spacious cricket, archery and croquet grounds. There was also an ornamental lake, a conservatory for floral displays and various other buildings designed to make the spot atractive to visitors.

The conservatory had a large glass dome, reminiscent of Hyde Park's Crystal Palace, built for the Great Exhibition of 1851. Not surprisingly it was given the same name. The area surrounding the Crystal Palace was sufficiently extensive to cater for a wide variety of tastes. Next to the Palace there was an hotel, with stabling for 50 horses; there were 30 acres of grass-land, where, in season, a military band played twice a week, and in 1880 it was claimed that: " Ample provision has been made for the amusement and recreation of the visitors. There are boats for sailing and rowing, canoes for paddling, and punts for patient fishermen on Wyndley Pool which adjoins the gardens." It was also claimed that there was: " a splendid bicycle track, swings for children, dancing ground for adults, shady avenues for ' spooning purposes ', and one of the best cricketing grounds in the district." Early in the present century the grounds acquired the additional attractions of Pat Collins' Fun Fair, and a miniature railway, built by Bassett-Lowke, a firm specialising in model-railway engineering.

For a period during the nineteenth century, the Birmingham Volunteers—predecessors of the Territorial Army—were annual visitors to Sutton Park, where they encamped at Streetly, and underwent military training. Reveille was at 5 a.m., and the military exercises were carried out in co-operation with regular army units. From a newspaper report we learn of the Volunteers leaving for one such camp in June, 1876:—

"Although it was somewhat gloomy on Saturday last at the appointed time for the start of the Volunteers for the Camp in Sutton Park, there was a good muster of men at Bingley Hall, for they were invigorated by the thought of the pleasant relief from the dreary monotonous drills in town, and also of a week's sojourn in the Park.

"The men numbered 709 strong, which is considerably in excess of last year . . . The Corps passed down Snow Hill, Summer Lane, along Aston Newtown, through Perry Barr, leaving Oscott to the right, and entered the Park at the Chester Road entrance.

"An assemblage of several hundreds had congregated in the vicinity of the Camp, when the strains of the band in the distance announced the approach of the warriors, and a few minutes before seven o'clock they marched into the Camp in truly soldierly order."

In 1880 the Streetly Camp was the scene of a terrific thunderstorm, when the officers' mess was struck by lightning, and in 1881, Major T. H. Gem, who was in command of the battalion at Streetly and apparently in good health, was taken ill in the saddle. He never fully recovered, and died the following November. Major Gem was very popular and well known, not only in the battalion, but among local people. He was a solicitor, a clerk to the magistrates, a cricketer and athlete, a writer of humorous verse and a raconteur. He was also the first historian of the Corps, who wrote "the account of the raising, progress and exploits of the battalion" up to 1875.

In 1869, the town had acquired its first newspaper—the "Sutton Coldfield and Erdington News"—which Riland Bedford says "was started by a few gentlemen, who thought that a local organ of public opinion would be useful." He added that, after a chequered existence of about fifteen years, it passed into the hands of the proprietor of the "Sutton Coldfield and Erdington Times", which, at the time of his writing the "History of Sutton Coldfield" in 1891, was published every Thursday under the title of the "Warwickshire Herald". Riland Bedford was said to have a financial interest in this paper, for which he wrote frequently.

In 1869 also, a proposal was made by the Birmingham Waterworks Company for obtaining their water supply from Sutton Park, but it was withdrawn on account of opposition from Sutton Coldfield Corporation. In 1875, Birmingham Corporation bought the Waterworks Company and acquired the powers which eventually enabled it to draw its water supply from the Elan Valley.

Although Sutton succeeded in avoiding Birmingham's water supply problem, it was caught up with another problem of its own—that of sewage disposal. Up until a century ago, each house had had sufficient land attached to it to absorb what Riland Bedford called " the legitimate overflow of malodourous matter ", and, since the streets had been kept clean by volunteer scavangers, there was, apparently, little to complain about. It was inevitable that the increase of buildings in the town should create new problems. In 1866, the lessee of the meadows between Park Road and the Ebrook objected to sewage from new houses in Station Street (formerly known as Hackett Street) being discharged into the brook. The Corporation became involved in the dispute and Riland Bedford mentions that several local landowners " took an intelligent interest in the sanitary question." Amongst these was Thomas Colmore, a magistrate and three times Warden of the Corporation. According to Riland Bedford, he " exercised great influence for good in the district." Thomas Colmore lived at Ashfurlong Hall, a predominantly Georgian House, where recent alterations have revealed Tudor masonry and a Vesey window—hence its having lately become a " listed " building.

At a meeting of the Aston Board of Guardians in 1870, it was claimed, in accordance with public opinion, that the Nuisances Removal Act threw responsibilty for sanitation on the Warden and Society of Sutton Coldfield. However, in the Public Health Act of 1872 the definition of " Council " did not include the word " Warden " and the Corporation were thus relieved, for the time being at least, of responsibility.

Birmingham's sewage problem also became a matter of importance, and the Birmingham Tame and Rea District Drainage Board was formed in 1877. In 1881, the Board bought from W. W. Bagot, a local landowner, one of whose family had once owned Pype Hayes Hall, 344 acres of land in Minworth. In 1888, a further 358 acres of Minworth land was sold by him to the Board, and the result of these transactions was the creation of the now familiar " Minworth Sewage Farm ". At that time however, Minworth was not a part of Sutton Coldfield, but within the administrative area of Meriden Rural District Council. It was acquired by Sutton Coldfield in 1931.

In 1967, Minworth was disrupted when the Upper Tame Main Drainage Authority—successors to the Board—laid a main outfall sewer. The excavations involved almost ruined the village

green of which Minworth was very proud. It was all that
remained of an eighteenth century common, and a resident, in
a letter to the press, declared:—

> " . . . we are deeply concerned and saddened by the
> mutilation of our village green and the uprooting of so
> many lovely trees."

Some effort, however, has been made in the ensuing years to
restore the green to its former pleasant state.

CHAPTER VIII

Racing at Four Oaks—The Charter of 1886 and Sutton's first
Mayor, Benjamin Stone—George Moore and "Corvo" at
Oscott—Alfred Antrobus and "Fernwood"—Riland Bedford's
"History of Sutton Coldfield."

NOT many people now remember Sutton's place in the ' racing
calendar ', but there have been two racecourses in Sutton
Park. The first was made on the north side of Holly Knoll, where
the Birmingham Races were held in 1847; the second, by Westwood Coppice, was made in 1868, and was in use for just over
ten years.

Sir John Hartopp sold the Four Oaks estate to a racecourse
company in the 1870s, and since the freehold of Four Oaks
Park's 246 acres realised £60,000, he may well have regarded
the transaction as being very profitable. The racecourse promoters spent an additional £40,000 on paddocks, stables, offices
and stands, including a club stand, a grandstand, a press and
jockey stand and a Tattersall's stand.

The company was incorporated on 9th December, 1879, and
the course was opened in 1881 with the Grand National Hunt
Steeplechase. The closeness of Birmingham, Walsall, Wolverhampton and Coventry to this picturesque spot was thought to
bode well for its popularity with punters and bookies alike, and
its early commercial success seemed assured. Unfortunately for
the promoters, however, the project failed to pay its way from
the start, for Four Oaks, we are told, did not attract " either the
best class of racegoers or the multitude."

Consequently, on Thursday, 28th August, 1890, Four Oaks
Hall—described in the sale catalogue as a grand pile, built early
in the eighteenth century and commanding extensive views for
many miles over Sutton Park, Birmingham and Barr Beacon—
was sold by auction. With it were also sold, Four Oaks Park,
the Dower House, cottages, race-stands and stabling. The equipment which had been provided by the racing promoters for
£40,000 was disposed of for the paltry sum of £300.

The estate was sold to the Marquis of Clanrikarde (an uncle
of Lord Lascelles), who immediately embarked upon a programme of development. A number of roads were cut and pur-
chasers of plots on the estate were each obliged to give an
undertaking to the Marquis as to how the land was to be
used. The restrictions, as someone commented, amounted to

" no business, no booze and no nuisance ", and their enforcement—which has continued to the present day—has played a considerable part in making the Four Oaks estate a bulwark against many of the noisy encroachments of the twentieth century.

In 1898 a Royal Show was held at Four Oaks, on a part of the estate not at that time developed, and Sutton Coldfield brought out its flags and buntings in honour of the Prince of Wales—later King Edward VII. The prince, wearing a grey suit and a pink carnation, rode in an open landau along a route heavy with decorations from Sutton Coldfield Station to Four Oaks Hall, where he had lunch before visiting the show.

When a landowner let his plot, next to the Royal Show, to an advertising firm, it was considered to be an infringement of the " no business " rule. A meeting of the other landowners was called, and a Four Oaks Land Owners' Protection Society was formed. The nucleus of the society's funds was given by the defaulting landowner—out of the money he had received from the advertisers.

Four Oaks Hall—demolished shortly after the Royal Show —stood on the site of the present Carhampton House in Luttrell Road. Deer from the estate were accommodated in a deer-shed which was near the spot where a house called " The Drift " in Wentworth Road later stood, but which has since been demolished. An ice-house, by means of which ice for preserving meat was stored in an underground chamber, stood near what is now the western entrance to " Redlands " in Hartopp Road. In an era before refrigeration had been developed commercially, this was a refinement enjoyed only by the occupants of large country houses. Ice collected in winter was packed in a brick-lined shaft, 20 feet deep and insulated with straw. A moderately hard winter would usually ensure a supply of ice lasting until the following winter.

These buildings, along with the racecourse grandstand, which stood near the present tennis-club in Bracebridge Road, have disappeared. The hall's vinery has survived and can be seen in a garden on the north side of Wentworth Road, near its junction with Lichfield Road. On the south side of Wentworth Road, almost opposite the vinery, stood—until a year or so ago— the crumbling ruin of the Dower House.

In the 1880s a number of golfers used to play in the Park, near the town gate, but it was not organised and there were, at first, no greens. On 7th October, 1889, a meeting was held at the home of T. S. Eddowes, when it was unanimously decided to form a Sutton Coldfield Golf Club. A plan was drawn up by a Captain Wilson. The course was one of 2,334 yards, starting near the town gate, crossing Holly Knoll, and turning near Blackroot Pool; the longest hole was 340 yards, and the shortest 160 yards. Members of the club were their own green-keepers, and it was not uncommon to see the club secretary pushing the club's lawnmower in a barrow from green to green. The club at that time had its own uniform which was defined as " a scarlet coat with grey collar and with brass buttons with ' S.C.G.C. ' thereon, the coat to be without cuffs."

In 1890 it was proposed that a course should be laid out on the Streetly side of Sutton Park. Permission was obtained from the Corporation to make the greens and fairways and the work proceeded with the minimum of delay. In 1893, with a membership of 160, the club members formed themselves into " The Incorporated Sutton Coldfield Golf Club ", when debentures were issued, with interest at four per-cent.

Sutton Coldfield's long reputation for being a healthy place was borne out by the 1889 report of the Medical Officer of Health of the borough, Dr. A. Bostock Hill. The population of Sutton at the census of 1881 had been 7,737. and it was estimated that, by 1889, it had increased to 9,100. During this year there had been 210 births, and 102 deaths, of which 20 were of children under one year of age, and twelve were of children between one and five. According to the statistics, Walmley and Hill were the healthiest parts of the borough, and the overall conclusion was that Sutton Coldfield was one of the healthiest towns in the United Kingdom. This fact spoke well, it was said, not only for the sanitary state of the borough, but for its salubriousness as a health resort.

Dr. Hill stated that he had no hesitation in saying that never had the borough been in a better sanitary state. Sewers had been made and houses re-drained; water supplies had been carefully tested, and when necessary and possible, purer supplies substituted. As County Analyst, Dr. Hill had had 100 samples of food and drugs submitted to him, and of these only four were adulterated. This, he said, conclusively showed that the quality of food supplied to the town compared very favourably with that of adjacent districts, the percentage of adulteration being about one-third of that of the county as a whole. Fifty-three sets of plans of new buildings had been approved by the Health and Highways Committee. They were for 37 houses; 2 houses and shops; and 14 alterations of premises, while two new roads had been laid out.

In 1896 a man named F. H. Cook opened a vegetarian health-food store in Sutton Coldfield. It was apparently so successful that he subsequently set up a factory at Four Oaks called " Vitaland ". He named his company Pitman Health Food Co., as a tribute to Sir Isaac Pitman, a vegetarian, whose system of shorthand bears his name.

Unsuccessful attempts were made in 1835, and again in 1855, to alter the administration of Sutton Coldfield under the provisions of the Municipal Corporations Act. Opposition to incorporation was, apparently, strong, one of the opponents being Doctor George Bodington, who was himself twice Warden of the Corporation. The Municipal Corporations (New Charters) Act of 1879 helped to clear the way for reform, and the Warden— Dr. Johnstone—promoted a petition for a municipal charter. This promptly brought forth a counter petition from the objectors, and a circular was written convening a meeting:

" You are requested to attend at the Royal Hotel, Sutton Coldfield, on Wednesday next, the 23rd of April at Two o'clock in the afternoon to meet other gentlemen who signed the Petition of Inhabitant Householders against the granting of a Charter of Incorporation to the Town, Manor and Lordship or Borough of Sutton Coldfield . . . "

The objectors won the day, and the promoters of the petition were unsuccessful in their attempts to obtain the grant of a charter. The victory, however, was short-lived, for in 1883, Sir Charles Dilke's Corporations Bill was enacted, and those Corporations not appointed by previous Acts, were extinguished. This was the end of the road for the Warden and Society, under which administration had been carried out since Vesey's day.

The Warden and Capital Burgesses continued to exercise magisterial powers until 1884, when their duties were taken over by the county justices. The office of Coroner was also transferred to the county, and Riland Bedford, in " Vesey Papers ", tells us that " the exemption from serving on juries at Warwick, claimed by Sutton inhabitants from their liability to their own sessions, was abolished, inasmuch as no such sessions had been held for more than a century." Sir Charles Dike's bill abolished what Riland Bedford called the " feeble autocracy " of the Warden and Society, and he went on to say: " It is for the Town Council to show that they can keep the grain of the judicious exercise of antiquated rights while winnowing the chaff of timid and corrupt administration. Sutton has glorious traditions and judiciously guarded privileges, but her word must be 'Excelsior!'."

In 1886 the town was granted a new Municipal Charter, under its first mayor, Benjamin Stone, who was to hold that office five times. In that year, also, the full-time employment of a Town Crier was first recorded, although it is thought that there had been one previously on a casual basis. The full title of the post was ' Pinner and Town Crier '—a pinner being one employed to catch and impound stray cattle.

*Sir Benjamin Stone—
Sutton Coldfield's first
Mayor—who is remem-
bered for his supreme
skill as a photographer,
was also M.P. for East
Birmingham from 1895
to 1909.*

Benjamin Stone was not only a successful businessman and politician, but also an artist. Although married with six children, he travelled the world, and became an author, yet still found time for what was then a comparatively untried art form—photography.

Benjamin Stone's status as a pillar of Victorian society is assured. Born in 1838, he became a successful glass manufacturer in Birmingham, and—before becoming the first mayor of Sutton Coldfield—was High Steward of the town. He was a Justice of the Peace, a Fellow of the Society of Antiquaries, and a Fellow of the Geological Society. He wrote books about his travels in places as far apart as Spain, Norway, Japan and Brazil; and in 1892, in recognition of his many talents, a knighthood was conferred upon him. Today we remember Benjamin Stone less for all these achievements than for his supreme skill as a photographer and chronicler of his environment. It has been said of him: " He was first to realise, in a serious way. the great service which the camera might render to the fullness and accuracy of history." His lasting memorial must be his gift to posterity of 26,000 photographs—all taken at a time when photography was a new-fangled, esoteric and—above all—laborious cult.

The invention of the gelatine dry plate a century ago saved photographers the task of preparing their own chemical materials every time they took a photograph. The dry plate did not come into general use until around 1880 in England, and considerably later in many other countries. Before that time, the meticulous preparation immediately prior to taking a photograph—the plate for which had to be exposed wet in the camera—was matched by the equally meticulous development of the picture immediately afterwards. This would have deterred all but the most dedicated. Benjamin Stone, whose photographic career started well before the introduction of the dry plate, had—in addition to dedication—skill, resourcefulness and tenacity, which were to single him out for recognition in his chosen art.

In 1890, Stone went with an expedition to Brazil to photograph a solar eclipse. There he arrived just in time for a traditional South American revolution, which enabled him to take photographs of a quite unexpected kind. When he saw rebels constructing a barricade in readiness to shell the governor's palace, he prevailed upon them to hold their fire until he had photographed them beside their guns.

At a time when photography entailed the use of cumbersome equipment, Benjamin Stone would sometimes climb a church-tower—or even the 250-feet tower of the Sir Josiah Mason's Orphanage, Erdington—in pursuit of panoramic views of a still semi-rural environment. His reputation as a photographer grew, and he was given authority to make a photographic survey of Parliament, the Palace of Westminster, Westminster Abbey and the Royal Palaces. He was quite prepared to give very long exposures to get the required results, as in the case of his wonderfully expansive interior of Lichfield Cathedral, which involved an exposure of 24 hours. He became president of the National Photographic Record Association and president of the Birmingham Photographic Society.

The culmination of his photographic career came when, in 1911, he was appointed as official photographer at the Coronation of King George V.

Among his published works were " A Summer Holiday in Spain " (1873), " Children in Norway " (1882) and a fairy-tale called " The Traveller's Joy ". Sir Benjamin's cheerful, avuncular countenance is, perhaps, an indication of his great love for children. This fact, combined with his absorption with the old customs and traditions of his native Warwickshire, may explain why, during his first year in office as Mayor of Sutton Coldfield, he found time to revive the ancient custom of maypole dancing.

Sir Benjamin Stone died at his home, the Grange, Erdington, on 2nd July, 1914—the same day as another famous local man, Joseph Chamberlain. Stone's wife, to whom he had been married for almost 50 years, died three days later, and following a double funeral, they were buried at Sutton Coldfield on 7th July, 1914.

On the occasion of Queen Victoria's Golden Jubilee in 1887, Benjamin Stone had taken many photographs of the festivities in Sutton Coldfield, including over 100 of the Maypole dancers in their picturesque costumes. It was arranged that these photographs should be presented to Queen Victoria at Windsor Castle by four little girls, representing the town's schools. On 29th November, 1887, these children, aged 10 to 11, accompanied by Benjamin Stone, set out by train at seven o'clock in the morning on their long journey.

At Windsor Castle, a great fuss was made of the little girls. One newspaper reported that: " In striking contrast to the uniforms of the distinguished persons present, the pretty costumes of the Sutton children were particularly noticeable, and from the moment they entered the drawing-room, their bright looks and modest behaviour attracted the favourable attention of all who were present." The pretty costumes referred to were those worn previously by the girls for the Maypole dancing at Sutton.

When the time came for the little girls to meet the Queen, one of them—Jane Rochford—fell sick and had to be taken away. After receiving the presentation album from the three remaining girls, Queen Victoria—having enquired if the fourth child was better and being told that she was ' somewhat improved '—saw Jane separately from the others, and according to the press account: " greeted her so cordially that her momen-

Sutton Coldfield had a traffic problem in 1887—the occasion was Queen Victoria's Golden Jubilee.

tary unhappiness, indeed her sickness, soon passed away."
Recalling this incident at a very advanced age, Miss Rochford
stressed that her malaise was not caused by nervousness, but by
train-sickness.

Among the many local commemorations of the 1887 Jubilee
was the lighting of a huge bonfire on Barr Beacon which had
previously been impregnated with 216 gallons of oil, tar and
creosote.

In 1897, Queen Victoria celebrated her Diamond Jubilee.
At Four Oaks, on the flat roof of a five-storey building, known
as the Tower or " Lewis's Folly ", which stood in Hill Village
Road, opposite Sherifoot Lane, there was a spectacular fire-work
display— and on the other side of the road, an ox-roasting. Not
everyone found the meat palatable, however, and there were
complaints of it being smoky and only partly cooked.

The tower had been built by a diminutive and eccentric
retired pawnbroker from Dudley, named Lewis. It was claimed
that, on a clear day, it was possible to see the Bristol Channel
from the top of the tower, and another of its interesting features
was the possession of wine-cellars. Mr. Lewis did not live there,
but at the other end of Hill Village, and when asked why he had
built the tower is quoted as having said: " Well, you can see from
the top what you cannot see from the bottom." This remark,
possibly, led to the belief that Mr. Lewis had built the tower so
that he could keep an eye on the comings and goings of his
wife. When he died he left £70,000 to Dudley Guest Hospital,
but the will was contested by his widow.

The tower was demolished c. 1905 at the order of the local
authority on the grounds that it was unsafe. Its remains and the
adjoining wall can still be seen in the front garden at 51a, Hill
Village Road.

When a successful Birmingham jeweller named Alfred
Antrobus decided to provide himself with a new home, he chose
a site at New Oscott, just off the Chester Road, where he built
" Fernwood ". In those days Chester Road was a quiet country
road flanked by fields and hedgerows and—with 8½ acres of
land of his own—Alfred Antrobus was able to live a retired
life, devoted largely to botany, and the culture of trees and
shrubs. He introduced all manner of rarities to his grounds, including some sub-tropical plants, and for years " Fernwood "
was the admiration of natural history societies.

When Alfred Antrobus died in 1907, " Fernwood ", with its
beautiful gardens, its stabling, carriage-house, kennels, cow-house
and piggeries, came onto the market. In their eulogy of the
grounds of " Fernwood ", the auctioneers claimed in their sale
catalogue that:—

"The garden, upon which the late Mr. Antrobus has, during the last 35 years, made a lavish yet well-considered outlay, is unique. It contains perfect specimens of an endless variety of choice trees, shrubs and ferns, and an enormous collection of rare herbaceous and other plants."

The estate eventually fell into the hands of a prosperous book-maker named Edward Beston—later nicknamed the "man in the moon"—who seems to have had exotic and expensive tastes. He considerably enlarged the house, adding to it a music-room, a cinema, an Abyssinian boudoir, a Chinese lounge and a ball-room. With a complete new wing, "Fernwood" boasted 20 bed-rooms, five bathrooms and a heated garage for four cars. The grounds, in which were incorporated a switchback railway and an aviary, were extended to cover several more acres, and in addition to peacocks, Beston kept four St. Bernard dogs which were housed in big cages.

One of Beston's friends, and a visitor to "Fernwood" was Horatio Bottomley, founder and owner of the once-famous weekly "John Bull". Bottomley was a very influential man in his day, but is now perhaps more often remembered as being a convicted swindler.

"Fernwood" disappeared over thirty years ago, and most of the grounds have been swallowed up by building develop-ments. However, many garden owners in the Antrobus Road and Fernwood Road areas have reason to remember Alfred Antrobus. Thanks to him, their gardens are still graced by beautiful trees, planted for a future which he could not have envisaged.

In the same locality, the Oscott Tavern, not the present building, but an earlier hostelry, was once called "The Brewery", and a cottage which stood beside it still survives. Next door was Cook's Farm, in front of which was a duck-pond. This lay back from the Chester Road, almost in line with the present Antrobus Road.

Oscott College stands imposingly on a beautifully wooded hill astride the Sutton—Birmingham boundary. It was built in 1838, and for over 50 years housed, under the same roof, a theological college and Catholic public school. One of the school's least honoured pupils was George Moore, the Irish novelist who, in his book, "Confessions of a Young Man" tells us:—

"Neither Latin, nor Greek, nor French, nor History, nor English Composition could I learn, unless, indeed, my personal interest was excited . . . I was a boy that no school-master wants, and the natural end to so wayward a tempera-ment was expulsion. I was expelled when I was sixteen, for idleness and general worthlessness, and returned to a wild country home, where I found my father engaged in training racehorses."

It is over a century since George Moore left Oscott under a cloud, following his expulsion. He returned to his home in County Mayo, where he took to riding, read the racing calendar, stud-book and latest betting and had aspirations towards being a steeplechase rider.

Before achieving success as a novelist, Moore started to train for the army—but disliked military discipline. He became an art student and lived in Paris for a while, where he turned from art to poetry and came under the influence of the novelists Balzac, Flaubert and Zola. He returned to London and took up journalism. By the age of 30, he believed himself to be a failure, but his novel, " Esther Waters ", was later acclaimed to be a masterpiece, and when he died in 1933, his obituary referred to him as " the last of the great Victorians ".

George Moore was not the only literary celebrity to have associations with Oscott College. Frederick William Rolfe— better known to posterity as " Baron Corvo "—came to Oscott as a divinity student in October 1887, and remained there until mid-summer, 1888. Some of his contemporaries there remembered him—years later—for a variety of reasons. One recalled him as a thin, somewhat emaciated, rather good-looking young man. Another recollected his eccentricity in stamping everything available with his crest, the raven (' Corvo ' is Italian for raven), and he even had a stuffed raven in the place of honour on his table. A future bishop who knew him at this time revealed that he was looked upon as a ' poseur ', and that many of his fellow-students were afraid of his caustic tongue and his unmistakable sense of superiority. He was depicted as a short-sighted, pipe-smoking young man, who invariably wore pince-nez.

The facts of Rolfe's life are well documented. " The Quest for Corvo " by A. J. A. Symons, published in 1934, gives a good portrait of this bizarre character, while a more recently published book, " Corvo ", by Donald Weeks, an American, has added some detail to the picture. At Oscott, Rolfe seemed to have a greater bent for art than theology. He became interested in the pre-Raphaelites, and the walls of his room were embellished with his own paintings of angels and saints, both singly and in groups. It has been said that he was expelled from Oscott, but this was not so. He had no-one to sponsor him for a second year there, and having no money to pay his fees, he did not return in the autumn of 1888. Shortage of money was to dog him all his life and there were, undoubtedly, people in Sutton who had reason to remember him on this account. One theological student who knew him at that time said of him " So far as I know, his chief offence in the eyes of the Oscott people was his propensity to run up bills which he had no chance of paying."

Perhaps typical was his relationship with William Wort, a local photographer. In the 1880s, Oscott College students were allowed out only on Sunday and Wednesday afternoons, expressly for the purpose of walking in Sutton Park. Rolfe, however, often took the opportunity of going into Sutton Coldfield, which was 'out of bounds' to students. Here he visited Wort for the purpose of obtaining photographic supplies, and he quickly ran up a bill, which remained unpaid when he left the district in 1888.

In his impecunious wanderings, Rolfe used the self-assumed title of Baron Corvo—possibly as an antidote to his feeling of failure. He tried his hand at a variety of things. In his own words:

> "I slaved as a professional photographer . . . I did journalism, reported inquests for eighteen pence, I wrote for magazines . . . I invented a score of things."

The vows of celibacy which he had taken—despite having been rejected by the Church—did not appear to add to his problems, for he described women as "superfluous."

By the end of the nineteenth century, Corvo became wholly dependent on writing for his livelihood, but his financial problems remained. He wrote several novels, but it is "Hadrian the Seventh", published in 1904, for which he is remembered. It is a thinly-veiled autobiographical phantasy, described as being of "audacious originality", "undeniably brilliant" and "an able satire". He died in Venice in 1913.

In 1891, the Rev. W. K. Riland Bedford, M.A.—Rector of Sutton Coldfield from 1850 to 1892—published his "History of Sutton Coldfield", which is still a source-book for all students of our ancient town. Riland Bedford was a good 'all rounder' —a sportsman as well as a scholar—who founded the Sutton Coldfield Cricket Club, and whose interest in archery also prompted him to found a Toxophilite Society, from among the numbers of which he formed a second cricket club, called the "Free Foresters". The "History of Sutton Coldfield" was not Riland Bedford's first book, for in 1889 he had written "Three Hundred Years of a Family Living", which was a history of his own family, showing how closely the Riland Bedford story is linking with the history of Sutton Coldfield.

The influence and standing of the Rilands seems to have increased greatly in 1710, when John Riland, the Rector of Sutton Coldfield, purchased the advowson from John Shilton, who was in financial difficulties. The rectory at that time, we are told, was "equal to the best of the residences then existing in the place." But it was not adequate for the needs of John Riland, who had another one built, half a mile east of the church. Sutton had long been of Puritan sympathies and the Shiltons, who for generations had owned the advowson of Sutton Parish Church, were supporters of that party. By the beginning of the 18th century, however, the pendulum of popular opinion in Sutton had swung in favour of the Tory and Jacobite causes, and the rector is described as being a high churchman, in spite of his connection with the Puritan Shiltons.

Succession at the rectory from Riland to Riland continued. One—in his dotage—set fire to his cauliflower wig with the altar candle; another of them is remembered for having planted a grand avenue of limes in front of the rectory. He was Richard Riland, whose proposal to a young lady from Bath has been preserved for posterity:—

" Madam,
     I intimated to you in my Last that I had an Offer of some considerable Importance to make, which I once intended to have mention'd sooner. Without any further Introduction, it is that of a Husband; if you are not better provided, I am at your service. I do not desire that any one should represent my Fortune, as it is usual on such Occasions to do, to better Advantage than it deserves; I think I may justly say of it myself, that it is neither small nor indeed very great, yet such, I doubt not, as might be abundantly sufficient to support a Family without the Addition of a plentiful Fortune with a Wife; but in Conjunction with yours (which what it is I am ignorant of) there will be enough not only for Convenience or Necessity, but ev'n for Pomp and Luxury, tho' I think neither of us will be so indiscreet as to Covet much of that . . . "

The proposal was accepted and the couple were duly married.

A non-clerical member of the Riland family—John, son of Richard—made his mark in partnership with John Gibbons and William Rawlins. They were responsible for damming Longmoor Brook, and so making Longmoor Pool. Riland's disinclination to take Holy Orders, we are told, was attributable to his conscientious objection to recognising the ruling sovereign. According to Riland Bedford (" Three Hundred Years of a Family Living "), his scruples were either partial, not extending to magisterial oaths, or subsided in course of time, for he took the oath and entered the Corporation in 1726. In 1728, he became Warden of Sutton Coldfield, a position which involved magisterial duties. He is described by Riland Bedford as " a respected and useful member of the community, though a sturdy specimen of a self-willed race."

The name Bedford was first linked to that of Riland in 1784, when a young Birmingham attorney of that name married into the family. This Mr. Bedford had a house in New Street, Birmingham, with a garden running down to Pinfold Street. His son, William, became the first Riland Bedford at the rectory, and, at the time of the Enclosure enactment, he planted trees extensively on his own land, and prevailed on many of his neighbours to do the same. He also wrote a book called " The Midland Forester " under the pseudonym " a Woodman of Arden."

The Riland Bedfords have gone, and the old rectory was demolished in 1936. But Rectory Park in early summer, with its oaks and great elms, is a pleasant legacy of the Riland Bedford era, and the whack of willow upon leather at the opening of the cricket season is a reminder of the sporting cleric whose anti-quarian interest influenced many.

CHAPTER IX

Sutton at the turn of the century—The Boer War—The end of the Victorian era—Some aspects of transport—The new town hall.

AT the turn of the century, England was embroiled in the Boer War, and at the top of Church Hill, Sutton Coldfield, there is a tablet which commemorates " the bravery, loyalty and devotion to their Country of those volunteers from the Royal Town and local company who served in the South African War, 1900-02."* Of the men named on the tablet—29 in all—only two were shown as casualties. One, a lance-corporal attached to the South Staffordshire Regiment, died on active service, and the other—a private in the Volunteer Medical Corps—died on his way home. Enteric fever was a frequent cause of death among the British troops serving in South Africa.

Patriotism was manifested by Sutton Coldfield school-girls who knitted socks and helmets for the soldiers. When British forces were besieged in the town of Mafeking from November, 1899 to May, 1900, patriotic feelings ran high. Not everyone, however, succumbed to the mood of " Goodbye, Dolly Gray " and " Soldiers of the Queen ", and among local people who were not convinced of the justice of the British cause was a Sutton publican, who became known as a " pro-Boer ". He was the landlord of the " Top Swan ", which stood near Bishop Vesey's Grammar School, and every time the Boers were victorious, he would hang a flag from his window. The relief of Mafeking, with its wild and exuberant celebrations, gave Sutton patriots the chance they had been waiting for. In what one writer called " the orgy of Mafeking night ", they caused so much damage to the " Top Swan ", that it was never repaired, and was eventually demolished. It did not pass unmourned, however, for someone wrote some verses in the form of a lament, beginning:—

Oh! a quaint little place was the old Top Swan
With its ales and its beer and its wine.
With its half-timbered wall and its gabled roof,
And the queer looking bird for its sign.

* This tablet was originally in the entrance-hall of the Town Hall.

Its parlour was low, and it billiard room small,
And the guests, when retiring to bed,
If they carelessly mounted the ricketty stairs,
Got some terrible bumps on the head.
But alack and alas! to think it is gone
For a quaint little place was the old Top Swan.

When, following the Boer War, peace was proclaimed by the Mayor from the Council House in Mill Street, crowds of towns-people stood singing in the street.

The turbulence of Mafeking Night was an unusual occurrence in Sutton Coldfield, and one man who appreciated the town's normal peace and quiet was James Fawdry, a property-owner, baker and corn-merchant, who had retired early to enjoy the idyllic setting of his house, " The Woodlands " in Manor Road. This house, which once had a large pool in its garden, and commanded a pleasant view across the valley towards Trinity Hill, was demolished to make way for the town centre redevelopment. James Fawdry is remembered for having given the Parade its name, prior to which it had always been known as the " Dam ". He was a keen gardener and a dog-breeder who won many prizes at Crufts.

Christmas, 1900 was one of the mildest ever recorded in Sutton, and some local people were able to pick chrysanthemums in their gardens on Christmas morning. The New Year, however, brought floods, when a part of Longmoor dam was washed away. This was followed by a hard frost, when the Park pools became sufficiently frozen for curling to be played on them.

When Queen Victoria died on 22nd January, 1901, a number of social events were postponed, but sport in the Park was unaffected, and the Birmingham Curling Club continued to take advantage of the cold snap. The death of the Queen—after over 60 years on the throne—was marked by the tolling of the parish church bell, and the hoisting of the Royal Standard at half-mast, both over the church and the town-hall. This, however, has been termed a faux pas, since the Royal Standard should only be flown on a building or ship where the Sovereign is present.

In 1901, an Irish farm labourer sued a Wishaw farmer at Sutton Police Court for overtime money, which he alleged was owing to him. It was revealed in the proceedings that the labourer worked from 6 a.m. to 6 p.m.—for 18/- a week. At this time, Sutton Coldfield building workers started work at 6 a.m. and finished at 5.30 p.m. (Saturdays: 6 a.m.—1 p.m.). Builder's labourers were paid sixpence an hour; scaffolders 6½d. an hour—the latter rate—according to the Sutton Coldfield Master Builders' Association—" to apply only in cases where in the erection of scaffolding a responsible scaffolder is necessary."

But if wages were poor, prices were low, too, by modern standards. In 1901, suits could be bought in Sutton Coldfield

" from 16/11d. "; a plate of bread and cheese cost 2d.; bacon was 4½d. a lb. and a gallon of best pale ale from the " King's Arms " in Coleshill Street could be delivered to the door at the cost of a shilling. For the privileged few who could afford a holiday in those days, board residence at Conway was advertised for two guineas a week. A villa residence, built by W. H. James of Whitehouse Common could be rented for £30 to £35 a year, and it was possible to rent a small house for 5/6d. a week.

The Coronation of King Edward VII was arranged for 26th June, 1902, but due to his contracting appendicitis, it did not take place until 9th August of that year. The decorations in Sutton Coldfield were put up for the original date, and remained up until the event took place, by which time they had become somewhat faded and bedraggled.

The annual report of 1899 on the management of Sutton Park, prepared by the Borough Surveyor, W. A. H. Clarry, had stated that " there is ample evidence of the increasing popularity of this delightful resort." There had been a record number of admissions to the Park during the period, those paying for admission being 301,163, which showed an increase of 31,989 over the previous year. This was the era of the cyclist, and 29,282 of them were admitted to the Park, a number said to be in excess of that for any two previous years added together. During the early years of this century, the Park was well served

Old cottages on Maney Corner (1892) showing, in the background, the site of the Odeon Cinema.

by tea-rooms. Blackroot Pool Refreshment Rooms were popular, and the Old White House Tea Room in Hollyhurst claimed that it could seat 700 people. Light refreshments were available at Longmoor Farm, and at the Keeper's cottage on the top of Rowton's Hill, it was possible to buy a draught of fresh milk. The Crystal Palace was a Mecca for thousands of visitors every year, and in August, 1906, it featured in an item of news in the national press, when the London " Daily Mail " proclaimed: " PANIC AT A CHILDREN'S TREAT ":

" A panic occurred yesterday (14th August), during the feeding of a large gathering of Birmingham's poor children at Sutton Park, a large common a few miles out of the city. The children, who numbered 5,000, were provided with tea in the Crystal Palace, and ate in batches of 1,000 at a time. As one section was leaving the hall, the floor collapsed, and thirty or forty children fell into the cellar. A good deal of alarm was caused, but the rush of children was checked by the attendants, and no-one was seriously injured."

The great increase in the numbers of visitors to Sutton Park since the building of the railway no doubt accounted for the disappearance of some of its wild life. In 1884, adders were numerous in Sutton Park, but the last one to be seen there was recorded ten years later. Birds, however, were the worst sufferers, for in the last century most rare birds fell victim to " the man with the gun ", and finished up in the hands of the taxidermist. Birds like the bee-eater, the hoopoe, the waxwing and the great grey shrike—all past visitors to Sutton Coldfield—were often to be seen in glass cases, adorning Victorian parlours.

The decline of the black grouse in the Park is a melancholy story. It was breeding there regularly in the early part of the nineteenth century, but was ruthlessly destroyed, the last pair having apparently been shot in 1871. In 1897, a pair revisited the Park, and reared two young, but by the November of that year, all four had been shot. A similar fate may have befallen the great crested grebes but, fortunately, following upon a long correspondence in the " Birmingham Daily Post " in 1886, the shooting there of those beautiful birds was finally prohibited.

In " A Short History of the Town and Chase of Sutton Coldfield " (1904), Midgley writes feelingly about the Park at the beginning of the present century. " The Park Committee," he says " seems to realise its responsibilty as trustee of one of the noblest public possessions in the Midlands, and would no more think of making a dividend-earning concern of it for the ratepayers than the Crown would of Hyde Park or Richmond ". The last sentences of Midgley's book are a plea for the Park:—

"'The encroachments and indifference of four hundred years have shorn it of some of its loveliness, but it still remains unsurpassed, perhaps unequalled in its gentle beauty. We may hope and believe that the unborn millions of our ever more and more densely peopled land will look back with gratitude to the men who hold today that beauty in trust for them."

William Charles Midgley (1865-1933), was an artist, portrait-painter, art-teacher, architect and medallist, who in early life had won a travelling scholarship, enabling him to study art in Italy. He was a small, bearded man, of great vitality who, in addition to his book, " A Short History of the Town and Chase of Sutton Coldfield ", was also co-author of books on " Plant Form and Design " and a history of the Royal Birmingham Society of Artists, of which he was an active member for many years. As an architect, he designed four houses in Richmond Road, Sutton Coldfield, living in one called " Rohedin " (No. 7), where, from both his attic studio and his beautiful garden he was able to enjoy vistas across the park which he loved so much.

On those occasions in the past when the inhabitants felt that the Park was under threat, they were swift to spring to its defence. Proposals to enclose, annexe or despoil it always met with implacable resistance. The rights and privileges of having the Park were worth defending—a fact that was made apparent in 1907. An abortive attempt was made in that year by Walsall Corporation to run motor 'buses through the Park. The response was overwhelming. A protest meeting was called, which packed Sutton Town Hall, and a broadsheet, captioned " Hands off the Park! " was distributed. A poem was written for the occasion, which began:—

> In days gone by,
> There's been many a try
> To steal our ancient right;
> But it always fails,
> And the Council quails,
> When the people start to fight!

Considerable indignation was felt among Sutton's neighbours when, in 1907, the Council announced that it was to increase the charge to non-residents for admission to the Park from one penny to twopence. In defence of the increase it was argued that the cost of the Park's upkeep had risen greatly, and that without an increased income the Council had been unable to carry out many necessary improvements. Young hooligans from Birmingham and the Black Country were accused of doing an immense amount of damage, the repair of which was a great drain upon the Park's finances.

The " Birmingham Daily Post ", however, claimed that the extra charge would close the Park to large numbers of working class families, and that it was calculated to produce a feeling of resentment on the part of many who might, although able to pay, be tempted to spend their money in going elsewhere. The decision of the Council, they claimed, was a retrograde step. The " Sutton Coldfield News " responded by pointing out that the Royal Town had a duty to itself, and could not afford to show unlimited magnanimity to its visitors. The increases, however regrettable, were, they felt, inevitable.

In a booklet published by the Health Resorts Association in 1913, it was said that " Among the many charming beauty-spots of mid-England, the Royal Town of Sutton Coldfield can well claim to hold its own." The advertisements included one for " Sutton Park rock ", and the " Horse and Jockey " public-house was described as " the finest *Country-inn* near Birmingham."

In the same year an advertisement proclaimed that Sutton Park was " The best place in the Midlands for school treats " and that " A splendid new motor-launch—' Nancy '—has just been put into service on Blackroot Pool." At Powells Pool—not at that time a part of the Park—there was a steam-launch called " Foam ", in which children, and their elders, enjoyed the scenic pleasures of circumnavigating the largest pool in the borough (28 acres—the next biggest being Bracebridge with 16 acres).

Sutton Coldfield was not just a place for day trips. Doctors sometimes recommended that their delicate patients should spend a month at Sutton—for the air. In a guide-book of the period prior to the first World War, under " Hotel Accommodation " it was said: " This is a very important item in the tourist's programme and so much of the success and pleasure of a visit to any town depends on the answer to the question, ' Where shall I put up? ' that we need offer no apology for giving the names of Sutton's excellent Hotels." Among those listed were the Royal Hotel in High Street (" with its dainty Coffee Room and splendid Billiard-tables "), the Temperance Hotel in Park Road (" in a delightful situation, and under capable management "), the Cup Inn, the Duke Inn (" the headquarters of the Town Football Club "), the Boot Inn, Rectory Road, the White Horse, Whitehouse Common, and the New Inn, Lichfield Road.

The town, having become something of a holiday resort, private houses as well as hotels were offered as accommodation to visitors from Birmingham and surrounding places. Holiday-makers were known to come to stay at Sutton year after year, and a popular place for lodgings was Park Road. One visitor recalled having spent holidays at Sutton as a child for seven consecutive years, covering the first World War period when there were military camps in Sutton Park.

At the beginning of the present century, there were an estimated 3½ million horses in Britain, and the demands upon
agriculture for the production of fodder was reaching saturation
point. No-one at that time could have guessed that the new-
fangled ' internal combustion engine '—the motor-car—still then
required by law to be preceded by a man on foot, carrying a
red flag, would make so explosive an impact on the dawning
century. Sutton people were still dependent on the horse in
every aspect of their lives. Births, marriages and funerals were
all accompanied by the rhythm of horses' hooves. The doctor
did his rounds by horse and carriage; the mail was delivered
by a smartly turned out horse-drawn mail-van; all domestic
deliveries were made by horse-vehicles and the fire-brigade—a
voluntary force in Sutton Coldfield—was served by horses
belonging to local tradespeople, but ' ear-marked ' for their fire-
fighting duties, as and when required. The modes of transport
were hardly less varied than their modern counterparts.
Broughams, landaus, gigs, traps, governess-carts, victorias,
waggonettes and a whole range of floats, drays, brakes and
waggons traversed the untarred roads of the borough.

The first sight to catch the eye of the railway traveller to
Sutton Coldfield was a small fleet of broughams and landaus,
which plied for hire outside the station. The brougham was a
closed, four-wheel carriage, closely akin to the old ' growler '
horse-cab; the landau was a more elegant carriage, with a fold-
back top, fore-runner of the ' convertible ' motor-car. On high
days and holidays, including May Day, it was customary to
decorate the horses. In Sutton Coldfield, the gala day of the year
was Trinity Monday, when a carnival procession of gaily
decorated horses and floats paraded through the town.

Even the farm-carts had their special occasions. When
Erdington children went on their annual outing to Sutton Park,
they were conveyed by local farm-carts, specially scrubbed and
cleaned for the event. The horses were brightly bedecked with
ribbons—even to a multi-coloured plaiting of their tails— and
local people turned out to watch them pass. Many such trips
were not to the Park itself, but to a farm at New Oscott, the
fields of which ran down to the reed-fringed edge of Powell's
Pool, where the children were able to pick bulrushes to take
home as mementos of ' a day in the country.'

Road transport at the beginning of the century was not
wholly monopolised by the horse. There were at least two people
in the town-centre with motor-cars—a man named Smith owned
a steam-car, and a grocer named Wodhams had a " de Dion
Bouton ". By 1901, there were said to be eight motor-cars in
Sutton Coldfield. The bicycle was obviously within the means
of a far larger section of the population and the rector (Rev.
W. C. Riland Bedford) was always to be seen on his bicycle,
wearing—summer and winter—a black straw boater.

The electric tramcar was also pushing its tentacular tracks out into the Birmingham suburbs and in 1903, a Bill was introduced to Parliament by Sutton Coldfield Corporation, seeking power to construct electric tramways within the borough. The proposed tramway was to run from the Birmingham boundary, just beyond Chester Road, to Watford Gap—a distance of 5¼ miles. There was also to be a branch line running in a loop along Chester Road, Boldmere Road and Jockey Road before rejoining the main road. It was said by the promoters that, though some people would prefer not to have tramways running past their houses, all were agreed that, tramways being inevitable, they ought to be in the hands of the Corporation. The Bill met with vigorous opposition, and the Rev. W. C. Riland Bedford, speaking as a property owner in Sutton Coldfield, gave evidence on behalf of the London and North-Western Railway (who operated the Sutton branch line), that none of his friends were in favour of the trams. The majority of the inhabitants of Sutton, he said, were people of a better class, who went there for the peace and quiet. The Bill, so far as it related to the proposed tramway, was rejected by a Parliamentary Committee. Their decision it was said, was not based on the alleged competition with the Railway Company, but on the grounds that the need for the tramway had not been proved to the satisfaction of the Committee. The 1903 Bill had also proposed that the Corporation should install electric lights in Sutton and, in the same year, Midgley tells us, the Corporation installed a municipal electric light plant at a capital expense of £32,000. " Unfortunately," he adds, " the townspeople have not yet thoroughly appreciated the advantages of this beautiful light " (" A Short History of the Town and Chase of Sutton Coldfield ").

Opponents of the tramcar in Erdington were not so successful as those in Sutton. On 22nd April, 1907—despite strong opposition from Erdington ratepayers and a call to " Crush the monster! "—the Erdington tram reached the Sutton Coldfield boundary, just beyond the junction of Chester Road and Sutton Road. This point is still known to older residents as " the Tram Terminus." Because of the large number of visitors who walked from the Erdington tram to the Boldmere entrance of Sutton Park, the council found it necessary, in 1912, to build a lodgehouse at Boldmere to deal with the increased business there.

The trams ran for 46 years, a period which included two world wars, and gave both a cheap and reliable service Many Sutton people, working in Birmingham, were glad to avail themselves of the " Workman's Return " tickets which, up to the late thirties, only cost four old pence for the double journey to and from Birmingham. The last tram to Chester Road—and, incidentally, the last one in Birmingham—ran on 4th July, 1953.

The coming of the railway in 1862 had resulted in trains doing the journey between Sutton Coldfield and Birmingham in an hour less than the time taken by the old horse-omnibuses. At the turn of the century there were 16 trains a day, each way, running between Birmingham and Sutton, and the journey took only 14 minutes. On Saturday evening, 12th April, 1902, a train from Sutton to Birmingham, with eight coaches drawn by a tanker, was in a head-on collision with a train from Birmingham to Four Oaks of the same description. The collision occurred in Sutton Coldfield Station and resulted in the death of a young waitress, and in 52 people being injured.

For almost half a century road travel had been in eclipse, despite the coming of the electric tramcars in 1907. By 1911, however, motoring was already creating problems. In a Council motion in the name of Councillor Rathbone in that year, it was resolved:—

> "That this Council call the attention of the Police Authorities to the necessity for closer supervision on the part of the local police, with a view to taking proceedings to prevent the dangerous, negligent or reckless driving of motor cars and motor cycles through the populous parts of the borough."

Then, in 1912, Sutton Coldfield Corporation entered into negotiations with the Birmingham and Midland Motor Omnibus Company (The " Midland Red "), and a number of other undertakings with a view to commencing motor omnibus services. One of the initial difficulties was the fact that, at the time, the Midland Red Company only had double-decker 'buses, and the Corporation were anxious to ensure the operation of single-deckers on the proposed routes.

Eventually the Midland Red undertook to comply with the requirements by providing single-deckers, and on 13th February, 1913, at a meeting of Sutton Town Council, it was decided that the council should grant licences to the company on the following terms:—

> "(a) the service to be daily, including Sundays, and to be run on such roads and to a timetable with such stages and fares as are approved by the Council;
> (b) the cars run to be new, 30 to 40 h.p., and single-deck;
> (c) the licences to be for 12 months only;
> (d) no goodwill or monopoly to be created and the Council to reserve the right to refuse to renew the licences or to grant others on the expiration of same;
> (e) the service to be commenced at Easter."

The proposed service was to be half-hourly (" to be increased as traffic warranted ") between Chester Road tram-terminus, Sutton Parade and the Barley Mow at Mere Green. There was also to be a service between Chester Road and the Park entrance, via Boldmere Road. Four 'buses were to be provided, with an extra vehicle on the Park route at holiday-times.

The 'Bus Company was unable to provide the single-decker vehicles in time for Easter, 1913, and the first to run were two 'buses hired by them from the British Automobile Traction Co. Ltd., and a limited service between Chester Road and Sutton was commenced on 10th May, 1913. The service to the Barley Mow started in August of that year.

Other services were inaugurated, although the work of consolidation was to some extent held up by the first World War. In 1919 a service commenced between Birmingham and Tamworth, and in 1920, Walmley and New Oscott were served by motor-'buses for the first time. The early " Reds " were 40 h.p. Tilling-Stevens, with solid tyres, seating 27 passengers, and with roof-racks for passengers' luggage.

On 19th September, 1906, Sutton's new town hall was formally opened by the Mayor, Councillor R. H. Sadler—an event which, it was said, was " distinguished by demonstrations of public approval ". This building, which adjoined the council house, was uniform in style with the fire brigade headquarters which, though opened a few months earlier, formed part of the same block. The clock-tower, fronting King Edward's Square. which was soon to become a familiar landmark, also served the purpose of a hose-tower for the fire-station, and a ventilating shaft.

The opening event at the new town hall was an evening concert, given by Sutton Coldfield Choral Society, the Principals being billed as:—

Miss May Seiber (Contralto),
Mr. John Ridding (The Celebrated Operatic Baritone),
and an excellent Orchestra with Herr Suck as Leader.
Prices of Admission: 2/-, 1/-, and 6d. Concert to Commence at 7.30.

The following night, an amateur dramatic performance of " The Duke of Killicrankie " (a Farcical Romance, in Three Acts), by Captain Robert Marshall was given by Mr. A. C. Fraser Wood and Company, which, it was said, was " witnessed by a crowded and enthusiastic house."

Following upon the opening of the new town hall, the former town hall in Mill Street was converted for use as a Masonic-hall, and the town's stocks, which had stood in what had been the council house yard, facing Mill Street, were, in due course, moved to King Edward's Square.

In 1907, Dr. A. Bostock Hill, the Medical Officer of Health condemned the " voluntary collection of refuse ", by which method a tenant could have rubbish removed on payment of a small fee. The system had resulted in accumulations of rubbish in garden pits to the detriment of health. But the Medical

Officer of Health said he did not think the borough needed a refuse-destructor.

A proposal made in the same year at the 15th annual meeting of Sutton Nursing Association to establish a Cottage Hospital in the town was made possible by the philanthropy of Lt.-Col. J. H. Wilkinson (1845-1931) of Ashfurlong Hall, who was also responsible for presenting Barr Beacon to the public as an open space in perpetuity. The proposal was carried out by enlarging what had previously been a Nurses' Home and transforming it into a hospital—so saving many sick people the necessity of being admitted to hospital in Birmingham. In 1924 the Wilkinson family defrayed the cost of enlarging the hospital and providing it with an operating theatre.

From the beginning of the century, communications in the district had been generally good. Roe and Yeomans, carriers, made daily trips to Birmingham from Sutton. There were 18 posting boxes in the parish, with sub-offices at Maney, Mere Green and Wylde Green, whilst letters to Walmley were delivered from Erdington. Sutton's Post Office was, originally, further up Mill Street than it is now. In 1909, it moved into the present premises, formerly the site of the "College Arms Hotel".* At that time postmen pushed the mail-bags up the Reddicroft on hand-trollies to the railway station. Eighteen postmen were employed at Sutton, and the mail-van was driven by a Mr. Pile of Duke Street, who took great pride in the horses and in having a smart turn-out.

The Coronation of King George V was celebrated with a full programme at Sutton Coldfield on 22nd and 23rd June, 1911. There was bell-ringing, street decorations and a procession which included the band of the Royal Army Medical Corps, the Sergeant at Mace, the Town Crier, Civic Dignitaries and Park Keepers with halberds. There were also sports in the Park, a Horse Show, Morris dancing and Maypole dancing—the first prize for which was won by the Boldmere Girls' School. For the old people, there was a dinner at the Crystal Palace, whilst the children were provided with tea. 3,200 Commemoration Cups and Medals were given to the children of the Borough. An avenue of limes, leading from the Town Gate towards Blackroot was planted in the Park and there was a Firework display and a Bonfire, which was lit on the hill between the Crystal Palace and Holly Hurst.

Poverty was rife in those early days of the century, and such an occasion as a Coronation no doubt gave many people the opportunity to forget for a short while the austerities of life. For those Sutton people who could afford a trip into Birmingham, however, there were glittering opportunities for entertain-

*Sutton Post Office has since moved to the Gracechurch Centre.

ment. The city boasted seven theatres and six music-halls (excluding those in outlying districts) and variety artists could be fully employed the year round without ever having to leave the Birmingham area. In 1901, a novel form of entertainment had come to Birmingham when, at Curzon Hall (later the West End Cinema), there was screened for the first time the " New Century Animated Pictures." The idea caught on rapidly, and in a few years ' picture houses ' were springing up over a wide area.

About this time, Henry de Vere Stacpoole (1863-1951), a physician and struggling novelist, was in lodgings in Jockey Road. Sutton Coldfield. While residing there it is said that, following a reading of Darwin's " The Voyage of the Beagle ", he conceived the idea for a novel which, when written, became a bestseller. The book was entitled " The Blue Lagoon " and the cinema version made much later proved to be as popular. Meanwhile, however, the film industry was still in its infancy and some years were to elapse before Sutton acquired its first cinema.

An occasional form of entertainment at this time was the appearance in the town of performing bears. A correspondent in the " Sutton Coldfield News " recalled having seen one tied to a five-barred gate opposite the " Park Hotel ", Boldmere, in 1904, where it was attacked by a large dog. Russian bears are remembered outside the " Beggar's Bush ", and performances by dancing bears were sometimes seen along the Parade.

CHAPTER X
The First World War years—The 'twenties and early 'thirties.

WHEN the first World War broke out in August, 1914, Sutton Park was placed at the disposal of the government and quickly became the training ground and camping site of the 14th and 15th Battalions of the Royal Warwickshire Regiment. These battalions—with the 16th Battalion, encamped at Moseley —were better known as the " City Battalions ". They were formed in the first weeks of the war, and represented the thrice-realised goal of raising in Birmingham a battalion of non-manual volunteers, in which friends could serve together. The response to the idea had been quite remarkable, and within eight days, 4,500 men had enlisted. It was widely claimed that the conflict would be over by Christmas, 1914, and for many of these young soldiers the likelihood of over four years of war must have seemed remote.

Horses, as well as men, were required for the war effort, and in the first 12 days after mobilisation, about 115,000 horses throughout the country were ' impressed ' for military service. Some of Sutton's horses finished up as far away as France, Egypt and Salonika. The best horses went to the cavalry and yeomanry regiments, and they were paid for by the government according to their usefulness in the field. Chargers fetched £75, troop-horses £40, and draught-horses, somewhat less.

The headquarters of the 1st City Battalion was at the Crystal Palace, and that of the 2nd was in huts near Powell's Pool. Prior to hutted accommodation being built in the Park the 1st City Battalion was billeted in private houses in Sutton and Four Oaks and the 2nd City Battalion was billeted in the Boldmere area, also in private houses. Training in the Park included bayonet drill, trench digging, target practice and route marches. In the winter of 1914, the cottage on Rowton's Hill was vigorously 'attacked' and 'defended' by elements of the 2nd City Battalion in a realistic military exercise.

Later in the war, after the departure of the City Battalions, the hutments in the Park, and at the Crystal Palace, were used to accommodate New Zealand troops and convalescing soldiers, discharged from military hospitals. At Sutton Coldfield, the 2nd City Battalion produced its own fortnightly magazine, which was brightly written and illustrated. No. 1 of the magazine—in April, 1915—ran to 10 pages. It later increased in size to 12 pages (for one penny), of which 5 pages were taken up by advertisements for local tradesmen.

The first World War lasted four years and the mood of the period is well captured in the yellowing pages of the " Sutton Coldfield News " for 23rd December, 1916—the third Christmas of the war. There was a front-page write-up for " the New Picture House " on the Parade. " Always a good clean entertainment " ran the advertisement. Its holiday billing was a four-reel comedy called " The Tailor of Bond Street ", with a supporting film, starring " the one and only Charlie Chaplin ", and for good measure there was a Christmas pantomime—" The Little Snow Waif."

Scattered through these now historic pages were constant reminders of the war, in pictures, articles and news-items. Photographs of " French troops in Monastir " and " Enemy material captured by the Serbs " jostled for position with items on " British troops trench raids " and " Further progress at Verdun ". Nearer home the problem of " Land cultivation around Birmingham " was considered in the light of a serious food shortage.

One item of news not related to the war was a charge of dangerous driving by a motorist in Slade Road, based on evidence that the defendant had travelled at " an estimated speed of 25 m.p.h." In his own defence, however, the erring motorist had said that his engine made a loud noise, giving the impression that he was going faster than he was. He was found guilty, fined 20s., and for not producing his licence, was ordered to pay a further 10 shillings. Motor-cars were rare in those days, and a lingering prejudice against them remained from the days when a man with a red flag had to walk in front of them. No-one could have known that, within 50 years, 74 per cent of all households in Sutton Coldfield would own cars, and that the " two car family " would be commonplace.

The editorial in that vintage newspaper dwelt on " another war Christmas ", and waxed eloquently in its sentimental appeal to readers to draw on their memories to help them to realise something of the old spirit of Christmas happiness. The mood was understandable, for 1916 had been a year of unsurpassed agony, perhaps typified by the great Battle of the Somme in July, with its colossal loss of life and limb. " Idealism perished on the Somme " declared A. J. P. Taylor, the historian, and so, too, did thousands of men. On one black day—1st July, 1916— the British alone suffered 60,000 casualties, 20,000 of whom were killed, including many men from the three Birmingham City Battalions. During that war, 561 officers and 10,891 other ranks of the Royal Warwickshire Regiment were killed in action.

Fortunately for the purveyors of good cheer at Christmas, 1916, it was not possible to see into the future. They were at least spared the knowledge that the sufferings of the past year would be eclipsed by those of the year ahead, for 1917 was to prove the blackest year of the war, with a growing risk of starvation at home to add to the continued frightful slaughter of the battle fronts.

Among the items of local interest at the bleak Christmas, 1916 was the award of the Military Cross to Lieut. C. G. Rathbone, R.E., son of Councillor and Mrs. F. Rathbone of Sutton Coldfield. According to the citation, he had used his trenchmortars to make a smoke barrage, and by his great courage and determination had prevented the enemy's observation, so materially assisting in the success of infantry operations. A comment from the Front was quoted: " But for a young fellow named Rathbone, we would have been wiped out."

Nearer home, the war effort took the form of a very successful concert, given by school-children in the Boldmere Parish Hall. Proceeds of this happy occasion were donated to Dr. Barnado's Homes and a fund for providing extra Christmas fare for wounded soldiers in Sutton Park. No doubt the gaiety and high spirits of those youngsters brought together in two laudable causes, also helped to brighten the lot of their elders and to take their minds away from the serious issues of the day, if only for a short while.

During the last harrowing months of the first World War —which ended on 11th November, 1918—local news reflected the growing threat of national starvation through the loss of shipping caused by the U-boat campaign. The need for growing as much food at home as possible was constantly being stressed, and garden produce was supplemented wherever possible by the creation of allotments on spare plots of land. One such plot was described enthusiastically in the " Sutton Coldfield News " for 8th June, 1918:—

> " New allotments at the corner of Chester Road and Sutton Road (near the tram terminus), are, so far as soil is concerned, about the best in the district. It is good, old virgin turf, well manured by horse pasturage for a long succession of years—it has been alike pleasant and encouraging in the last few days to see in so comparatively short a space of time, such wonderful progress on them."

But even the threat of starvation failed to have the desired effect on one lantern lecture at Sutton Coldfield Town Hall. Its subject was " Potato Diseases and the new Wort Disease Order ", given by a District Inspector of the Food Production Department. The lecture was described as being " well illustrated by exceptionally clear lantern slides." Attendance, however, was reported to have been " very poor."

Not only home grown food, but other native resources were being drawn upon for assisting the war effort. In response to a government request for ash trees in 1918—ash, presumably because of its lightness, being essential for certain parts of aeroplanes at that time—over 650 ash trees in the neighbourhood of Sutton Coldfield were earmarked for this purpose. The government at that time had an option on 70,000 ash trees throughout the country, and further offers were being asked for. Fighter aeroplanes were used in the Park at this time for machine-gun practice on ground targets along the line of the old Rifle Range, between Banners Gate and the foot of Rowton's Hill.

Just a week before the end of the war in 1918, a Sutton Coldfield man—Major Arnold Waters, D.S.O., M.C. of the 218 Field Company, R.E.—won the Victoria Cross. The citation in " The London Gazette " read:

> " For most conspicuous bravery and devotion to duty on the 4th November, 1918, near Ors, when bridging with his Field Company the Oise-Sambre Canal.
>
> " From the outset the task was under artillery and machine-gun fire at close range, the bridge being damaged and the building party suffered severe casualties.
>
> " Major Waters, hearing that all his officers had been killed or wounded, at once went forward and personally supervised the completion of the bridge, working on cork floats while under fire at point-blank range. So intense was the fire that it seemed impossible that he could escape being killed.
>
> " The success of the operation was due entirely to his valour and example."

The officer concerned—now Sir Arnold Waters—lives at Four Oaks.

Earlier in the year 1918, Flight Lieutenant Alan Jerrard had also won the Victoria Cross for his daring exploits against enemy planes on the Italian Front. He was the son of Mr. H. Jerrard, headmaster of Bishop Vesey's Grammar School from 1902 to 1926. His citation in " The London Gazette " read as follows:

" When on an offensive patrol with two other officers he attacked five enemy aeroplanes and shot one down in flames, following it down to within one hundred feet of the ground.

" He then attacked an enemy aerodrome from a height of only fifty feet from the ground, and, engaging single-handed some nineteen machines, which were either landing or attempting to take off, succeeded in destroying one of them, which crashed on the aerodrome. A large number of machines then attacked him, and whilst thus fully occupied he observed that one of the pilots of his patrol was in difficulties. He went immediately to his assistance, regardless of his own personal safety, and destroyed a third enemy machine.

" Fresh enemy aeroplanes continued to rise from the aerodrome, which he attacked one after another, and only retreated, still engaged with five enemy machines, when ordered to do so by his patrol leader. Although apparently

Flight Lieutenant Alan Jerrard, of the Royal Flying Corps, whose daring exploits against enemy 'planes on the Italian Front in 1918 won for him the Victoria Cross

wounded, this very gallant officer turned repeatedly, and attacked single-handed the pursuing machines, until he was eventually overwhelmed by numbers and driven to the ground.

"Lt. Jerrard had greatly distinguished himself on four previous occasions, within a period of twenty-three days, in destroying enemy machines, displaying bravery and ability of the very highest order."

Mr. Alan Jerrard died at Lyme Regis in 1968, aged 70.

In July, 1919, a dinner and entertainment was given in Sutton Coldfield Town Hall " to discharged and demobilised men who have served with H.M.'s Forces, on the occasion of a Victorious Peace." Music was provided by the Royal Sutton Brass Band, and a choir.

Sutton's first picture-house was on the first floor of the Masonic Buildings, and was known as " Roselle's Cinema ". From a 1915 advertisement in the " Sutton Coldfield News " we learn that " Roselle's Pictures at the Electric Theatre, Masonic Buildings, Sutton Coldfield " showed " . . . a wide selection of the best pictures only." The needs of wartime were met by a top-of-the-bill film, referred to as " an allegorical patriotic subject ". It was entitled " England's Call." The proprietor of " Roselle's Cinema " also held twice-weekly moving-picture shows at a public-hall in Mere Green.

The town's next picture-house was in the building on the Parade now occupied by Sutton Market— "the new Picture House " referred to in the Christmas, 1916 advertisement. It was built on piles, because of the close proximity of the Ebrook, which, after passing under the Parade, flowed almost beneath the building itself. In the 'twenties, before the shops were built between this building and the corner of Queen Street, it was possible to see the stream from the road. This picture-house appears to have provided the town with film entertainment until the building of the " Empress Cinema " in the Lower Parade in 1922. The builders of the " Empress " also had structural problems arising out of Sutton's watery surroundings. There were, in fact, two ponds in the vicinity of the site proposed for the " Empress "—Skinner's Pool and Jerome's Pool—the latter being named after Sutton farmers of that name, who were related to Jerome K. Jerome, the Walsall-born author of " Three Men in a Boat ". The drainage of the water nearest to the cinema site was not, apparently, the end of the problem, for even after the cinema had been built, regular checks were necessary to ensure that it was not subsiding into the mud!

The " Empress ", which cost £40,000 to build, was opened on Monday, 1st January, 1923, by the Mayoress in the presence of the Mayor, Councillor W. Harrison. The opening film— ' silent ', of course—was " East is West " starring Constance Talmadge. Prices of admission were 6d., 9d. and a shilling (balcony 1/6d., children half-price). On 5th March, 1923 the " Empress " acquired a cafe, restaurant and ballroom, which were situated under the cinema, with additional access from South Parade. The dance-hall accommodated 200 dancers.

Silent films were popular for almost 30 years before the coming of the ' talkies ' in the late 'twenties, during which period ' sound ' was provided by the cinema orchestra, with music appropriate to the theme of the film. When Al Jolson, crooning " Sonny Boy " in " The Singing Fool " was first heard in English cinemas, the impact was considerable and the queues for admission were almost as long as those forming outside the labour exchanges at that time. The ' talkies ' were not always an immediate success, however. At the " Empress " the installation of British Talking Pictures sound equipment in 1929 was a failure, and the cinema reverted to silent films. Perhaps some Sutton cinema-goers of that era might have agreed with the sentiment of Aldous Huxley, who, on seeing and hearing his first talkie described it as " the most nauseatingly luscious, the most penetrating vulgar mammy-song that it has ever been my lot to hear." But in 1930 the ' talkies ' were finally accepted by " Empress " audiences. After a complete re-decoration and re-installation of sound equipment, the cinema re-opened on Boxing Day of that year, with a film called " The Love Parade ", starring Maurice Chevalier and Jeanette McDonald.*

In the early years of the uneasy peace between 1918 and 1939, Sutton Coldfield, although growing rapidly, was still a semi-rural community. Between Sutton and Erdington there remained many acres of farmland, over which the horse still drew the plough, followed by flocks of rooks and lapwings. In unkempt hedgerows there were numerous trees, and in summer, along the Sutton and Four Oaks line, trains drawn by ancient tankers hissed and puffed their way to and from Birmingham between banks blue with field-scabious. The 10.37 a.m. from Wylde Green to Birmingham was different from the rest, for it was always " two behind and two in front "—the diminutive engine pulling two carriages, and pushing two as well.

In August, special trains brought 3,000 of Birmingham's poorest children for a sponsored annual day out in Sutton Park. They were the " Royal Robins ", sometimes referred to as the " Ragged Robins ". According to a contemporary account of one such visit " the appearance of the little folk evoked warm commendation, for if their clothes were poor and the worse for wear, their faces were clean and it was evident that care and

*The site of the Empress Cinema is now occupied by the Central Library.

attention had been bestowed upon them. The trains steamed out of New Street Station with their happy little occupants waving cheery farewells and lustily singing snatches of popular choruses." On reaching Sutton Park each child was given a bag containing a buttered roll, a baker's bun and a piece of cake, together with a liberal supply of ginger beer. Once within the Park, Punch and Judy Shows and a variety of organised games ensured that not many of the Robins wandered too far from the Town Gate.

In 1920, civic pride in Sutton Coldfield was concentrated on a new motor turbine fire engine which was bought that year. It was tested, both in Sutton Park and in King Edward's Square, when it fulfilled all expectations. Its acquisition may have been hastened by a tragic event in the previous year, when a fire in a house in Park Road resulted in the death of two of the occupants, and injury to five others. At that time there was only a volunteer fire brigade equipped with a horse-drawn engine and the service was operated on a tight budget. The Park Road tragedy was in no way due to negligence on the part of the Brigade, but since the horses for the engine were hired from local farmers and tradesmen, and only brought from their stables or place of work after the alarm was sounded, improvement was due. The new, mechanised fire-engine no doubt demonstrated the resolve on the part of the corporation to bring the service up to date.

In 1921 there was a great drought, which resulted in a number of serious Park fires. These were impossible to extinguish entirely due to the fire spreading beneath the ground in the peaty soil.

History was made in a small way at Sutton Coldfield in the early 'twenties—with a tin of white paint. This was when the first-ever central white-line was painted in the road at Maney Corner. A correspondent in the " Sutton Coldfield News " a year or so ago recalled the day when he watched workmen carrying out the task. " The line was put down as an experiment " he said " as there were a lot of accidents there, even in the early days of the motor-car. The experiment proved to be so successful that the whole country adopted it as a standard road safety device, and later foreign countries put white lines on their roads, too."

The authorities, its seems, were well aware of the traffic problems at Maney Corner, for at a council meeting in June, 1923, consideration was given " to the reckless way in which motorists continued to drive near the bottom of Jockey Hill." It was suggested that a policeman should be placed on point-duty there, to regulate and check traffic.

In continuation of an old tradition, Sutton Coldfield at the beginning of the 'twenties had a flourishing week-end street market which was held under the trees of the Lower Parade and beneath the arches of Victoria Road Girls' School. At night the stalls were lit by naphtha flares, and the merchandise was varied. There was meat—English and foreign—fruit, vegetables, farm produce, cakes, sweets, hardware, crockery and fancy goods. The meat was both good and cheap. One man was reported to have said: " I have bought my meat here for three weeks, and have saved three shillings on each joint." Someone else claimed that, by visiting the market, the saving on the purchases had been sufficient to pay the rent.

Another still honoured tradition of the period was the Trinity Monday celebrations, which were during the week following Whitsun. The origins of this event date back to Tudor times, when a licence was given for a fair on the " eve, day and morrow of Holy Trinity ".' In the last century, Trinity Monday started with cattle being grouped along the High Street, pigs and sheep being penned in Coleshill Street, and horses being tethered in what is now the Lower Parade. By mid-day, the buyers and sellers had departed, and the beasts, having changed hands, had been moved by drovers. Then came the fair, for which stalls and booths were set up all around the top of Mill Street and well down the hill (sometimes referred to as Oker Hill). On the stalls—according to the author of the " Holbeche Diary "—there was yellow-rock, gingerbread, brandy-soup and nuts. There were shooting galleries, roulettes and merry-go-rounds and " all the vendors had strident voices and I remember well, a very red faced lady, who had a long booth, and Charley Smith (from Erdington), who had an iron hook for a hand like Captain Cuttle."

" If you desired to see real pomp you should have seen the fair proclaimed " continued the " Diary ". " The Sergeant at Mace, certain old crippled friends with halberds and the crier, undertook this responsible duty." Riland Bedford gives a similar picture when he speaks of " a certain dwindling pomp symbolized by a town guard of tottering alms-house men, each hanging on to a halbert " which heralded petty sessions or the proclamation of a fair.

With the passage of time, the day's events of Trinity Monday were modified into the form of a carnival, which many people still remember. It is recalled that in the 'twenties it was " a very jolly affair with all sorts of fun, such as climbing a greasy pole and catching a pig." Decorated horse-drawn floats paraded through the streets, which were hung with flags and buntings. The day's events were rounded off with Sports at Rectory Park.

In July, 1923 a severe thunderstorm caused the dam at Longmoor Pool to burst, resulting in a great rush of water into the brook. This quickly made its way down stream to Powell's and Wyndley, through the Crystal Palace grounds and onwards to cause flooding and considerable damage in the town. A meeting was later called of tradespeople of the Parade who had suffered loss as a result of the raging torrent, and approaches were made to the council to consider the question of compensation. But it was pointed out by the Town Clerk, Mr. Reay-Nadin, that without proof of negligence on the part of the corporation, it would be useless for the tradespeople to seek compensation.

A now almost forgotten anniversary—Empire Day (24th May)—was marked with great enthusiasm in the 'twenties and 'thirties. In 1924, beneath banner headlines, the " Sutton Cold-field News " proclaimed that, despite inclement weather, the day was celebrated " most loyally by a large gathering in King Edward's Square." This gathering, which included many of the town's school-children, amounted to almost 3,000, among whom were the Mayor and Mayoress (Councillor and Mrs. W. Harrison), the Town Clerk, members of the council and local dignitaries. Speeches, declarations of loyalty and public singing were somewhat marred by heavy rain.

Councillor J. E. Willmott, the Chairman of the Education Committee, was asked by the Mayor to say a few words. The Councillor, in his oration, spoke of the map of the world with its " wonderful pattern of red splashes representing the different parts of the great Empire " and he declared there never had been in the history of the world an empire so extensive or so splendid. The Mayor, in conclusion, announced—as was customary after such assemblies—that the children would be given a half day's holiday on the following Friday. He thanked them for coming in such large numbers on such a wet morning, and hoped none of them would suffer any ill-effects from standing so long.

Other outside school activities included nature lessons in the Park; swimming instructions in Keeper's Pool; visits to the cinema to see films of an educational or patriotic nature; and, between 1929 and 1934, visits by older girls to the town hall to see plays, including " The School for Scandal ", " The Merchant of Venice " and " A Midsummer Night's Dream."

In 1925 the healthy condition of the borough was once again proved by the fact that in the five months ending 11th July, only eight deaths were recorded out of a population of nearly 25,000. Of these, three were aged over 80. The town was claimed to be one of the most healthy in the country.

During the municipal year to 16th July, 1925, there were 164,261 admissions to Sutton Park, as against 160,795 the previous year. The Park, it was said, had lost none of its popularity, even though the Lickey Hills had become more accessible to Birmingham people through the improved tram service.

At a meeting of the town council in 1926, the Mayor (Councillor H. E. Beach), speaking of the General Strike of that year, said that this was a subject on which there must perforce be many divergent views, and it was, therefore, important that no opinions or expressions voiced should be either political or provocative in any way. He said that a recruiting office for public service volunteers had been opened in the town, and that results were very satisfactory. All necessary steps had been taken to maintain food supplies and other essential services, and inhabitants were called upon to " remain cool."

In 1926 a well-known clothier's shop in the town announced its Whitsun bargains::

Sports coats	15/6d.
Tennis shirts	3/11d.
Men's Blue Blazers	12/11d.
Boy's flannel 2-piece suits	7/11d.

and in 1927, in a campaign to boost Sutton Coldfield as a shopping centre, it was said that " the Royal Town claims that it is able very effectively to hold its own in the matter of shopping facilities, and that, value for value, and price for price, its leading business houses can offer a service equal in every respect to that of the great city store."

Early in 1928 public attention was drawn to the fact that Sutton Coldfield was that year celebrating its 400th anniversary as a corporate body, and the mayor (Councillor T. W. Lawrence), said: " I think the whole of the inhabitants should take part in this celebration." Subsequent discussions in the council chamber, however, revealed a sharp division of opinion, particularly when the recommendation was made known that a sum not exceeding £1,000 should be allocated in respect of expenses involved in the commemoration. " Absolutely a waste of money " was Alderman Cartwright's verdict on the proposal. Some of the £1,000, he said, would be better spent on the latrines on the Parade. Councillor James said: " We have a population of 27,000, and we have no public baths and no public library for them. There are a hundred and one things on which we should spend this £1,000." Despite heated exchanges, however, the recommendation was finally adopted.

A Pageant was decided upon as being the most suitable form of celebration, and Councillor (later Alderman) J. E. Wilmott undertook to be the producer and writer of the episodes of the Pageant, which, he pointed out, would result in " the quickening of local patriotism, and the deepening of interest in the town's history." The event, which marked the 400th anniversary of the granting of the Royal Charter to the town by Henry VIII in 1528, was enacted in Sutton Park in July, its opening being attended by a number of distinguished visitors and about 6,000 spectators in all. Almost 1,200 performers took part in the Pageant, which told Sutton Coldfield's story through the centuries from Roman times. One commentator on the event said that the Pageant was much more than a loosely connected series of tableaux, representing episodes in the Royal Town's history. the episodes, he claimed had been chosen and handled in a manner " distinctly reminiscent of the great masters of stage-craft." The event was considered to be a personal triumph for Councillor Willmott who, it was pointed out, was a student of literature and of the great classics of the theatre.

John Willmott, despite his long service on the council, which he joined in 1924, was unable to accept the office of Mayor owing to business commitments, but was made a Freeman of the town. The John Willmott School is named after him. In a book called " Tales of a Bishop and a Royal Town ", John Willmott said of Vesey, who was instrumental in the town receiving its Royal Charter:

> " Though assessments of Vesey's merits as a prelate and statesman and judgments of his character may disagree, the immense value of the lasting benefits he rendered to his native town is beyond all cavil or dispute and should make his name for ever honoured in Sutton Coldfield."

There is a full-length portrait of John Willmott, dressed as Bishop Vesey, hanging in the council chamber. Alderman Willmott died in 1957.

News was made in 1929 by what was then something of an innovation: the installation of automatic traffic-signals. These were at the junction of Chester Road and Sutton Road, and it was reported in the press that " One of those rather fearsome looking controllers, with their alternating red, yellow and green lights, now stands sentinel at each of the four corners involved at the junction, and, should they justify their existence by the adequacy of their control, will presumably replace the familiar white-coated figure who, from his isolated stand in the middle of the road, has in time past raised a warning hand or waved the ' All Clear ' signal to oncoming travellers."

In 1930 the Moor Hall estate, covering 291½ acres came on to the market and was sold—for £35,000. In the same year the Trinity Monday Carnival was proclaimed to have been the best for many years, thanks, it was said, to the energy and enthusiasm which the Mayor (Councillor J. A. Oldbury), had infused into all those responsible for the arrangements. During August, 1930 a local botanist, John Evelyn, collected no less than 108 different varieties of wild flowers in and around Sutton Coldfield, and in that year the growing scarcity of the red squirrel—once common in the Park—was remarked upon.

This was the era of mass unemployment and the problem was reflected in the 1930 Christmas appeal of Mr. Leonard Ganley, the manager of Sutton Coldfield Labour Exchange for discarded clothes for unemployed men. " Sometimes " he said " a badly worn mackintosh will cover a jacket so full of holes that necessary identification papers have to be carried in the hand. I have begged of friends and I have helped hundreds of cases; but now I have exhausted all my resources." " Is there anyone " he pleaded " who could give me any discarded suits of clothes, hats, or boots, so that I may help some of these hard cases to regain their self-respect?" The passing of 1930 was not lamented. The " Sutton Coldfield News " commented: " The conditions which troubled and perplexed and dismayed us in 1929, in 1930 became more and more critical. Trade has slumped to an almost unprecedented depth, and unemployment has risen to corresponding proportions."

In 1931, Dr. Barnes, Bishop of Birmingham, and well known for his ' advanced ' views, visited St. James' Church, Hill for the purpose of dedicating an extension of the choir panelling. During his sermon, at a point when he claimed that man had descended from the apes, a young woman cried from the gallery " I don't believe you!" and when she continued to protest, she was escorted to the door by the verger and church wardens.

At a meeting of the Sutton Coldfield Licensing Justices in February, 1931, permission was given for the rebuilding of the New Oscott Tavern, a house which the licensee claimed was "not fit to be inhabited." The old inn, with its own malt-house, recalled the era of home brewing. On a building to the rear of it—used as a smokeroom—there was some interesting carved stonework, and in another apartment there was a quaint, open fire-place with a roasting spit.

Sutton Coldfield in 1931 was said to be less crowded than elsewhere in the Midlands. With a proposed density of four houses to the acre on land adjoining the Four Oaks estate; eight houses to the acre on land adjoining first class roads, and not more than 10 to the acre elsewhere in the borough, it was confidently forecast that Sutton would become second to none in the country as a residential town.

Pacifism was very much ' in the air ' in 1931 and Mahatma Gandhi, the architect of ' passive resistance ' visited Birmingham. Sir Norman Angell, a famous author and advocate of disarmament and world peace, spoke at a crowded meeting at Sutton

Coldfield Town Hall, promoted by the local branch of the League of Nations Union, and a " No More War " demonstration was held in the Congregational Schoolroom, Sutton Coldfield. The annual Drumhead Service in Sutton Park, in honour of the war dead, was better attended than ever.

In December, 1931, a one-way traffic system was put into operation in the centre of Sutton Coldfield, affecting the area between the " Empress " Cinema and the corner of Park Road and the Parade. This was designed to avoid traffic congestion on the Parade and was claimed to be a step made " for the convenience of all the townspeople." The system involved traffic coming down Mill Street having to proceed into the Lower Parade, and traffic coming from Park Road to the Parade having first to negotiate the island.

An event of outstanding importance during 1931 was the acquisition, under the Sutton Coldfield Act of 1930, of a strip of land alongside the Chester Road, near the Birmingham boundary, at Kingstanding. This ensured that Sutton Park became, for the first time in the history of the borough, entirely surrounded by land within the Sutton boundary. Thus, it was said, the safeguarding of the amenities of the Park—the cherished possession of the residents—was ensured. This acquisition was the fulfilment of one of the greatest ambitions of the Town Clerk (the late Mr. R. A. Reay-Nadin). One of his first acts on taking office in 1904 had been to discuss with Sir Benjamin Stone the advisability of having the Park completely surrounded by borough land. He was congratulated for having worked so hard towards this end, and by his success it was said that he had earned the admiration and thanks of the inhabitants. In 1966, however, land on the Streetly boundary of the Park was transferred to Aldridge-Browhills Urban District Council, following upon a recommendation by the Boundaries Commission.

Another acquisition during 1931 was a large part of the parish of Minworth, which had previously been a part of the Meriden Rural District Council.

At the beginning of 1932, Sir Alfred Evans (a Freeman of Sutton Coldfield), in sending his best wishes for the New Year to the town's inhabitants, said that his greatest wish for the coming year was that a free library would be provided. The wish was not to be fulfilled for another five years.

The opening of the links and club-house of the new Moor Hall Golf Club, Sutton Coldfield in the spring of 1932 led to a press comment that the town " had added a further attraction to its various claims as a Midland holiday centre and in the ' golfing world ' had become a place of considerable significance." The course—the fourth eighteen-hole one within a short radius of the town—was described as being " wonderful " and " situated amidst fine old park land and typical Warwickshire countryside."

In 1932, some misgivings were expressed in the council chamber over a proposal that the nurse-midwife should be provided with a car to replace her push-bike. It was pointed out that the nurse worked under difficulties in having to go to various parts of the borough by cycle, and it was important that she should be in the very best physical condition. It was in the interests of true economy that the car should be provided. The question of the cost was raised by Councillor Cobb. A car, he observed, might mean any car—perhaps a Rolls-Royce. Mrs. Lowe, Chairman of the Maternity and Child Welfare Committee, said that the car would not cost £100—it was an Austin Seven. Approval was given for the purchase.

The sale of " The Beeches " at the corner of the Birmingham Road and Jockey Road in 1932, led to petitions being submitted from residents in the Maney district, asking the council to endeavour to prevent the estate being developed in any manner which would be contrary to local amenities. Shops there, it was felt, would result in lowering the value of property in the area, and the petitioners were also satisfied that existing shopping facilities were adequate. The property, which was sold for £3,700, was later developed as " Beeches Walk."

Regrets were expressed in 1932 over the cutting down of the beautiful woodlands surrounding " Fernwood Grange ", New Oscott. It was said, in defence of the developers, that wherever practicable, trees had been preserved, including a whole coppice which, it was pointed out, still remained to give joy to tree-lovers. That part of the estate fronting on the Chester Road had been cleared so that a number of houses could be built there. One of the ' casualties ' of the period—the date is uncertain—was the original " Beggar's Bush " at New Oscott, which was a gnarled and knotted thorn bush, standing in the middle of the Chester Road and protected by iron railings. It was destroyed by workmen when widening the road, and the present bush was planted because of the indignation of local people over its destruction. According to legend, a tramp, or beggar, had died under the original bush, and because the bush marked the boundary of the parish, there was a dispute as to who should defray the cost of his burial. Such disputes were not uncommon. On one occasion a beggar was found dead on Four Oaks Common. Sutton Coldfield declined to pay for his burial, and as a consequence the cost was defrayed by the neighbouring parish of Shenstone. This resulted in Shenstone successfully laying claim to a substantial area of waste-land formerly belonging to Sutton.

CHAPTER XI

The years of the " gathering storm "—1933-1939.

PAST events, intermingled with personal recollections, are always vivid and memories of our youth merge with the cataclysmic eruptions of history. Many people will remember the early weeks of 1933, not only as the time when Hitler came to power, but also for its heavy snowfalls which gave a great opportunity to young people in Sutton to enjoy winter sport in the Park.

Sutton Coldfield, in common with many other places, was, at this time, in the grip of an influenza epidemic. Doctors were working overtime in the district and some were even presented with ' the key of the door ' to households where all the occupants were bed-ridden. A Midland coroner recommended fresh air and gargling as aids to keeping fit.

By the end of January, 1933, many people were taking more fresh air than usual for the time of year. After heavy snow and frost, Sutton was ' first in the field ' with skating in the locality. Despite a few early casualties when skaters fell through the ice, the Park pools were soon in excellent condition, with a fine covering of ' snow ice '. There was a run on local iron-mongers for skates; ice-hockey and figure-skating came into their own, and several of the pools were illuminated at night by flares and car-headlights. Biting east winds were no deterrent, though hot coffee was in great demand. At Keeper's Pool the fire brigade obligingly sprayed a film of water over the ice, which imparted a wonderfully smooth surface.

These were lean years, and many people could not afford holidays. But even Birmingham's poorest managed the occasional trip to Sutton Park or the Lickeys. A sense of remoteness in the Park was easier to experience in those days, when expansive views of open country still extended beyond its confines. A good summer always drew the crowds, and at a time when relatively few people had cars, most visitors came by public transport, or on foot or cycle. During the wonderfully hot summer of 1933, there was a record Whit Monday ' gate ', when over 50,000 visitors paid their entry fee to the Park.

In the 'thirties, noise from 'planes was being complained about. Walmley residents spoke of Sunday afternoon disturbance by fliers from Castle Bromwich Aerodrome, and complaints of a similar kind followed from Wylde Green. Stunting by pilots on Sunday, when many people were taking a well-earned rest was annoying, but—it was pointed out by the press—as the country as a whole was being asked to become " air-minded ", the only answer was for people to " grin and bear it." It was not clear whether, nuisance-wise, the R.A.F. or members of the Midland Aero Club were the worst offenders.

Maney Hill in the early 'thirties was a place of some beauty, being still undeveloped. It was an open expanse of upland, with a ridge of trees across its top, where men with nets came to snare the rabbits. There were many other still rustic areas in the Borough, but, during that decade, various changes took place, and the rate of house-building increased. The council made its own attempt to combat the Depression. It built roads—Monmouth Drive and Antrobus Road amongst them—and the work upon them helped to employ many men who would otherwise have been ' on the dole '. For this project it received financial help from the Unemployment Grants Committee.

Some old landmarks disappeared, among them the spade mill in Stonehouse Road, the mill and farm at Longmoor Pool, the old rectory and the Georgian cottages and other buildings in front of the church—where the Vesey Gardens were subsequently laid out. In 1934, 430 new houses were built in Sutton Coldfield, and the population rose to 31,000. In 1935, the Council sold for scrap the first World War tank and guns which had stood for many years in a small enclosure in Sutton Park, by the Town Gate. The tank raised £40, and the proceeds were given to the British Legion.

In 1935, the Birmingham Municipal Bank took the steps necessary to establish a branch of the bank within the Borough of Sutton Coldfield—where, at the time, almost 4,000 people had accounts in that bank. The proposal raised what, even in those days was a highly inflammable subject—" annexation ". A lively discussion in the Council chamber had the effect of highlighting Sutton's nightmare fear of being taken over by Birmingham. The council was divided as to whether a written guarantee on " annexation " should be obtained before agreeing to the proposal, or whether a gentleman's agreement would serve the purpose. It was claimed that a branch of the Municipal Bank in the town would be " one more link in the chain which Birmingham is forging in Sutton, to be used ' when the time for annexation comes!' ". A spokesman for Birmingham retorted that there was no thought of annexation, and that the general view was that, if Birmingham wanted Sutton, it had long since had enough interests in the borough to overcome even the most fiery opposition that such a demand would evoke.

Public disquiet on the question of annexation was well expressed by a correspondent in the " Sutton Coldfield News ": " . . . Surely, apart from those with long experience of Sutton and its amenities," he said " there must be thousands of the younger residents, whose pride in the traditions of the Royal Borough has descended from their forebears, who will come into the open and lend their youthful enthusiasm to this fight." " It is quite probable " he continued " this danger will not develop for some years, but believe me, Mr. Editor, it will come sooner or later unless the proper steps are taken effectively to prevent the grip of the octopus, when the octopus thinks the time is ripe."

Monday, 6th May, 1935 was a National Holiday for the Silver Jubilee of King George V. Sutton Coldfield was lavishly decorated for the event, and the fine weather brought huge crowds to the Park to celebrate the occasion. Following colourful displays of tableaux and Maypole dancing in the Park by local school-children, 2,980 youngsters were given tea in marquees erected near the Crystal Palace. The nearby Fun Fair and the boats at Blackroot Pool did a roaring trade, and Punch and Judy shows were popular. At night there was a firework display on Holly Knoll, and the Boy Scouts lit a beacon on Maney Hill—one of the 2,000 beacons to be lit on prominent heights all over the British Isles. The streets of the town were thronged until a late hour with spectators, looking at the decorations and brilliant illuminations, and the Jubilee in Sutton was considered to be an unqualified success. The " Sutton Coldfield News " declared that as far as the Sutton celebrations were concerned " there was a concensus of opinion that no better, more beautiful or more dignified effects were obtained in Birmingham or in any other Midland town."

The popularity of " Sutton Coldfield " as an address continued to grow, and new houses being built in Clarence Road, Four Oaks were advertised as being " within easy reach of Four Oaks Station and a few minutes from Midland Red 'buses." Price: £425, leasehold for 99 years, ground-rent £5. Homes overlooking Sutton Park were very much sought after. New houses for sale at Boldmere were advertised as having " guaranteed unrestricted views of the Park—rising in price from £600."

Coinciding with the increasing prestige and popularity of Sutton Coldfield as a residential area, approval was given by the College of Arms in 1935 for the Borough to have a new Coat of Arms, which was described in the following terms:—

" The design is exceedingly attractive and colourful, and has been widely approved. The shield is composed of the Arms of Harman with the addition of a mitre, in special allusion to Bishop Vesey (Harman), and an upper division of the shield (called a " chief "), which is green, on which there are stags " courant ", representing Sutton Park.

As to the crest, a " mural coronet " is a suitable emblem for a town. Arising out of it is a demi-stag, based on the Crest of Harman, which holds the cross keys and sword from the See of Exeter—a sufficient representation of that See. The helmet is customarily placed to support the crest, and the mantling, which is gold and red, forms the livery colours of the town.

There are " Tudor supporters " in allusion to Henry the Eighth's Charter, and they are necessarily " differenced " with mural collars (civic emblems), from which depend small shields charged with Tudor roses. The green mound (termed a " compartment "), upon which the supporters rest, is the usual practice, and in this case is a further reference to the Park."

The seal of approval was placed on the new Coat of Arms by a letter in the " Sutton Coldfield News " from Mr. W. F. Carter, Chairman of the Dugdale Society—a prominent historical society —in which he said: " . . . I am greatly pleased with the Arms— especially with the Stags courant—they enliven the bearings and typify the Park most pleasingly. They have certainly ' done you proud ' in the matter of the supporters. It is satisfactory to have a confirmation of the fact that you are a Royal Town." This confirmation helped, no doubt, to quell the fears of one member of the council, who had previously stated that Sutton's right to call itself a Royal Town had been " seriously questioned " and had expressed the view that the borough was not strictly entitled to the arms then in use.

1936 brought, as one national newspaper put it, " a deepening sense of gathering storm." War, however, was still three years away, and local interest was centred on a variety of things, not associated with the deteriorating international situation. In January, 1936, it was announced that special classes were to be held at Sutton Coldfield for maids and servants to be instructed in the use of domestic electrical appliances. It was stressed that no attempt was to be made to train the girls in the repair of any damage to electrical equipment, but merely to instruct them in its correct use—so preventing the necessity for repairs. During the same period Sutton Coldfield was in the process of changing over from direct current to alternating current.

In February, 1936 the reconstructed and enlarged Empress Cinema was formally opened by the Mayor of Sutton Coldfield (Councillor W. A. Perry), who, deprecating what he called " those films of the vulgar or gangster type ", said that he understood that nothing but the highest standard of films would be shown there. The re-opening of the Empress, it was said, was welcomed by local shopkeepers, who claimed that trade had been badly hit during the time of its closure, owing to the fact that shoppers from surrounding areas, wishing to combine shopping with " going to the pictures ", had transferred their allegiance elsewhere. On Saturday, 18th April, 1936, the Mayor was again called upon to officiate at a cinema opening—this time of the Odeon Theatre, with seating capacity for 1,636. The architect was Harry W. Weedon, a Birmingham man, who was also the designer of the Odeon, Leicester Square.

One of the lamentations of 1936 was that Sutton, in becoming a modern residential town, was out of touch with its old customs. The town's great historical traditions were losing their meaning. The celebration of Trinity Monday—a traditional day of festivities in Sutton—had died out, it was claimed, through lack of public interest, as people who worked in Birmingham could not be expected to attend sports or other functions in Sutton on a Monday.

The need for a library in the town had been felt for a long time. In 1876, an anonymous letter-writer, signing himself " Grumbler ", had written to the local paper, protesting that: " . . . we want something more than public-house knowledge . . . we have an idea that a portion of the town's wealth should be expended in a free library." Nothing had happened, and when the matter had been discussed in 1908, objections had been raised on the grounds that the council could not afford a free library. The matter had again lapsed, but in the early 'thirties, someone proposed that Vesey House in the High Street might be suitable for conversion into a library. The idea was not acted upon. In 1935, Mrs. F. Lowe offered her home—" Oakhurst ", Anchorage Road—as a library, but the council turned down the offer.

It was not until March, 1937, after the conversion of a Wesleyan Chapel on the Parade, that Sutton Coldfield acquired its Central Library. This was the first of a number of public libraries to be opened in various parts of the town. By the 1960s, over a million books were being issued annually, and at the present time the library service consists of—in addition to the Central Library—full-time branches at Boldmere and Mere Green, and part-time branches at Banner's Gate; Harrison Road, Four Oaks; Falcon Lodge; Walmley; Minworth and Wylde Green. Sutton Coldfield was one of the first places to acquire a gramophone record library—in 1947—and framed pictures are also issued, on loan, to the public. The libraries are also responsible for the service to schools in the Borough. A new Central Library of much larger proportions is at present being built.*

In 1937, both Wyndley Pool and Powell's Pool came into the possession of the Corporation and became part of Sutton Park, together with a parcel of land on the Park's perimeter. The conveyance of the property from the Somerville Trust contains a covenant by the Corporation to use the land on the north side of Monmouth Drive as an addition to the Park. The trustees, however, declared in a separate document that this covenant did not prevent the playing of open air games on the land, or the erection of suitable buildings in connection with those games. The total area transferred to the Corporation under this agreement was 152 acres.

*Completed in 1974.

In May, 1937, the main thoroughfares of Sutton Coldfield were transformed into avenues of red, white and blue when decorations were put up for the Coronation of King George VI. Over 11,000 bulbs of seven different colours were used to illuminate the town. On Coronation Day, despite poor weather, a large number of visitors came to Sutton Park where, at the entrances, men engaged in controlling traffic, used miniature Union Jacks for signalling purposes. Colourful displays were given by the town's school-children, nearly 2,800 of whom were provided with tea, and there were massed choirs and community singing in the Park. The day was also marked by the formal opening of an extension to the Town Hall by the Mayor, Councillor W. A. Perry. This was to provide a new lounge, costing £6,000, which the Mayor said would be of great use and service to the town. A new Mayor's mace was presented to the borough by Councillor Perry.

Coinciding in time with these celebrations came the news of measures to be taken in the face of the still-deteriorating international situation. Sutton Coldfield Fire Brigade Committee made a statement on Air Raid Precautions: " Volunteers are required as Aid Raid Wardens, First Aid Workers (men and women), and for the Fire Brigade Emergency Service . . . a course of instruction in anti-gas training will be instituted." A Sutton Councillor said he thought each householder in the Borough should be provided with a gas-mask, so as to be acquainted with its use, and to instruct other occupants of the house.

At Christmas, 1937, in continuation of an old tradition, 2,231 bundles of holly were distributed from the Park to residents, schools, churches and other institutions, in addition to which 30 Christmas trees were given away, mainly to hospitals and schools. Rabbiting in the Park was popular, and 160 permits were issued over the holiday period, resulting in 450 rabbits being caught.

In January, 1938, Councillor W. G. H. Seal, Chairman of the Air Raids Precautions Committee, said there was evidence that public interest in the proposed precautions against any possible attack from the air was being stimulated and that the apathy which previously existed was being gradually overcome. In the same month, Belisha-beacons were introduced in Sutton Coldfield. The first to be erected was at Mere Green, to mark a crossing between Belwell Lane and Mere Green Road. In the town centre a lorry-driver pleaded guilty to driving without due care and attention, following a collision near the " Empress Cinema "—with a horse-trough.

During 1938, there was a strong move locally against the running of double-decker 'buses in various parts of the town. The issue was raised by the Midland Red 'Bus Company, who applied to the Traffic Commissioners for permission to run double-deckers over certain of their routes within the Borough. At the hearing of the application it was mentioned that Walsall Corporation double-deckers already ran from Walsall to Streetly. The Sutton authorities replied that there was no reason why they should have a red nuisance as well as a blue one. The Mayor, Councillor W. Bigwood, supporting the objection said that he occupied a corner house in Four Oaks Road, and that anyone on a double-decker 'bus would be able to see into his garden, dining-room, drawing-room—and bedroom. Double-deckers, in his opinion, would be urbanising the rural advantages of the Royal Town. In due course, however, the application was granted and the Commissioners expressed the view that the 'buses would not interfere with the privileges or the pleasures of the inhabitants, nor injure the beauty of the town; nor would they, they said, unduly interfere with the privacy of houses or gardens along the routes.

In the autumn of 1938, two large school-blocks, consisting of four new schools, for Senior Boys, Senior Girls, Junior Mixed and Infants, were opened at Boldmere by Mr. Kenneth Lindsay, M.P., Parliamentary Secretary to the Board of Education. This followed a re-organisation of local schools. The Mayor, Councillor W. Bigwood said at the opening ceremony that many improvements had been made in the Borough during the last few years, particularly with regard to education. These improvements included the founding of the Girls' High School (now the Girls' Grammar School), the development of a Public Library, and the extension of the Vesey Grammar School at a cost of £49,000. He thought all would agree, however, that the re-organisation of the elementary schools was one of the most important developments in the history of the town. The districts of Boldmere, Wylde Green and New Oscott, he said, were to be envied, since they would be the first to receive the benefits.

Many local events and news items of 1939, prior to the outbreak of war, in no way reflected the impending crisis. Sutton Coldfield Golf Club held a Ball to celebrate its Golden Jubilee and the Vesey Memorial Garden—laid out on the site of two old public-houses and other property demolished two years previously—was officially opened by the Deputy Mayor, Councillor Wilfred Bigwood. The " Sutton Coldfield News " declared that completion of the scheme would: " perpetuate for all time the name of the town's great benefactor, Bishop Vesey."

There was a sharp decline in 1939 in the number of " Poor Maidens " applying for marriage portions. One applicant, a ' general maid , aged 23, produced a testimonial from her former Headmistress:

> " She will regard home as a sacred charge and make it one which follows worthily the tradition of English home-life."

Her application was successful.

In 1939, the Air Ministry built a Balloon Barrage Depot at Whitehouse Common where, in July, hundreds of people turned up to see the ascent of the first balloon. The event must have symbolized a new era for many Sutton people, particularly the younger generation. Within a few months young men were to be donning uniforms and breaking-in boots in route-marches on unfamiliar English roads to the strains of " Bless 'Em All!", " Roll out the Barrel!" and other, less respectable, refrains. The tethered balloons, high above many towns and cities, became— like respirators, sandbags and the blackout—tokens of the " phoney war ", so soon to fan out into a state of total war, engulfing the world.

CHAPTER XII
The second World War years.

THE first three days of September, 1939 were memorable. On Friday, the first, German troops crossed the Polish border, one million British children were evacuated from " vulnerable areas ", and the piled sandbags around public buildings rose higher and higher. On Saturday there was General Mobilization, and on Sunday, the third, at 11.15 a.m., Neville Chamberlain, the Prime Minister, in a terse broadcast, announced that England was at war with Germany. Sutton Coldfield children were not evacuated, but some Birmingham evacuees came to Sutton and, at a later period—when the aerial war developed in ferocity— there was a sudden influx of Coventry children into the town.

Those early days of hostilities soon accustomed Sutton people to the silver barrage-balloons, glistening in the September sky, but the Blackout was a somewhat different matter. In Sutton Coldfield there were 200 special constables to enforce the Blackout Regulations and, not surprisingly, there was a great scramble in the shops for the limited amount of blackout material available. The first batch of prosecutions for blackout offences brought forth a warning from a magistrate that what had been tolerated in the First World War would not do in the Second. In a letter to the " Sutton Coldfield News " a corres- pondent posed the question: " Are Wardens officious?" He des- cribed how a warden knelt on a lawn in front of a house, trying to catch a glimpse of lights through a chink in black curtains. Pleading for a common-sense interpretation of the regulations, the correspondent pointed out that the Blackout was designed to baffle aircraft—not submarines!

Within a few days of the outbreak of hostilities, Sutton Coldfield had formed its own wartime Citizens' Advice Bureau, the official purpose of which was described as being " the dissemination of information on the many questions that may arise during the war . . . " Except for a great increase in military traffic, the roads became quieter—petrol rationing was claimed to have kept 70% of private vehicles off the road during the first month of the war. Cars were going for a song, but an enterprising Sutton garage proprietor advertised: " More miles per gallon—have your engine tuned to the new pool petrol."

Land came into its own. A local estate agent, proclaiming that it was the safest investment, intimated that he was in a position to offer several plots. Sutton people were exhorted to grow their own potatoes, as in wartime, it was claimed, a potato-patch was of more credit to a gardener than the finest bed of roses.

The Germans had made plans for the aerial destruction of a number of local objectives as early as June, 1939—three months before the out-break of war. Their objectives included Fort Dunlop, Bromford Tubular Rolling Mills and Hams Hall Power Station. They soon became aware of Sutton's Balloon Barrage Depot, which they photographed from a reconnaissance 'plane in October, 1939. During the ' Blitz ', Sutton Coldfield fared somewhat better than its neighbour, Erdington. What bombing there was was inclined to be haphazard, and on one occasion several bombs dropped harmlessly on Echo Hill (near Bracebridge Pool), in Sutton Park. In 1940 an attempt by a German raider to sever the railway line to Sutton and Four Oaks almost succeeded. A bomb just missed the bridge in Station Road, Wylde Green, leaving a huge crater in the road, a few yards west of the bridge.

Some 70-80 bombs were dropped on Walmley, causing damage to property but no loss of life. One bomb fell in the garden of Maney Vicarage and another caused slight damage to the Co-operative premises on the Parade.

During the most crucial phase of the war, the driving force behind the frenzied building of 'planes was provided by Lord Beaverbrook, Minister of Aircraft Production, and at Castle Bromwich, the premises now belonging to Pressed Steel Fisher became the biggest aircraft factory in Europe. Beaverbrook's impassioned plea to housewives for pots and pans to turn into Spitfires met with an immediate response, and production went from strength to strength. At Castle Bromwich alone, over 12,000 'planes were built. Although all this activity lay beyond Sutton Coldfield's boundaries, Minworth—within the borough —had the distinction of being the site of an aircraft storage depot with hangers so high that pilots, while testing Spitfires, habitually flew straight through them!

Sutton Park, as during the 1914-18 War, played an important part in the war effort. A great amount of tank testing took place there; a Civil Defence camp was built near Powell's Pool; an aliens' internment camp was sited at Longmoor Pool; 95 acres of heathland were put under cultivation near Streetly; and considerable amounts of timber were felled at Westwood Coppice,

Upper and Lower Nuthurst, Holly Hurst and the New Plantation.

In the grim days of 1940, the Park's internee camp was in the news when, seemingly, several hundred people, mainly over 50, had to march about 1½ miles to the site, carrying their belongings, because of a misunderstanding over the 'buses which were to have met them at the station. On arrival at the camp it was alleged that the internees found nothing for their comfort other than tents and groundsheets. The Home Secretary (Sir John Anderson), was asked questions in the House on the subject by Sir Richard Ackland, M.P.

Probably more fortunate than the internees were those German P.O.W.s who found themselves in a working party supervised by the late Mr. Alfred Warren. When they were repatriated, they presented him with an inlaid box made out of oak taken from the Park as a tribute of their regard for him. Among the many anecdotes and reminiscences of the Park which we owe to Mr. Warren is one relating to the keeper's cottage on Rowton's Hill, which he tells us was damaged during the war, although it is not clear as to how it became a casualty. He claimed that, due to the damage to the cottage—which was built in 1853—it was necessary to evacuate the family living there to Mere Green. Afterwards it fell into the hands of vandals, and eventually had to be demolished. Later, Mr. Warren said, he took a party of about 20 P.O.W.s to the cottage to salvage the best of the bricks, which were taken to Darnel Hurst to build a temporary dutch-barn for the War Agricultural Authority.

During the war, the pursuit of victory manifested itself in many different ways at Sutton Coldfield. In October, 1940, £6,000 was raised by the Sutton Coldfield " Spitfire " Fund, a cheque for which amount was despatched to Lord Beaverbrook, the Minister of Aircraft Production. Between May and December, 1940, knitters at Hill Village produced 379 articles as part of their war effort, and at a later date they made up a parcel of 15 pullovers for British prisoners of war, and pyjamas, socks, cuffs, mittens and helmets for a local regiment. In Walmley, too, hundreds of knitted comforts were provided in the village, though at one stage the problem of obtaining wool put a brake on these activities.

Corporation workmen attached to the Highways Depot formed a Pig Club, and in March, 1941 they were keeping 14 pigs at Whitehouse Common. Also in 1941 it was reported that Sutton Coldfield Photographic Society had assumed the responsibilty of taking something in the region of 100 photographs of buildings of historical interest in the borough. The object of this scheme was to keep pictorial records of as many historical buildings as possible before they were either destroyed by enemy action, or removed during the carrying out of future town planning schemes.

All military news during the war was subject to rigorous censorship, but in 1941 the authorities saw fit to release news of demonstration exercises in Sutton Park by members of the 6th Warwickshire (Sutton) Battalion of the Home Guard, when it was said that, during a three hour period " specially trained units demonstrated tactics which are calculated to defeat the machinations of any would-be invader."

Sutton people were urged to step up their fund-raising efforts with more and more salvage, and great enthusiasm was being shown by local allotment-holders. At Sheffield Road one of the allotments was worked by a woman of 84, who dug and planted it herself, in addition to which she helped her ' young ' brother, aged 65, and her son aged 58, with their allotments.

In wartime it was unpatriotic to travel more than was absolutely necessary, which may have accounted for the big wartime ' gates ' at Sutton Park. The searching question which would-be travellers were urged to ask themselves: " Is my journey really necessary?" could hardly be applied to the Birmingham munition worker, contemplating a day in the Park. Many took an August Bank Holiday Monday break in 1940, when 26,000 visitors paid admission to Sutton Park, and on the corresponding day in 1941, over 25,000 visitors paid to enter the Park.

After the United States entered the war in 1941, large numbers of American troops came to England, and at Sutton Coldfield, beside Sutton Park Railway Station, they built their main American Army European Post Office. This project employed a great many American G.I.s who were, at first, billetted on local inhabitants. Later on, camps were built for them at Penns Lane, on the Streetly side of Sutton Park, and at Minworth. Not surprisingly, a number of local girls became " G.I. brides " and embarked, with their husbands, on a new life in America after the war.

In February, 1942, King George VI and Queen Elizabeth visited Sutton Coldfield, where they inspected members of the National Fire Service in Sutton Park and watched a demonstration of fire-fighting. Before the departure of the Royal Party, the King was presented with copies of the town's charters by the Mayor (Councillor Cobb).

One of the minor irritants of that year for Sutton Coldfield housewives was the fact that, despite the town's hard water, they only had the same ration of soap as Birmingham housewives, who enjoyed soft water. One woman who did all her own washing claimed that she would be driven to using her husband's shaving soap to wash herself with, because the week's wash would take all her ration.

In May, 1942 a young woman of 23—Miss Eileen Kirkham —became the first woman to be engaged in operating signals on the then London, Midland and Scottish Railway system, when she took up duties in the signal-box at Sutton Park Station. She was one of three signal-operators in the same box, and her job involved working eight hours at a stretch.

It was perhaps a happy coincidence that, at a time when there was a renewed interest in music and the arts, sparked off by the rigors and hardships of war, the curtain of the Highbury Little Theatre went up for its first production—Shaw's "Arms and the Man". This was in May, 1942, although in fact the "Highbury" had been conceived much earlier. The group was founded in 1925 and since 1937, when the Highbury Players had decided to purchase the Sheffield Road site, fund-raising had been their constant preoccupation. Bazaars, treasure-hunts, tennis tournaments, rambles, whist-drives and other appropriate ways of raising money were employed, and patrons, enthusiastic at the prospect of the best in drama to follow, gave generously to the cause. It was pointed out at the opening that Mr. John English, the arts director, had kept doggedly on in spite of air raids, black-outs, members being called up for the Forces, civil defence duties, bad weather, shortage of material and other difficulties. The theatre itself, compact yet comfortable, was highly praised, as was the stage, which—it was claimed—would be the envy of many amateur and professional companies alike, both as regards its capacity and its equipment.

On 1st May, 1943, the "Wings for Victory" Week was inaugurated by the Mayor of Sutton Coldfield, Councillor W. Moss, when there was a procession through the town of nearly 2,000 people in uniform. The subsequent programme included entertainments, dances, a football match, and displays by the R.A.F. and the local Squadron of the Air Training Corps. The fund-raising target for 'planes was exceeded, and after expenses had been met it was still possible to make a donation to the R.A.F. Benevolent Fund. Other fund-raising activities were also carried out for the Merchant Navy Comfort Services, and for the proposed auxiliary hospital at "Good Hope", Rectory Road, the former home of the late Mr. Ramsay Winter, and later to be the site of the Good Hope General Hospital. The house, which stood in 17 acres of parkland and garden, was built in 1880. Before becoming known as "Good Hope" it was called "Broomie Close". A former owner of the house had had the ground hallowed and a vault built in the garden to enable a burial to take place there. When the house was sold, the new occupants did not like having a body buried in their garden, so they obtained permission to move it. This act took place in the middle of the night, when the body was reburied in the nearby cemetery. A dog and some musical instruments were also found buried in the vault.

A British Restaurant was opened in South Parade in 1943, and it was reported by the chairman of the Emergency Feeding

Committee (Councillor W. F. Taylor), that during the first six months trading, 62,016 meals were prepared and supplied at the restaurant, and 39,099 school meals were prepared there during the same period.

The next year—1944—was described as " Sutton Coldfield's Red Cross Year "—a year in which, throughout the borough, a variety of events were organised for that cause. They included exhibition matches and auctions by Walmley Golf Club and Sutton Coldfield Golf Club, by means of which nearly £10,000 was raised, the annual allotment produce show and food exhibition at the town hall, a billiard and snooker exhibition, dog and horse shows, fetes, entertainments and dances. In addition, children sold toys and gardeners their vegetables; ladies raffled their treasures; and motorists placed boxes in their cars and collected from people to whom they gave lifts.

The " Sutton Coldfield News " declared at the end of 1944 that the year's events " clearly reveal that the unrelenting strain of war has not begun to impair the resolute character of the people at home."

During the latter part of the war there was a tank-testing site along the rising ground on the Canwell side of Camp Road. Here the testing was carried out, not by the army, but by civilian testers. Amphibious tanks also underwent their first tests on water in a disused brickyard in Barnard Road.

Victory in 1945 brought relief to millions of war-weary people throughout the world. The end had been anticipated for some time before the termination of hostilities, and a few of the war-time restrictions were already being relaxed, when—in May—the cease-fire in Europe finally came. In Sutton Coldfield, the spontaneous relief of the inhabitants was emphasised by the flood-lighting of buildings, fireworks, bonfires on every spare piece of land, dancing and parties in the roads, and a big display of flags and buntings. Three months later, in August, 1945, there was a repeat performance to mark " V.J. " Day—the end of the campaign against Japan, and the end of the war.

CHAPTER XIII
1946-1954.

A MONG the numerous post-war problems was a nation-wide shortage of bricks. As a consequence of this, Sutton Coldfield, in common with many other places, went into the ' prefab. business '. The first prefab. was formally opened in January, 1946 at Four Oaks and in April, that year, it was announced that the Council was to purchase 50 permanent prefabricated houses at a cost of £65,350. Many people were desperately anxious to forget the war, which may have been one of the reasons for there being no great enthusiasm for the official Victory Celebrations of 1946. At a meeting of the Town Council, the Deputy Mayor, Councillor F. W. Terry, expressed the view that, with the various troubles existing in the country, it was hardly a time for general rejoicing. Nevertheless a sum not exceeding £300 was allocated for the purpose of entertaining the school-children of the Borough, and an additional sum was provided for illuminating the town on 7th and 8th June, 1946.

Polling took place in 1946 on the question of whether Sutton Coldfield's cinemas should continue to open on Sundays, as they had done under special licences during the war years. The result was 3,243 votes in favour of Sunday opening, with 936 against. In 1946 Sutton also had its first woman Mayor, Councillor Mrs. K. M. Garrard, who—in accepting the office—declared " I am a very proud woman."

The New Year of 1947 was heralded with optimism, and locally an almost pre-war air of festivity showed itself, with people buoyed up by the hope that conditions were improving, despite the parlous state of the economy. Soon, however, the country was in the grip of one of the harshest winters in living memory, and between the beginning of January and early March, a total of 27 inches of snow was recorded in Sutton Coldfield.

The post-war housing programme was held up by the extreme weather conditions, and all available workmen were engaged in clearing snow-drifts in all parts of the Borough. Every effort was made to keep all north-bound traffic moving along the Chester Road where, on Welshman's Hill, New Oscott there was, at one time, a snow-drift eight feet high. The available snow plough proved to be quite inadequate to the situation and men had to be transferred from other tasks to clear the road. The corporation was reported to have run out of salt.

Some of the highlights of entertainment in Sutton Coldfield during April, 1947 were represented by Turgenev's " A Month in the Country " at the Highbury Little Theatre, while at the Odeon, Sutton's native-born film-star, Hazel Court, was seen starring in a film called " Meet me at Dawn." In the Town Hall, the Sutton Coldfield Photographic Society held its 8th Annual Exhibition which, according to one critic, was marked by a " pleasing freshness and originality."

War time shortages, with rationing of both food and clothing continued, and periodic guidance was given in the local press to Sutton Coldfield residents on " How to get your new Ration Book ". One of the pre-requisites of getting the ration book was the possession of an identity-card. The German prisoners-of-war were still in Sutton and many of them were entertained by local people. The Rev. W. Salmon, Minister of Park Road Congregational Church wrote to members of his church: " We wish that all prisoners could be sent home, but since the authorities have decreed otherwise, we must make their stay as happy as possible."

At Christmas, 1947, the German prisoners-of-war at the Penns Lane Camp sent a Christmas-card to the Mayor of Sutton Coldfield, Councillor C. H. Dainty, with the message " May the joy and peace of Christmastide remain with you through the year ", and inside the card was written: " We wish to extend our sincere thanks for your warm and generous hospitality, and to take this opportunity of expressing our common friendship, together with best wishes for a happy Christmas and a prosperous New Year." The Mayor sent a card to the prisoners, and visited the camp, expressing " on behalf of the burgesses of the Royal Town sincere good wishes and goodwill to all mankind."

In 1948, Sutton Electricity Department, which had opened at the turn of the century with 70 consumers, became a part of the Midlands Electricity Board. Some progress was made during that year with the building of the Falcon Lodge Estate, despite the acute post-war shortage of both labour and material. More than 2,000 people attended the opening of a " Thanksgiving Garden " at Boldmere Junior School.

In that year, the Corporation bought Park House—the only privately owned property in Sutton Park—for £19,250. This estate, consisting of 19 acres and a house, had been retained when the exchange of Park-land was made with Sir Edmund Hartopp in 1825. The Civil Defence Camp, later a National Fire Service Training School, at the Boldmere end of the Park was given a new lease of life as a European Volunteer Workers' Hostel, which brought many Latvians and Lithuanians to the district. Warwickshire Agricultural Committee at that time still had 256 acres of land under cultivation in the Park.

On 5th July, 1948, the National Health Act came into force —and Sutton Coldfield Dispensary became redundant. The dispensary had been founded in 1888, and within a year of that date, 1,279 people were subscribing to receive medicine and medical attention. Some of the doctors associated with it were Sir Alfred Evans, Dr. Chavasse, Dr. Jerome and Dr. Knott. The assets of the dispensary were handed over to Sutton Coldfield Municipal Charities for general purposes.

Sir Alfred Evans, who had been given the Honorary Freedom of the Borough in 1931 for his long and distinguished public service to the town, was a relative of George Eliot (Mary Ann Evans), Warwickshire's most famous novelist. In his study, Sir Alfred is said to have had books, photographs and other items showing his connection with George Eliot. His affection for her does not appear to have been lessened by her unorthodoxy, despite the fact that he was a life-long member of the Church. Sir Alfred Evans is said to have been knighted for treating the children of Princess Alice Orphanage free of charge.

Dr. Chavasse was a tall, immaculately dressed man, who always wore a silk hat, top coat and morning suit—at whatever time of the day or night he was called out. He was a great horse lover—and owner. His home was in the High Street, but his stables were in Anchorage Road. He was a nephew of Sir Alfred Evans.

In the 1948-49 season Sutton Town Football Club had been the winners of the Walsall Senior League Cup. At the Club's annual dinner in 1949, the Mayor, Councillor H. Hothersall—replying to the toast of " The Royal Town "—said that he did not think that there was any danger of the town losing its independence, as was once imagined by some people. On another occasion the Mayor declared that it was the Council's wish " to preserve the Royal Town as a delightful and pleasant place." Although many Birmingham workers lived there, he said, the word " suburb " should not be applied to it. Councillor H. Bladen Jones, speaking at a meeting of the Town Council, lamented that, ever since the death of Sir Henry Cameron-Ramsay-Fairfax-Lucy in 1944, the Royal Town of Sutton Coldfield had been without a High Steward, and he stressed " the importance of filling this ancient and historic office." In his plea he referred to " these swiftly changing days, when old institutions and customs are passing away." He pointed out that before 1528 the holder of the office had been appointed by the Crown, and since then he had been appointed by the Corporation. " As it is now, the office is an honorary one," Councillor Bladen Jones added " There will be no addition to the rates, but it will add to the greater dignity of the town." The question was referred to the General Purposes Committee, and in 1951 the vacancy was filled by the 4th Lord Leigh.

On 17th December, 1949, an event took place in Sutton Coldfield which was to affect the leisure habits of a great many Midlanders. On that date the first television transmissions were made from the new station at Hill Village, where a 750 foot mast had created some considerable interest prior to the event. This was the first high-powered television station to be built outside London, and by its means the ' small screen ' was introduced to regions as far apart as Shropshire, the eastern borders of Wales, the Potteries, Oxford, Leicester and Nottingham, as well as places nearer at hand. Sutton Coldfield became overnight a place known by name to thousands of people who had never before heard of it, and its transmitting station was the prototype for future stations.

A contract won by Mr. Pat Collins in 1950 led to the disappearance of a local landmark—the Big Dipper in the Crystal Palace grounds. It was dismantled and removed to supply the need for a Big Dipper on the Thames Embankment for the Festival of Britain, which took place the following year.

In December, 1950, following a public meeting at St. Peter's Hall, Maney, a Sutton Park Protection Association was formed, which became the Friends of the Park. Some acrimony had been aroused by an earlier proposal to use war-time hutments in the Park for housing purposes. One speaker said that the aims of the new body would be to maintain the Park as it was gifted to the townspeople by Bishop Vesey, and to ensure that the Town Council became "trustees of the Park and not land-owners as they seem to consider themselves to be." Efforts to prevent conversion of the huts into temporary housing accommodation were unsuccessful.

In 1951 the census established that Sutton Coldfield's population had risen by 59 per cent in 20 years—from 29,928 in 1931 to 47,590. A notable achievement of 1951 was the continuing growth of the Falcon Lodge estate. Sutton's post-war building programme, according to statistics, suggested that its efforts compared favourably with those of other local authorities up and down the country. In 1952, however, it was claimed that shortage of bricks was slowing up house-building in the Borough. One of the causes of this was said to be the fact that many brick-yards had been closed during the war, and had never been re-opened.

In July, 1952, there was an unprecedented thunderstorm, in which six houses in Sutton Coldfield were struck by lightning. Two of these were severely damaged. There was also wide-spread flooding and disruption of telephone services. In November of the same year a gale reaching over 80 miles per hour caused hundreds of pounds worth of damage throughout Sutton Coldfield. The roof of the newly erected stand at Boldmere St. Michael's Football Ground in Church Road, Boldmere, was torn off and completely smashed by the force of the gale, and a number of roads were made impassable by fallen trees.

Early in 1953, concern was expressed on behalf of Sutton Coldfield farmers over the amount of agricultural land in the borough being taken over for building purposes. The government, it was said, was appealing for more food to be grown in the country, yet land was continually being taken from farmers. Some farmland in the borough was used for playing-fields and—what was worse—a farmer claimed that about 20 acres of his best land had been taken over by the Town and Country Planning Authority, then left untouched until it became over-grown with docks.

Despite cold, wet and windy weather, the Coronation of Queen Elizabeth in June, 1953, was celebrated in a wide range of activities in Sutton Coldfield. The Town Council's programme on the Meadow Platt included a display by the Sutton Coldfield branch of the Women's League of Health and Beauty, precision drill by a local R.A.F. unit, community singing and dancing, followed by a spectacular firework display and bonfire on Holly

Knoll, whilst children's parties took place all around the town. To commemorate the Coronation, a coppice of mixed hardwoods and conifers was planted overlooking Longmoor Pool. This was called, appropriately, Queen's Coppice. The mound in this coppice is shown on old maps as a tumulus and nearby there is reputed to be an unexploded bomb dropped by a German 'plane during the last war.

A few days after the Coronation, the Mayor of Sutton, Councillor C. Stephens, formally opened the garden at the junction of the Driffold and the Birmingham Road as a memorial to Dr. George Bodington. A number of members of the Bodington family attended the ceremony. The Mayor described Dr. Bodington as " an acute observer, a vigorous thinker and a fluent speaker; but he was best known as one who devoted all his life to the general treatment of consumptive cases."

In 1953, Miss Diane Leather, the daughter of a surgeon— Mr. J. B. Leather—from Little Aston, achieved the distinction of running the world's fastest mile for a woman at the White City, London. Miss Leather, a member of the Birchfield Harriers Athletic Club, ran the mile in 5 min. 2.6 sec., beating the previous record by 7.2 sec. The following year, running at the Midland Women's Athletic Championships at Perry Barr, she cut her time for the mile run to 4 min. 59.6 sec.

In January, 1954, following upon a proposal that Walsall Corporation should extend trolley'bus routes into surrounding districts, a Parliamentary Bill was promoted by that authority. Sutton Coldfield Town Council voted unanimously in favour of opposing that part of the bill which sought powers to extend Walsall's transport system. A spokesman for the Council said that Sutton Coldfield must protect itself, and trolley-'buses were never seen in Sutton streets. A few months later, the Council instructed the Town Clerk to lodge objection to the Boundary Commission's proposals that the Borough should be combined with the Erdington Ward of Birmingham to form a new Parliamentary constituency. " We should be concerned only with the preservation and independence of this Royal Town," declared Councillor W. F. Taylor, Chairman of the General Purposes Committee.

The proposals, however, were carried, and at a crowded adoption meeting of both Sutton and Erdington Conservatives in April, 1955, Mr. Geoffrey Lloyd, the then Minister of Fuel and Power, was unanimously adopted as Conservative candidate for the new constituency, and at the General Election of the following month became its Member of Parliament.

With the de-control of the sale of meat in July, 1954, food rationing was finally abolished—nine years after the end of the war. The " Sutton Coldfield News " commented " The national larder is now well stocked with sugar, butter, meat, eggs, tea and most of the other commodities we need, or like to have, but prices are high—far too high for comfort . . . "

Following upon a nation-wide Civil Defence recruiting campaign in 1954, efforts to enrol over 700 volunteers in Sutton Coldfield met with no success. Twice in one week the Civil Defence Corps held public demonstrations of their work in the town, but the Civil Defence Officer commented afterwards: " They were of no benefit at all. The public never came."

During the summer of 1954, local naturalists were intrigued by a strange diving bird with white under-parts and russet flanks which appeared on Wyndley Pool. This rarity prompted the late Mr. Roland Antrobus to write to the press on the subject: " It will no doubt interest many of your ornithological readers to know that black-necked grebe have visited a pool in Sutton Park," and he went on to describe how he had watched a pair of them there.

Roland Antrobus, who died in 1962 at the age of 84, was a surveyor and estate agent who lived for many years in the Driffold. He was a sportsman-naturalist, and a great lover of Sutton Park, who was to be seen walking there every morning with his dogs. The trees at the western end of Keeper's Pool were given to the Park as saplings by Roland Antrobus. He was a gifted artist who, until an advanced age, was still painting accurate water-colours of British birds. He was a son of Alfred Antrobus, who had built " Fernwood " at New Oscott.

CHAPTER XIV
1955-1965.

ON a late Sunday afternoon in January, 1955, the nine-coach York-Bristol express was roaring through the deserted Sutton Coldfield Station under a full head of steam, when the engine left the rails. Coach after coach piled up and the first coach was sandwiched between the engine and the second coach. The fourth coach reared in the air and tore down a part of the station roof and the platforms were ripped up on either side of the shattered track.

Police, firemen, ambulances, doctors and surgeons rushed to the scene; the mobile surgical unit from the Birmingham Accident Hospital attended, together with 40 extra ambulances from surrounding districts, and servicemen from the R.A.F. Camp at Whitehouse Common also rendered aid. Seventeen people died in the disaster, and many more were injured, but it was pointed out that the casualty rate would have been higher had it not been for the prompt help rendered immediately after the accident.

In recognition of their efforts in stopping an oncoming train after the disaster, Mr. and Mrs. Norman Fairey of the Driffold received a silver tea service from British Railways, and at the same ceremony, two railway employees who were travelling on the ill-fated train—Fireman Derek Smith of Derby and Ticket-collector George Attenborough of Lichfield—were presented with gold watches for their part in stopping the train. Mr. and Mrs. Fairey, on hearing the crash, had rushed down the embankment from their garden, towards the station, when their young son, James, shouted to them that another train was approaching. They waved to the driver of the oncoming train, and after he had stopped, they dashed on to help the injured. The two railwaymen each made their separate ways to the signal-box after the accident, and in a joint effort of telephoning, putting the signals at danger and placing detonators on the track, showed great presence of mind—particularly as Fireman Smith was injured and shocked as a result of the accident.

In 1955, in an article in the " Municipal Review "—the monthly journal of the Association of Municipal Corporations —Sutton Coldfield was compared favourably on its health statistics with four other Midland towns—Wednesbury, Oldbury, Stafford and Kidderminster. The town was described as " a dormitory borough of considerable charm with a cross-section of all social groups in the population, but with an unusually large percentage of well-to-do business and professional people. Moreover, it is of large phsyical size, covering 14,000 acres, of which 2,400 are parks." Sutton's exceedingly low infant mortality rate was commented upon, as was its significantly lower rate of tuberculosis compared with the other towns.

" In fairness to other authorities " the report continued " it must be conceded that Sutton Coldfield is of very recent growth, and therefore has a high percentage of modern houses. The town has increased ten-fold since 1861, and by one-third since 1938. It appears to have been consistently healthy, and in the early years of the century had a death rate of under ten for six years running."

In 1956, Sutton Coldfield lost several familiar landmarks. Early in that year demolition of " The Rookery ", an ivy-covered Georgian house, was commenced, in preparation of the site for a new police-station and court-house. Before demolition had proceeded very far, however, the work was held up for a while on Home Office instruction because of a government credit squeeze. A site was cleared on the Birmingham Road from nearly opposite the Wylde Green Hotel for some 300 yards towards Sutton, which entailed the demolition of a number of large, older houses. One of the house demolished there was " Marchmount ", a house of some distinction, with a large, peaceful garden. Many new houses were eventually built on the plot, which was leased by the developers from the seventeenth century Stanley Trust, the founder of which was Walter Stanley, Lord of the Manor of West Bromwich, who had also acquired land in Sutton Coldfield and Erdington.

During 1956, an unsuccessful campaign was mounted to save the Vesey Cottage at Little Sutton—a building listed as being of special architectural and historical interest. The late Alderman (then Councillor) Harry Herringshaw, and three other local business-men offered £300 to the demolition firm in a bid to save the cottage, but the offer was rejected. Councillor Herringshaw stressed the need for the town to preserve its old buildings if it was to retain its identity.

In March, 1956, the diesel train service between Birmingham and Lichfield, calling at Sutton Coldfield, was inaugurated, and the "Sutton Coldfield News" commented shortly afterwards: "Suttonians have made good use of the new speedy service, which bids fair to become increasingly popular."

In September, 1956, Dr. Violet Parkes, J.P. was appointed World President of the Soroptimist International Association—a post she held until 1960. Dr. Parkes, a general practitioner in Wylde Green for many years, despite her busy professional life, has found time for many socially beneficial activities, including membership of the British Council for Aid to Refugees and aid for the Margery Fry Memorial Fund, which looks after the welfare of ex-prisoners. She was awarded the O.B.E. in 1968.

Many of Sutton's older residents must have felt that Wylde Green lost its last symbol of rural life when Stud Farm was demolished in 1957. Built in the early seventeenth century, possibly from some of the remains of the manor house, its history is obscure. At the time of its demise it was still lit by oil lamps, and although its extensive lands had dwindled to a mere 50 acres, it was still very much a working farm, with pigs, dairy cows and the horses and foals of the stud, from which the farmstead took its name.

One celebrity who loved the place was James Agate, a regular visitor there at week-ends and a frequent attender of horse shows in Sutton Coldfield during the 25 years prior to his death in 1947. Agate—author, essayist and drama critic—was also an exhibitor of show harness ponies, so it was natural that he should have much in common with Albert Throup of Stud Farm, who bred and showed horses.

When in Sutton Coldfield, Agate liked to stay at the "Three Tuns", which he once described as "the most comfortable inn I have ever struck." In April, 1935, he was the guest of honour in Birmingham at the Shakespeare Dinner of the Central Literary Society. This was no mean achievement for a man who had spent almost 20 years of his early life in his father's cotton mill in Manchester, where he sold millions of yards of calico, "hating every yard of it" as he put it, because of his great urge to be a writer.

James Agate's sentiments on Albert Throup and Stud Farm were expressed in an entry in his published diary for 8th May, 1944, which reads:

"Albert Throup was thrown out of his trap yesterday and is in hospital with a fractured leg. A great artist with horses; whatever a nagsman can do in the way of coaxing action out of an animal, displaying its qualities and hiding its defects—that Albert does to perfection.

"I suppose I shall never again know such happy hours as those I spent at Wylde Green before the war, watching the horses at work on that raised plateau. To the left the farmhouse built in Shakespeare's time, to the right and below one, the rich Warwickshire plain."

On a clear day, the rich Warwickshire plain is still visible, though the cooling towers at Hams Hall Power Station have increased in numbers since Agate's day, and tend to dominate the scene. Were he alive today, he would have some difficulty in recognising the site of Stud Farm, since the junction of Kempson Avenue is now situated where previously a drive had led from Wylde Green Road to the farm. The farm itself, with all its out-buildings, has completely disappeared, and only some of the bigger trees remain, scattered around a wide area of suburban development. A walk down Kempson Avenue, however, brings one to a turning on the right, leading to a narrow, winding lane, heavy with foliage. This is Cow Lane, frequented by generations of courting couples, and once the cart track leading from Wylde Green Road to the distant fields of Stud Farm, extending then far over the present Walmley Golf Links. To walk along Cow Lane is a stepping back in time—to a period when to stand and stare upon the highway was neither as difficult nor as dangerous as it is today. Throughout England there can be few quieter ways than this, with its overgrown hedgerows, high banks and narrow, winding course. Here, in summer, nettles, bracken, wild roses, elders and oak saplings effectively conceal the close proximity of bricks and mortar.

In Sutton Park, on high ground at the junction of the Boldmere and Keepers Pool roads stands a stone monument and bronze plaque, recalling a big event of 1957. The inscription reads:

"This plaque commemorates the World Jubilee Jamboree of the Scout Movement which was held in this Park from August 1st to August 12th, 1957 and was opened by H.R.H. the Duke of Gloucester. 32,000 scouts from 87 parts

153

of the world came here and were visited by Her Majesty Queen Elizabeth II and H.R.H. Prince Philip, Duke of Edinburgh, and many other distinguished persons."

During those 12 days, the smell from a thousand pungent wood fires filled the air of Sutton Park, and along the Parade strolled the scouts of many nations, all apparently with money to spend on souvenirs. Shops in the town did a roaring trade. When Sutton Park was hit by a very bad thunderstorm, hundreds of scouts were driven from their tents and had to take up quarters in the town, where schools, houses and even the town hall were pressed into service as billets. But on the day that the Queen and Prince Philip visited Sutton Coldfield, the weather was fine, and the occasion was marked by an easy informality, appropriate to an out-door event focusing on a large natural park.

The holding of the Jamboree in Sutton Park had met with some prior opposition on the grounds that it would do long-term harm to the wild life and natural beauty. As one newspaper correspondent put it:

> "The park is utterly unsuitable for this kind of mass invasion, if its wildness is to be preserved. But Sutton now is overrun by the sort of people who complain if they see a cow-pat where they have designed to picnic; who wish in their hearts that horses were other than as their Creator designed them; and who are all for draining marshes and reedy pools, no matter at what cost to wild life."

Some of the opponents' misgivings were apparently justified. Although the event did not involve the draining of any marshes or reedy pools, it was claimed by the Nature Conservancy in a report on the Park in 1965 that the heathland, with its flora and fauna, had been affected: "Much of the heather," it pointed out "is sparse and mixed with other vegetation, and a large proportion of it is young growth resulting from clearance and trampling at the time of the 1957 Scout Jamboree." The disappearance of at least one unusual bird from the Park—the nightjar—is thought to date from that event, possibly due to the wide use of insecticides.

Early in 1958, the newly formed Sutton Coldfield Civic Society had its first general meeting, under the chairmanship of the late Councillor H. Herringshaw, who described the aims and objects of the Society as being five-fold: :

> To maintain and foster historical interest in the borough and to seek to preserve all sites and buildings of historical worth.
>
> To preserve objects of beauty and character and to oppose acts of vandalism.

To encourage civic pride and a sense of beauty.

To initiate schemes of civic and artistic interest.

To adopt suitable measures to interest all citizens in these aims and objects.

More than 40 people, representing many facets of local life, attended the meeting to offer support to the Society. Councillor Herringshaw pointed out that Sutton's population had grown from about 4,000 in 1861 to 56,000 in 1958.

"This makes it only too easy to realise how Sutton Coldfield buildings and traditions have disappeared in the great surge forward " said Councillor Herringshaw. " There are many citizens " he continued, " who can remember Sutton Coldfield as it was at the beginning of the century. This change brings to them some pangs of regret, but it has to take place and we must be thankful that so much is left to us. It makes us realise what a great debt we owe to the past."

Following the revelation in 1958 that there was not so much as a silver spoon at the council house, gifts of civic plate were forthcoming from a number of quarters. The Mayor, Councillor Mrs. Grounds, said: " Any other gifts of silver would be welcome. I would like anything at all that can be added to the present array of plate so that a collection can be built up truly representative of Sutton Coldfield." By May, 1959, the corporation had acquired 16 pieces of civic plate in all. These included a silver tray, made by Matthew Boulton, and inscribed: " Presented by the inhabitants of the Royal Town of Sutton Coldfield to William Webb as a tribute of gratitude for the able, diligent and conscientious discharge of his magisterial duties as capital burgess during the period of forty-one years." The recipient of the tray—William Webb—was headmaster of Bishop Vesey's Grammar School from 1766 to 1817, and was Warden of the Corporation in 1772. The tray had lain, almost forgotten, in a Streetly storeroom for 20 years.

Building developments in 1959 included Moor Hall estate; shops and flats in the Boldmere shopping area; and, close to the town's boundary, the Lyndhurst estate high-rise flats neared completion. The chapel house on the Birmingham Road, Maney, was demolished in 1959, and the death knell was sounded for the nearby tiny chapel, built for the Independent Calvinists in 1848. It was not until May, 1961, however, that the building was demolished. A campaign was launched by the Civic Society to save another old Sutton building—No. 1, Trinity Hill—but to no avail.

By 1960 the question of multi-storey flats had become a ' live ' issue. Strong feelings were aroused when it was first proposed to build high flats near the junction of Boldmere Road and Fir Tree Grove, and reference was made to " great ugly monstrosities looming out of he sky." The other view was that, with both a serious housing shortage, and an acute shortage of municipal building land, the need to build upwards was obvious. "You can't stop progress," it was pointed out. Fears were expressed that the Georgian character of the area around the parish church would be defiled by skyscraper flats on the site of the old, dispensary at the junction of Coleshill Road and Rectory Road. Assurances were given by the council that such fears were groundless.

In 1960, Sutton Coldfield's new Petty Sessional Court-house and Divisional Police Headquarters were completed at a cost of £175,000. Police Superintendent G. F. Bailey, in inviting the ratepayers to inspect the new premises, said: "We are giving the people of Sutton Coldfield an opportunity to see round the building they have supplied for their police-force." The move to the new headquarters ended a long occupation by the police of cramped premises in Station Street, a part of which had once been a public-house.

It became known in 1961 that Sutton Coldfield was to be a garrison town. The announcement that the Fusilier Brigade was to take over the camp, formerly occupied by the Royal Air Force, gave concern to some residents. Someone remarked: "It is not so much the men in the camp, but the camp-followers we do not want." A housewife commented: "I don't particularly relish the idea of being awakened in the early hours of the morning by the sound of bugles and the clatter of hob-nailed boots." Another resident said: "I have lived in garrison towns before, and I can say from experience that a garrison in Sutton Coldfield will have an adverse effect on the town." Most of these fears, however, proved to be groundless.

In 1961, Sutton Coldfield acquired its first betting shops, two of which were opened in the town on the same day. During that year, in a blaze of light and with a fanfare of trumpets, a ten-pin bowling centre—the first in the Midlands and the biggest in the country—was opened on the premises formerly occupied by the Wylde Green Pavilion Cinema. In 1961, the Somerville estate, covering about 45 acres of land between Somerville Road, Monmouth Drive and Stonehouse Road, was in the course of being developed. It entailed the disappearance of Stonehouse Farm, whose farmhouse had previously been demolished, following which the farm tenant had occupied premises once known as Jockey Lane Farm Cottage.

During 1961 a ban was put on fishing in Wyndley Pool. In imposing the ban, the council made it clear that they were not trying to deprive the fishermen of their sport, as there were plenty of other places in the Park where they could go to fish. One correspondent in the local press referred to the ban as a token of further enlightened action on the part of local officialdom. "Can we hope" he asked "that the council will now take up the logical next step of dedicating Wyndley Pool as an absolute sanctuary for wildfowl for all time?"

In a review of "The Natural Resources of Sutton Park" prepared by the Nature Conservancy Council in 1965, it was claimed that of the Park pools, Wyndley was by far the best. "The breeding population" it said "includes great crested and little grebes, mallard and tufted duck, moorhen and coot. In the marsh bordering the alder carr both reed and sedge warblers nest." Mention was made of the black-necked grebes there in 1954, and of an osprey in 1963. The review added " Bracebridge Pool also supports a pair of great crested grebes, and so did Longmoor Pool before it was dredged and the small island cleared."

Between 1951 and 1961 there was a ' population boom' in Sutton Coldfield, with a 25,000 increase in the number of inhabitants, and between 1952 and 1962, 8,563 houses were built, most of which were occupied by people working outside the town. The new municipal estate at Falcon Lodge was completed in the early 'sixties, and at the more expensive end of the housing spectrum, building took place on the Park's boundary in what had been the large gardens of old houses in Hartopp Road, Four Oaks. Suburbia was stretching out into the surrounding countryside, and by 1962 it was estimated that there were only about 135 acres of land available for development within Sutton Coldfield's boundaries. Enterprising estate agents catered for all needs—one even planned a small development at Four Oaks, designed—he said—to appeal to wealthy widows. With a 500% increase in population in just over 60 years, the inevitability of high-density building became obvious.

In 1962, Sutton Coldfield celebrated the centenary of its local railway line. The event was marked by a special celebration run of a steam train over the route of the first train in 1862 from New Street to Sutton Coldfield, organised by the Stephenson Locomotive Society. The train—which was full of railway enthusiasts—was pulled by a 1903 locomotive. Heading the large crowd of townspeople and others waiting to receive the train at Sutton Coldfield Station, was the Mayor and Mayoress, Councillor (later Alderman) and Mrs. Frank Brassington. The Stephenson Locomotive Society also staged an exhibition in the central library at Sutton Coldfield, consisting largely of a pictorial display, designed to show how the town had grown following the coming of the railway.

The summer of 1962 saw the demolition of another familiar landmark—the Crystal Palace—and there were complaints among some visitors that Sutton Park would never be quite the same again. Later in the same year the Crystal Palace fun-fair closed down. Demolition work was going on all around the borough, and the "Sutton Coldfield News" declared in August, 1962: "All over Sutton Coldfield, stately Victorian houses are being demolished to make way for modern flats." Growth and redevelopment was very much in the air. A report by Max Lock and Partners, town planning consultants, on redeveloping the central area came before the borough council and was reproduced in the local press for the information of residents. A forecast was made in 1962 that within the next five years, 1,000 extra homes would be provided in the borough—by means of building multi-storey flats. At Hundred Acre Wood, Streetly—where copses of silver-birch trees swept down to the Chester Road from the gentle slopes of Barr Beacon—a new housing estate came into being, named, appropriately, Hundred Acre estate.

In his annual report as Medical Officer of Health, Dr. J. R. Preston commented upon "individuals who come for a day's outing and consequently seem to be in their most destructive mood." Vandalism in public conveniences, Dr. Preston said, was particularly bad, and he added: "abuse by those using them is such as to make their use objectionable to normal civilised human beings."

In December, 1962, Sutton Coldfield once again paid tribute to its benefactor, Bishop Vesey, on the occasion of the 500th anniversary of his birth. But at a special service at the

The Crystal Palace, Sutton Park, built in 1868, became a familiar landmark to Park visitors. This photograph was taken in May, 1962, just before its demolition.
Photograph: D. J. Cadwallader, A.R.I.B.A.

parish church, the Bishop of Birmingham (the late Dr. J. L. Wilson), started a controversy by saying he had no great opinion of Vesey as a bishop, and he referred to his " ill-gotten gains ". The Mayor, Councillor Brassington, who was at the service, afterwards defended Vesey, saying that, prior to his time, the town had been in a shocking state.

The winter of 1962-63 was one of unabated severity, which started before Christmas and continued well into March. Members of Sutton Coldfield Winter Swimming Club were unable to enjoy their annual Christmas Day swim in Blackroot Pool. Instead, those members so inclined " took the plunge " through a small hole in the thick ice. During week after week of intense cold, the regular bathers kept the hole open, even when the ice was a foot or more thick, and the deferred Christmas swimming race could not take place until 7th April!

In May, 1963, the old building known as the Smithy at Maney—which had belonged to the corporation since 1944—was first opened to the public on two days each week, it being the council's aim to preserve it as a period house with suitable furnishings.

The official opening by Earl Jellicoe of the new £81,000 fire-station at Sutton Coldfield in 1963 meant that, for the first time since the brigade was formed almost a century earlier, it had a purpose-built headquarters with facilities that befitted the needs of a modern fire service. Earl Jellicoe (the First Lord of the Admiralty), said in his speech: " Modern development, for one reason or another, brings an increased fire-risk, and I think you are wise to provide yourselves with really up-to-date facilities." He added that: " Many people quite often thought of the fireman as a person who squirted water on fires, and occasionally risked his life to rescue pretty young things in night-dresses." " In these days " Earl Jellicoe continued, " the fireman's job requires much more skill, and he needs a great deal of technical knowledge, and he also needs to know a lot about fire prevention. That is why, in this respect, good training facilities are very important." The new station was provided with three double bays, housing three appliances, a spacious drill-ground, a hose-drying and drill tower (65 feet high), supplementary garages, workshops and space for auxiliary fire services.

Some excitement was caused in September, 1963 by the appearance of a large, unfamiliar bird, wheeling and turning over Wyndley Pool, after which it flew off in a southerly direction. The " Sutton Coldfield News " office was inundated with 'phone calls from people who had seen the bird, the identity of which had mystified them. It was an osprey—a bird normally associated with the more remote parts of Scotland, and there usually only as an irregular passage-migrant.

159

In 1964, 'the orphanage'—a landmark which had been familiar to generations of local people—disappeared from the skyline. Although it stood in Erdington it was, because of its height, quite as well known in Sutton. The Josiah Mason Almshouses and Orphanage had been conceived under the constitution of an "Orphanage Trust". Their building and endowment, at an estimated cost to Mason of £30,000, was said to have been one of the most munificent acts in the annals of charity. Josiah Mason, a poor boy from Kidderminster, whose only formal education had been at a dame school next door to his home, acquired immense wealth in Birmingham from the trades of steel-pen making and electro-plating. In his orphanage he made provision for the education, as well as the feeding, clothing and housing of the children, of whom it was claimed that he knew each one personally.

When, prior to the redevelopment of the site, the 250-ft. tower of the Sir Josiah Mason Orphanage was felled in 1964, demolition workers chipped away half the base of the tower, substituted beams for bricks, then set fire to the beams. The tower—estimated weight 2,500 tons—collapsed in clouds of smoke and dust. "It fell smack on the target" said master-steeplejack, Mr. J. Clover of Sutton Coldfield, who was in charge of the operation.

There were several innovations in 1964. The town acquired its first multi-storey council flats—at Park Court, Boldmere Road—and a crematorium, costing £125,000 was built in Tamworth Road. Following three years of effort by volunteer workers, a Citizens' Advice Bureau and a Marriage Guidance Centre, both under one roof, were also opened at Sutton Coldfield. In opening the premises, the Mayor, Councillor (now Alderman), C. F. Beaumont-Edmonds, M.C., said that the centre should assist people, both in understanding modern legislation and in stabilising family life.

Earlier in the year, speaking at the Mayoral Banquet in the town hall, Councillor Beaumont-Edmonds referred to the town's need for men and women "who could rebuild it with character and individuality." He also high-lighted the need for courage and resolution "because there is much to be done in our town." Courage and resolution are characteristics readily associated with Alderman Beaumont-Edmonds. He was blinded by enemy action while serving with the eighth army in Tunisia in 1943, but—as the "Sutton Coldfield News" said of him when he came to office—"Townspeople who have been in contact with him have always admired the cheerful manner in which he faces up to the handicap and the alertness and efficiency he has shown in the council chamber and formerly as secretary to the local association of the Scout Movement."

160

In the early hours of a July morning in 1964, firemen from two brigades—the Warwickshire and the Birmingham—were called to St. Michael's Parish Church, Boldmere, the roof of which was ablaze, almost from end to end. The scene was described, graphically, in the local press:

" Hidden behind the tall trees in the full leaf of summer the burning church emitted a sort of ghastly beauty as if, even in its death throes, the building was determined to retain the grace and splendour it had borne through life. In the grave-yard a hotch-potch of hoses, white at first, but soon stained by leaf-mould, lay over old tombs. A sizeable crowd of onlookers, some strangely garbed in anoraks and pyjama bottoms, swiftly formed on the pavement in Boldmere Road. Most looked on dumbly, with sleepy eyes, as if not comprehending that this could happen to a place that had been there for as long as they could remember."

The church was completely gutted by the fire.

In 1964, Ken Matthews of Sutton Coldfield became the supreme world champion in his class, when he beat his nearest challenger by a quarter of a mile in the 20 kilometre walk at the Olympic Games at Tokyo. For his achievement he was awarded Great Britain's second gold medal of the Olympics. On his return to Sutton he was given a civic reception and an enthusiastic welcome by a large crowd of local people.

What was described at the time as the last remaining large plot of building land in Sutton Coldfield was sold in March, 1965 for £685,000. It was the 56 acres of farmland at Princess Alice School, and the purchaser said that it was proposed to build about 350 homes on the site, fronting on to Chester Road North, and commanding open views across Sutton Park.

At the official opening of " Greenacres "—the Sutton Coldfield Cheshire Home—in May, 1965, the founder, Group Captain Leonard Cheshire, V.C., spoke of the huge waiting list for the home. " This waiting list of over 700 proves that we are only touching the fringes of the problem presented to us by the chronically sick " he said. " Sutton Coldfield obviously realises the need for help " continued Group Captain Cheshire " and has been enthusiastic in efforts to fulfil it."

In a report by the Lichfield, Sutton Coldfield and Tamworth Hospital Management Committee in 1965, the Committee's Chairman, Mr. R. T. Salt, referred to great strides being made at Good Hope, and stated: " I am happy to say that the immediate future will result in even greater development and culminate in the expansion of Good Hope into a fully comprehensive general hospital."

Some nostalgic sentiments were aroused in 1965 by a letter in the " Sutton Coldfield News " from the late Mrs. Olive Norton, the well-known novelist and writer from Four Oaks:

" . . . How many readers remember The Tank?" she asked. " And has anyone a photograph of it? Not, of course, in its later fenced-in state, when it was temporarily a memorial, but swarming with children as it used to be. Dirty, rusty, greasy— and horribly smelly, too—but never for a moment striking us as a death-dealing implement, only as a fascinating mechanical cave."

"Does this same nostalgia still sometimes prick other respectable Suttonians in their staid fifties? Those who also remember ponies in the pound, an electrocuting lamp-post in Trinity Hill, the game called 'Old Man Dogherty', and the ghastly tangle we made of the maypole dancing behind Holly Knoll? And fishing for bullyheads in the Crystal Palace grounds, and playing in the Queen Street field and the derelict house on the Co-op site? And gathering bilberries in Nuthurst?"

Another correspondent was prompted to recall his boyhood memories of the osier beds where the Midland 'Red' Garage now stands: "Many a safari was enjoyed, making tracks in the five feet high reeds and bulrushes, culminating in a swim in the small pool formed by damming the stream which flowed through the middle. The long summer days seem to have been always hot, and how fortunate we lads were who made friends with the boy whose father ran the 'pop factory' which stood at the corner of Upper Holland Road and Lower Queen Street!"

During the 'sixties the "improvers" became particularly vocal on the subject of Sutton Park. A scenic railway was proposed; a race-course, it was said, would be a gold-mine; a sale of "perimeter" land for building purposes would raise a million pounds; a face-lift, entailing a large-scale clearance of undergrowth would be a remedy for the Park's alleged ills and motel-type chalets could help in creating "an inland resort". The people for whom the wind of change could not blow fast enough were often more vocal than those who had no wish to see any further whittling away of the Park's amenities. But spokesmen for the cause of conservation were not missing, and one Suttonian, in a letter to the press, wrote:

"People of Sutton Coldfield prefer a natural park, as free as possible from man's improvements, where one can still at times snatch a brief respite from getting and spending, watch the miracle of a heron's flight and walk on fallen leaves."

Miss H. M. Moss, secretary of the Sutton Coldfield Friends of the Park Association declared: "We are very much against anything that would affect the natural condition of the Park." On another occasion, Alderman Frank Brassington—a member of the Parks and Open Spaces Committee—after listing some of the threats to the Park by would-be "improvers", added his own plea: " . . . let us leave this wonderful heritage alone so that it can be enjoyed by our children's children. Let us hear the old rallying cry of 40 years ago—'Hands off the Park!'."

*High Street, Sutton Coldfield, showing the Three Tuns Hotel and,
adjoining it, Ennis House, which was demolished in 1971.*
Photograph: Douglas V. Jones

CHAPTER XV
The immediate past.

EARLY in 1966, Mrs. Wendy Cooper, a writer, playwright
and freelance journalist from Wylde Green won the distinction of being named as " Woman journalist of the Year "
by the Hannan Swaffer award committee. Mrs. Cooper, who
was born at Sutton Coldfield, is a frequent contributor to both
the national and local press. She is a former Warwickshire
County tennis player and she also played at Wimbledon in
1949 and 1950.

During National Nature Week in 1966, over 4,000 people
visited a " Living with Nature " exhibition which was held under
canvas on the Meadow Platt, Sutton Park. This exhibition—the
emphasis of which was on the natural history and other aspects
of the Park—was sponsored by the Borough Council, and
arranged by the Sutton Coldfield Natural History Society for
the Parks Advisory Committee. In conjunction with the exhibition, and for those more energetic people wishing to increase
their knowledge of natural history in a practical way, a nature
trail was laid out in the Park.

In 1966, Sutton Coldfield Civic Society called for " a
thorough survey of existing trees, a tree care programme, tree
planting and a plan for tree preservation." Mr. J. H. Olsen,

secretary of the Trees Sub-committee of the Civic Society, declared: "It will cost money, but if Solihull can afford £1,500 annually, surely Sutton Coldfield can. With its immense advantages of natural landscape and mature trees, Sutton must never be allowed to fall back into a treeless conurbation. This could happen gradually if there is not constant vigilance." The implementation of such a policy, it was pointed out, would be greatly strengthened by the Civic Amenities Bill, which was at that time passing through Parliament.

A press release from the Civic Society presented a very clear picture of ' leafy Sutton ' in the year 1966:

> "The number of English towns identifiable by their own special characteristics, such as Bath and Cheltenham, Warwick, Tewkesbury, Chester and Shrewsbury, is dwindling quickly.
>
> "Very soon, if present trends continue, all our towns will look very much alike all over the country. Today's ideas of town planning seem based on replacing the heart of even historic towns like Worcester with box-like buildings that have no local personality in form or colour.
>
> "Sutton Coldfield as yet still retains very much of its own identity. It possesses a natural park where people can see the peace of an unspoilt countryside of woods, copses, lakes, streams, parklands, fields and heath.
>
> "Rectory Park still retains sufficient trees to be called properly a park. There are few more pleasant places in the Midlands on a summer's day when cricket is being played against a backdrop of trees that catch the eye for their character, maturity and beauty . . .
>
> " . . . From Birmingham Road, between the "Odeon" and Manor Hill, an inviting prospect of rising fields and trees is surprisingly discovered when looking down the roads near the Sutton Coldfield Hospital . . .
>
> " . . . The view of the Parish Church set on a hill, surrounded by trees, is a picture of serenity.
>
> "Trees on the level, even in the heart of the town, characteristically soften the effects of brick and pavement. For example, Birmingham Road from Wylde Green Post Office to Greenhill Road; Lichfield Road from Doe Bank to Four Oaks Station; in Rectory Road, Penns Lane, Manor Road, Weeford Road, Chester Road from the "Pavilion" to Oscott College; and Wyndley Lane, Somerville Road and Clifton Road."

The growth and changing character of the English village —particularly when the village happens to be within easy reach of a large city—is characterised by a description of Shenstone in 1966. In the local press it was described as "a high-income commuter village, with less than one-tenth of its occupied popualtion engaged in agriculture. Almost half (49%) of its population is in the managerial and professional classes." '

Road widening in 1967 resulted in over 150 houses in Jockey Road losing a part of their front gardens, while opposition to the widening of Walmley Road, between the junction of Wylde Green Road and Penns Lane stiffened during that year. In taking up the cause of the Walmley Residents' Association, the Sutton Coldfield Civic Society pointed out that the proposed widening of Walmley Road would " bisect the community with shops and amenities on both sides of the road. It would also destroy the village atmosphere which, it is argued, the people of Walmley wish to retain, and would be strictly against the spirit of the Civic Amenities Act."

Building activities in 1967 continued to make the headlines. In July, an impressive new extension, costing £220,000 at Bishop Vesey's Grammar School was opened by Sir Edward Boyle (now Lord Boyle), Member of Parliament for Handsworth. " We look for further great things from this school, which has always had such a distinguished record," he said, and in the course of his speech he high-lighted the great need for more trained and qualified people than ever before.

A few days later, at the opening of a £27,000 Post Graduate Medical Centre at Good Hope General Hospital, Sir Max Rosenheim, President of the Royal College of Physicians, declared: " Medicine is advancing at a pace which has never been known before. Recent advances based on research centres should be transferred to patients as soon as possible."

In September, 1967, following the destruction by fire of St. Michael's Church, Boldmere, three years earlier, the rebuilt church, costing £105,000 was consecrated by the Bishop of Birmingham, the late Dr. J. L. Wilson. When it had been found by experts to be practically impossible to reconstruct the church as before, Canon J. C. McCallum, the Rector, expressed the view that the design should follow a modern trend. The main material used for the rebuilding was Staffordshire blue brick, and the roof is supported by four cross-section pillars, with a ceiling described as being of ' umbrella ' design.

A few months later, Dr. Sidney Campbell, organist of St. George's Chapel, Windsor Castle, gave a recital on the new organ at St. Michael's Church. Canon J. C. McCallum commented: " This is the beginning of a series of concerts in which we shall try to make use of the Church for musical entertainments, both classical and romantic." Dr. Campbell described the tonal range of the new organ as ' exciting.'

The last noteworthy " opening ceremony " of 1967 was a dual-event, when the Duchess of Kent visited Sutton Coldfield for the purpose of opening the £417,000 Mount Development Reddicap Hill and the Good Hope Maternity Hospital. The occasion according to the " Sutton Coldfield News " was characterised by:

" a delightful atmosphere of informality and in consequence, an absence of that feeling of ' stiffness ' which, with
the best of intentions, is apt to surround such visits."

Strong protests from local shopkeepers in 1968 failed to
deter the Ministry of Transport from confirming an order
placing a complete ban on parking along the trunk road
through the centre of Sutton Coldfield. " This is the last straw
to break the camel's back " declared one irate shop-keeper.

In 1968, it was found necessary to provide " Vigilante "
patrols at Sutton Coldfield Parish Church as a counter-measure
to vandalism. " It is an empty church which tempts the feeble-
minded and immature to vandalism " said the Rector, Canon A.
P. Rose.

During August, 1968, after years of waiting, ministerial
approval was given for the building of the town's swimming
baths in Clifton Road. Before the end of the year, however,
inflation had been responsible for the estimated cost of the
project rising from £400,000 to £480,000. The completion of the
town's new, £50,000 Central Youth Headquarters at the old
Crystal Palace site in September, 1968 satisfied a long felt need.
The centre incorporated an assembly hall, covered sports area,
a coffee bar and various activity rooms.

In January, 1969, a 50-year-old Sutton Coldfield man, Mr.
Sidney Genders, made known his intention of rowing across the
Atlantic, single-handed. He admitted to not having rowed
seriously for about 25 years, but added that he occasionally
took a boat out in Sutton Park. Just over a year later he made
headline news by completing his long voyage from Sennen
Cove in Cornwall to Antigua in the Caribbean. In a serialized
newspaper account of his epic journey, the man who became first
to row from Britain to the Americas, admitted that he found
it hard to contemplate a return to the West Midlands weather
and said that he had had enough of the nine-to-five, nose-to-tail
style of living in a crowded island.

The demolishers were again busy in the spring of 1969.
Walmley House—one of the best known buildings in Walmley
—the site of which had been sold for £142,000, was demolished
to make way for new homes. The house, which was about 100
years old, belonged to the Horsfall family, being originally a
part of the Penns Hall estate. A week or so later, the cluster of
little buildings in Mill Street, backing on to the Reddicroft, fell
victim to the bulldozer.

In June, 1969, when the recommendations of the Maud
Report on the Reorganisation of Local Government Structure
were made known, the chronic fear in the minds of many Sutton
people of being " swallowed by Birmingham " became acute.
Serious misgivings were widely expressed over the report, which

the " Sutton Coldfield News " referred to as the " proposed rape of Sutton."

During the past decade the problem of litter has become much more widespread. Increased mobility and greater prosperity have contributed to the dismal trail of discarded television sets, refrigerators, gas-stoves, beds and other large household objects which defile the English country-side. More and more people, it seems, use their own transport to cart away almost any of their bulky possessions which have become victims of their own " built-in obsolescence." Even the vehicles sometimes suffer the same fate, resulting in their being dumped in unexpected places when they have outlived their usefulness.

The expenditure of £430,000 on a new refuse destructor in 1969 may have prompted a Councillor to declare that Sutton Coldfield had become a tidy place. Presumably, however, he had not included the Park in his assessment, for he would only have had to take a walk around the perimeter of Holly Hurst to see just how untidy Park visitors could be. A random survey made there in 1969 revealed some interesting finds. Secreted in the thick undergrowth were a wide range of articles, including bricks, tin-cans, cartons, plastic bags—some of them full of unsavoury matter—broken porcelain, concrete, garden refuse, a six-pint beer tin, a butane gas container, a car-bumper and a variety of " deleterious substances ", which probably only a public analyst could have identified. The range of bottles was impressive. Wine-bottles, beer-bottles, milk bottles and orangeade-bottles told a mute tale of innumerable picnics, while a whole box of " baby " champagne and British champagne perry with Jamaican orange-juice " empties " must have been a memento of a more than usually convivial visit to the woods.

In April, 1970, details were released of the proposed Town Centre Relief Road to run from Jockey Road to Tamworth Road, which would necessitate the demolition of a large number of properties. Opposition, both from organisations and individuals, was widespread. It was pointed out by Mr. J. Harrison, Chairman of Sutton Coldfield Civic Society, that it was a moot point whether the road would be necessary when nearby motorway schemes and the eastern by-pass were completed. Serious misgivings were felt at the thought of this £2,000,000 one-mile stretch of super-highway, snaking its way through an established residential area, destroying innumerable houses, rendering many people homeless, detracting from community life and involving rate-payers in another round of increases.

There was also considerable opposition in 1970 to the proposed six-mile Sutton Coldfield Eastern By-pass, but following an enquiry, the Minister of Transport approved the scheme, despite objections, because the route chosen " reduced interference with properties to a minimum consistent with the need to construct a high-standard, large capacity road ". It was said that the road would relieve Sutton Coldfield of much of the heavy traffic which was having a damaging effect on the town centre.

Following upon a remark by Mr. Leo Abse, M.P. for Pontypool, in 1970, that some of Britain's register offices were " little more than shabby holes in the wall " it was claimed that the dreary surroundings of Sutton Coldfield's Register Office in Riland Road was responsible for a good many couples going elsewhere to marry. Mr. R. E. Langley, the registrar, commented that quite a number of people, on seeing the situation of the office, decided to marry in Birmingham instead of Sutton Coldfield.

The problems of neighbouring villages were high-lighted in 1970. Due to the withdrawal of Middleton's 'bus service the year before, villagers without cars wanting to go shopping complained that they had to walk a mile and a half to the nearest 'bus route. The sense of isolation was increased by the closure of the village post office and the pending closure of the village school. At Curdworth, Sir William Dugdale—county councillor for Meriden—spoke at the annual meeting of Curdworth parish council, when he warned listeners of the risk to the village if the Maud Report were to be implemented. Curdworth, being on the very edge of a great city, Sir William said, could suffer the fate of Aston, which before becoming a part of Birmingham, had been an independent village. " Major amenities " he continued " will remain in the city centres, while only the ' fringe benefits ' will come to the outlying areas."

A seven-week dustman's strike in the autumn of 1970 led to many local people having to take their rubbish to the Withy Hill tip, for which purpose plastic sacks were made available by the council. Mr. H. T. Mitchell, the Borough's Chief Public Health Inspector commented: " Compared to other places, Sutton Coldfield has really been let off quite lightly during the strike, thanks to the co-operation of the public."

Despite sweeping reforms in 1968 the Municipal Charities still continued to provide a supplement to the social services. In a review of these charities in 1971, Mr. J. P. Holden, the Town Clerk, said: " It is a very long time since anyone took advantage of the poor maidens' grant," and added: " No-one seemed to wish to admit that they were either poor, or a maiden." It was stressed, however, that although the charities no longer gave out doles of bread to the needy or provided young maidens of the town with enough money to catch themselves husbands, they still had a vital role to play in the community. One of their major functions was the provision of almshouses, and in the spring of 1971, the completion of Sutton Coldfield's newest almshouses at Walmley was the occasion of a visit by Princess

Anne, when she unveiled a commemorative plaque at the opening ceremony.

A week or so later another commemorative plaque was unveiled—this time by the Mayor of Sutton Coldfield, Alderman Mrs. Ethel E. Dunnett, on the occasion of the opening of the long-awaited Wyndley Swimming Baths. One of the first people to take a dip in the new pool before the official opening was a " Sutton Coldfield News " reporter, who, commenting on its panoramic view over the Park, described the design as impressive and the layout as faultless. He added that, most important of all, it was a nice place in which to swim.

The growing fear in 1971 was that Sutton Coldfield would soon be " swallowed by the big city." The theme was taken up by Mr. Enoch Powell who, in addressing a capacity audience at Sutton Coldfield Town Hall in July of that year, said: " I wonder how many people in Sutton Coldfield know that they are to form part of a unit of local government which will stretch from Wolverhampton on one end to Coventry on the other." Mr. Powell continued: " The current trend of bigness, the cult of size, is becoming a fetish. The presumption is everywhere supposed to hold good in favour of bigness: big units of production, big units of government. We live in the age of gigantism, the superstitious worship of giants." "This superstition " he added " was powerful in the minds or sub-consciousness of those who favoured Common Market entry to form a European super-state."

By early 1972 it was clear that Sutton Coldfield was at serious risk of losing its identity under the government's boundary reorganisation plans, and the help of Mr. Geoffrey Lloyd the town's M.P., was enlisted for the inevitable battle which was to follow. Protest followed protest, and on one occasion a party of 500 Sutton residents organised a protest march through the streets of London as part of their campaign. At an appropriate time during the Local Government Bill's Report Stage, Mr. Lloyd tabled an amendment to put Sutton Coldfield into the administrative county of Warwickshire, when he said that the Birmingham merger plan had provoked " a sense of overwhelming outrage " among his constituents.

Mr. Lloyd asked " Why should this established, efficient local authority—strongly against the wishes of its inhabitants—be merged with the city of Birmingham to form a metropolian district within the West Midland Metropolitan County?" and added: " Birmingham already has a very large population, and if the two are conjoined the metropolitan district will have a population of 1.1 million. This is far too large in population and area for a local authority to give the kind of personal service to its residents that the people of Sutton Coldfield have been accustomed to."

It was all in vain. Mr. Peter Walker, the then Environment Secretary blandly rejected the amendment, and commented that Sutton Coldfield was not an area which had natural unity of population, but an area which had a close but distinct connection with Birmingham, where more than half the working population were employed. The long-persisting fears of annexation had been realised. Alderman R. H. Phillips, Chairman of Sutton's Re-organisation Sub-Committee, described the decision as " a political carve-up to help the government to try to retain political control of the West Midlands."

An unofficial strike in 1972 brought work almost to a stand-still at Sutton Coldfield's £6,000,000 shopping centre develop-ment. Nearly 2,000 children in the town had to stay at home because of school heating systems being put out of action by a coal strike, and as a result of power cuts, Good Hope Hospital was placed on a " red emergency ", restricting admissions to urgent cases only. Pedestrians were urged to take extra care at night in unlit roads; and there was a brisk trade in candles.

Following upon a heavy rainfall in September, 1972, flooding once again caused chaos in the lower part of the town. In Fawdry Close, hundreds of pounds worth of damage was caused to residents' furniture and carpets. A consultant engineer was called in to investigate the flooding on behalf of the owners of the flats, and the Deputy Borough Surveyor, Mr. C. F. Everett, confirmed that the problem was not the council's responsibility. but that of the riparian owners—the developers.

In December, 1972, Sutton Park had an unusually high number of visitors for the time of the year when almost 20,000 spectators came to watch a R.A.C. rally. About 130 competitors took part in the event, but there were no accidents. The rally brought about £1,500 profit for the borough council. The official view was that the occasion was a great success, but Miss H. M. Moss, Secretary of the Friends of the Park, said her association would oppose any future plan to hold the rally in the Park again.

CHAPTER XVI
Sutton Coldfield—today and tomorrow.

WE live in an age of vast and unprecedented changes. Our amenities, both natural and historical, are being lost to us at a phenominal rate. The problem is, of course, widespread —in fact, international—and is all a part of what Aldous Huxley once called the " organised lovelessness " of modern society. The threat of an impending steel and concrete wilderness, with a continuing diminution of natural beauty around us, cannot be dismissed lightly. The growth of huge conurbations in the present century has been accompanied by large migrations of people, and in Sutton Coldfield the population has almost doubled within 20 years.

Many changes have taken place in the town's appearance, and the shortage of building land in recent years, plus the astronomical prices asked for the least promising plots, has led to some upward growth in the building line. Every available pocket of land has been winkled out, and plots previously considered to be not worth developing have found a ready market. In 1971 a record West Midlands price of £34,425 an acre was paid by a Sutton Coldfield developer for a 4.7 acre site at Streetly. By 1973, the value of land had so much increased that a plot in Four Oaks realised £88,000 an acre, and a few weeks later another 1½ acre site at Chester Road North, overlooking Sutton Park, was sold for £136,000. The same plot had been bought in the 1920s for £100, and sold a few years later for £250.

Both the builders and the demolishers have been busy during the early 'seventies. Some familiar landmarks have disappeared, including many of the shops on the Parade, the "Empress" Cinema and the string of old cottages in Mill Street. A number of the houses in Manor Road have gone, too, and across the valley below Manor Hill, once occupied by a chain of reed-fringed pools, a new complex of buildings on an unfamiliar scale is growing steadily.* Even the High Street has not been sacrosanct: Ennis House (No. 17), next to the Three Tuns, and in joint ownership with it—despite being 200 years old and listed as a building of special architectural interest—was demolished in 1971, leaving an unsightly gap where it stood.

In the past, the inhabitants of Sutton Coldfield have shown a great loyalty to their town and park. This loyalty, in more recent years, has been reflected in the activities of two societies in the town—the Civic Society and the Friends of the Park—which, between them, have been able to do much to influence both the authorities and public opinion. Under the new administration it is important that more local people than ever should be aware of the nature of our inheritance in all its aspects, so that any future threat to it can be countered. Identity and a sense of 'belonging' is an attitude of mind, not to be easily eradicated by governmental decree. A widely disseminated knowledge of the history and traditions of the town and the park can only serve to strengthen this attitude.

Under the provisions of the Civic Amenities Act (1967), local authorities have the power to designate areas of architectural or historic interest for preservation—as distinct from individual buildings. No-one has a better claim to a say over environment than those people who have to live in it, and individuals should make their voices heard whenever their surroundings are at risk.

Sutton's High Street, together with Coleshill Street and Trinity Hill, embodying so much of the town's history, is an obvious choice for a 'conservation area.' The wooded escarpment of Manor Hill should be preserved—both for its historic

*Now the Gracechurch Centre.

171

associations and its natural beauty—and so, too, should that small scattered group of old buildings at Maney. A sentimental tour of old Sutton could well be started from Trinity Hill, which stands 400 feet above sea level. The churchyard of Holy Trinity Church, in accordance with the prevailing practice, has been cleared of the majority of its old grave-stones, which are now lined up along the wall, and the cleared area turfed over. It is a pleasant spot, offering momentary escape from the noisy twentieth century. Peaceful and leafy in summer, the only reminder of the motor car is the subdued sound of distant traffic in Mill Street, mingling with the rustle of foliage in the breeze. It is not ,however, a place without danger—for young children, at any rate—as there is a sheer and unfenced drop of many feet from the churchyard into the road below (Trinity Hill).

Through the trees are glimpses of Holly Hurst and Barr Beacon and, nearer to view, rising beyond the town and the valley of the Ebrook is Manor Hill's tree-covered mound. To the east of Manor Hill, and further away, Sutton's third hill at Maney presents a more urban vista having been largely built over in the last 25 years. In the middle of the churchyard stands an eighteenth century sandstone-based sun-dial—chipped, dilapidated and defaced, its Roman numerals obscured by verdigris. Nearby is the grave of Mary Ashford.

The church interior is rich in colour and interest. Nave and chancel roofs gleam and sparkle in the light of a sunny day, whilst gilded angels, heraldic shields and decorated panels reflect a whole galaxy of colour. The Tudor Rose, not surprisingly, is a constantly recurring *motif*, while the Vesey Chapel, with its carved oak screen, rose and thistle roof-panels and striking effigy of Bishop Vesey in his coloured vestments, create an atmosphere worthy of a benefactor's memory. The pulpit is tall and elaborately carved, with a canopy patterned in inlaid wood. The Norman font is twelfth century. After being discarded from Over Whitacre, at the time of the demolition of the old church there, it was for a time used as a horse-block outside an inn at Shustoke, before its restoration to a place of honour in Sutton. Perhaps the most striking impression is that of all pervading silence, for whatever the density of the traffic on the roads outside, none of the sound penetrates the inner sanctum of these solidly enduring walls.

The best way to see Maney is to walk down the hill from the " Horse and Jockey " passing on the way Beeches Walk shopping centre before reaching Bodington Gardens, where a commemorative plaque tells us that:

This garden is a memorial to George Bodington, M.D., a Warden of the Town, the first Doctor to treat pulmonary consumption by means of sunshine and fresh air, and who practised this form of cure in a small sanatorium nearby.

Lying back from the road, the garden—with its spacious flower-beds—is a pleasant place to sit on a sunny day. At its lower end stands the Smithy which, like some other properties in the town, once belonged to Emmanuel College, Cambridge, from whom it was bought by Sutton Coldfield Corporation in 1944. It is now a small museum, containing some interesting historic bric-a-brac, and a number of water-colours of Old Sutton. * At the rear of the building can be seen the Smithy's immense supporting cruck-frame—its real claim to antiquity.

Opposite the Odeon Cinema stands a seventeenth-century stone building which was once a farmhouse, and in Maney Hill Road, recent redevelopment has opened up a view of a Vesey Cottage—one of the few remaining of the 51 stone houses built by Vesey, four centuries ago.

Sutton Coldfield once had thirteen water-mills, most of which were used for a variety of industrial purposes. The only surviving mill is at Newhall, which for almost three centuries supplied one of the most basic of human needs: flour. The bread produced from its flour was, by repute, of an excellent quality.

The production of flour at Newhall ceased some years ago, but it is still a working mill, with its own resident miller, Mr. Ben Davis, who operates it as a diesel-powered grist-mill. In 1972 it was proposed to raise £40,000 under a trust for the purpose of restoring the mill and setting in motion once again its fine, overshot wheel. The idea may appeal to many local people—providing, of course, that none of the building's distinctive character is lost in the process.

In 1903, Benjamin Styles, the miller at Newhall, and grandfather of Mr. Davis, the present miller, wrote a poem:

I am an old Water Mill—in the Royal Town of Sutton,
    I do my work well, and don't care a button.
I've stood all my life on this very same spot,
    I use the Park Water, and don't waste a lot.
I've a fine Water Wheel, which is termed overshot,
    And the stones turn round just like a top.
I have a good friend in the Squire at the Hall,
    I supply all the flour as fast as they call.
I grind for the Farmers and others besides,
    I give them good weight, and measure likewise.
I ground some Wheat once, that was reaped the same day,
    And in less than six hours it was bread on the tray.
There were seventy nice loaves, so good to digest,
    And everyone said 'twas a very good test.

*The museum has since closed.

173

The demand for the bread, which was very keen,
  That a loaf was sent to our late belov'd Queen.
I make a good picture, I wish you to know,
  I've hung in the Art Gallery three months for a show.
I'm hundreds of years old, if my days were all numbered,
  I've always stood firm when its hail'd, rain'd, and thundered.
I had a severe test when Wyndley Pool burst,
  Of all the great floods, this was the worst.
In conclusion I ask you to give me a call,
  And leave some good orders for the Mill at New Hall.

The Vesey House in Wylde Green Road—just a stone's throw from Newhall Mill—was once a ford-keeper's cottage. The ford-keeper was one of Vesey's ' trusty guides ', who conducted travellers across the nearby Ebrook on their way between Sutton and Coleshill. The stream, in former times, was treacherous, and Riland Bedford relates in the " Vesey Paper " that: " Peat, running sand and clay faults are to this day (1893), the cause of stagnation in the flow of the stream, and consequent percolation of the soil. One of the few sound crossing places over the stream of the Ebrook, was close to this cottage . . . "

Newhall itself—the home of Lady Owen—needs no introduction to Sutton people. Moated and splendidly set amid its own woodland, it is claimed to be the oldest inhabited house in England. Together with its mill, its Vesey cottage, its farms, and the picturesque black and white, timber-framed "Wincelle" (brought from Wiggins Hill and rebuilt here in 1910), the whole group proclaims itself worthy of preservation.

Most unusual among Sutton Coldfield's possessions is its 2,400 acres of parkland which—merely by its amazing survival as a region of relatively unspoilt natural beauty—probably makes it unique. The sad decline in wild life generally, however, is reflected in that of Sutton Park. It has become increasingly rare to see the kingfisher in flight, watch a heron, flush a snipe or hear the cuckoo, and it would probably be difficult now to find more than a few of the 16 species of butterflies which once bred there.

Any future plans for the Park should not clash with its role as a conservation area. Spraying and drainage should both be recognised as threats to this role. As a spokesman of the Nature Conservancy has commented: " It seems a basic component of the wild character of the Park that some spots should be difficult to reach." There are so few boggy and marshy areas left in the West Midlands that those surviving in Sutton Park, with their varied flora and fauna, are doubly precious. Perhaps nowhere else in the region can acres of cotton-grass still be seen in flower, and comparable areas of heathland on the scale found in the Park would be difficult to come across.

Sutton Park has the dual-attractions of natural beauty and a long history to commend it to the visitor. Even the banks around the enclosed woods of the Park are 'historical monuments', probably dating from the period following the granting of the Charter in 1528. At that time, Miss Bracken tells us, Vesey: "At his own cost of £43 2s. 6d. he inclosed the coppices called the Seven Hayes, i.e., Ladywood, Pool Hollies, Streetly Coppice, Darnelhurst, Upper and Lower Nuthurst and Hollyhurst, and added gates and locks; and towards the ditching and quicksetting of the park fences, at one time gave £16 8s. 10d., and at another, £10 16s. 8d., and then he stocked the park, at the cost of £40, with mares, colts and horses."

Perhaps there is no better way of first seeing the Park than to walk across its western fringe, along the course of the Roman Road, from near the "Parson and Clerk" Hotel, towards Streetly Village. From one elevated spot just inside the Park, the Roman road rolls away splendidly towards the golf course at Streetly. Its overgrown but clearly discernible route is now bounded by saplings on either side, recently planted as a memorial to the late Alderman Harry Herringshaw.

Not far from where the Roman road leaves the Park at Streetly, rises that little stream which runs across the Park and through the Town, known in former times as the Ebrook—now Plants Brook. Unlike that part of the brook beyond the confines of the Park which, in the process of being 'improved', has lost all its character and most of its wild life, those stretches within the Park are still largely in a natural state.

In 1972, when the presence of the fresh-water crayfish in the Park's streams was commented upon in the local press, a spokesman of Sutton Coldfield Natural History Society said: "It is gratifying to know that our Park has, so far, escaped the sort of pollution which may have resulted in the disappearance of crayfish from many Midland streams. It emphasises the importance of its role as a conservation area."

During the summer of 1973, a survey of Sutton Park's streams was made by Mr. H. A. Hawkes and students of the Applied Hydrobiology Section of the University of Aston. Their findings confirm that the streams there are relatively unpolluted, and that the well aerated, soft acid waters support a variety of aquatic life, including nymphs, stoneflies, mayflies and fresh-water shrimps. Along the stream between Blackroot Pool and the Town Gate, in addition to crayfish, there are minnows and sticklebacks to provide fishing for the young. The survey emphasised the problem of maintaining a balance between providing amenities for the general public and conserving some natural habitats in the midst of an area where both man's increasing population and his technology are affecting both his own environment and that of other forms of life.

Sutton Coldfield in the last year of its civic existence, continued to function in traditional ways. In May, 1973, Lord Justice James, in proposing the toast to the " Royal Town " at the last Mayoral banquet, said that there were few royal towns which could produce such pride and character. The town had not rested on its laurels, he asserted, and the list of societies alive in the town was evidence of the interest in the arts, culture and nation-wide subjects. " They cannot wipe off the slate a way of life, the loyalties and the belief in the town. They will surely remain," he added.

The newly installed Mayor, Alderman Donald Mills, in his reply, said: " Change there must be, and change there will be. It is nevertheless important that this corner of local government, a proud and ancient town, should not be forgotten."

The Mayoral year for Alderman Mills and his wife, the Mayoress—County Councillor Mrs. Julia Mills—was 10½ months, at the end of which time, on 1st April, 1974, Sutton Coldfield was merged with the Birmingham Metropolitan District.

Rev. W. K. R. Bedford, M.A.
Author of "History of Sutton Coldfield" published 1891

William C. Midgley
Author of "A Short History of the Town and Chase of Sutton Coldfield" published 1904

APPENDIX I

Below is a selection of dates, taken from a comprehensive indexed Chronology of Sutton Coldfield's History, prepared by Mr. Norman Granville Evans for the Borough Librarian, which can be made available by arrangement with Mr. R.M. Lea at the Central Library in Sutton Coldfield.

In view of the lack of precise dates for earlier events, the Chronology is confined to dates following the Norman Conquest.

1071   Edwin, Earl of Mercia, was put to death. Sutton Coldfield, as part of Mercia, passed to the Crown.

1086   In Domesday Book, Sutton was rated at 8 hides; the woods were 2 miles in length and one in breadth. There was no church.

1126   Roger de Newburgh, Earl of Warwick, acquired the Manor of Sutton Coldfield from Henry I in exchange for the Manors of Hockham and Langham in Rutland.

1300   Guy de Beauchamp, Earl of Warwick, obtained a Charter for a market every Tuesday at Sutton Coldfield and a fair on the eve of Holy Trinity and for the three days following.

1353   Thomas de Beauchamp, Earl of Warwick, obtained a renewal of the Charter for markets and fairs and for an additional fair on the eve and day of Saint Martin.

1471   Death of Richard Nevil, Earl of Warwick ("the King-maker") at the Battle of Barnet. Sutton Coldfield reverted to the Crown.

1528   Charter granted by Henry VIII to John Harman (alias Vesey) Bishop of Exeter, placing the Chase and Manor in the hands of a local body, known as "the Warden and Society."

1662   New Charter granted to Sutton Coldfield by Charles II.

1759   By Act of Parliament the whole of the road between Castle Bromwich and Chester was made into a turnpike road.

1801   Population at first census 2,847.

1811   Military camp established at Sutton Coldfield, commemorated in the name of Camp Road.

1825   An Enclosure Act for Sutton Coldfield, excluding the Park, was passed, when 3,500 acres of common land were conveyed to the chief landowners.

1853   The Sutton Coldfield Gas, Light and Coke Company was formed, and a gas works built at the corner of Riland Road and Coleshill Road.

1859 New Town Hall built in Mill Street (now the Masonic Hall).

1862 Opening of railway between Birmingham and Sutton Coldfield (L. & N. W. Railway).

1869 Sutton Coldfield acquired its first newspaper, " The Sutton Coldfield and Erdington News ", later taken over by the proprietor of " The Sutton Coldfield and Erdington Times."

1879 Opening of railway through Sutton Park (Midland Railway).

1881 Population 7,737.

1886 Under a new Municipal Charter, Sutton Coldfield became a Borough with six wards, a Mayor, five Aldermen and 18 Councillors.

1906 The present town hall was opened, also a fire-station and clock-tower, which served as a hose-tower and ventilating shaft.

1913 The B. & M. M. O. Co. (the " Midland Red ") first ran a 'bus service between Chester Road and Sutton Coldfield.

1914 At the outbreak of World War I Sutton Park was placed at the disposal of the government and became a training ground and camping site for troops.

1931 Sutton Coldfield Corporation acquired a strip of land to the west of the Park, thus ensuring for the first time in the Borough's history that Sutton Park was entirely surrounded by land within the Sutton boundary.

1934 Population 31,000, and in that year 430 new houses were built in Sutton Coldfield.

1937 Following upon conversion of a Wesleyan Chapel on the Parade, Sutton acquired its first Public Library.

1938 Four new schools—Senior Boys, Senior Girls, Junior Mixed and Infants—opened at Boldmere.

1939 Balloon Barrage Depot at Whitehouse Common opened in July by Air Ministry.

1942 Opening of Highbury Little Theatre.

1946 First " pre-fab " completed at Four Oaks in January. Later that year the Council bought 50 permanent prefabricated houses at a cost of £65,350.

1949 Opening of B.B.C. Television Station at Hill Village on 17th December.

1956   Diesel-train service between Birmingham and Lichfield, through Sutton Coldfield, inaugurated in March.

1960   Sutton Coldfield's new Petty Sessional Court-house and Divisional Police H.Q. completed.

1963   Opening of Sutton Coldfield's new fire-station by Earl Jellicoe.

1964   Sutton Coldfield acquired its first multi-storey council flats at Boldmere—and a crematorium, costing £125,000.

1968   Completion of Sutton Coldfield's £50,000 Central Youth H.Q. on old Crystal Palace site.

1971   Opening of Wyndley Swimming Baths.

1972   Mr. Geoffrey Lloyd, M.P., tabled an amendment during the Local Government Bill's Report Stage with a view to putting Sutton Coldfield into the administrative county of Warwickshire. Amendment rejected by Mr. Peter Walker, the Environment Secretary.

1974   (1st April) Merger of Sutton Coldfield with the Birmingham Metropolitan District.

Wall plaque at Hill Hook
Photograph: Douglas V. Jones

MAYORS OF SUTTON COLDFIELD

1886-90	Alderman	J. B. Stone, M.P.
1890-91	,,	A. H. Evans
1891-92	,,	J. T. Glover
1892-93	,,	J. Conchar
1893-94	,,	E. T. Walters
1894-96	,,	W. J. Seal
1896-97	Councillor	F. W. Brampton
1897-98	Alderman	A. L. Crockford
1898-1900	Councillor	S. C. Emery
1900-02	Alderman	J. T. Glover
1902-03	Councillor	C. Vale
1903-06	,,	R. H. Sadler
1906-07	,,	Jos. Appleby
1907-08	,,	William Randle
1908-09	,,	John Norris
1909-12	,,	T. H. Cartwright
1912-13	,,	C. F. Fiddian-Green
1913-16	,,	J. H. Parkes
1916-20	Alderman	W. J. Seal
1920-21	Councillor	G. F. Pearson
1921-22	,,	G. R. Hooper
1922-25	,,	W. T. Harrison
1925-27	,,	H. E. Beach
1927-29	,,	T. W. Lawrence
1929-31	,,	Joseph A. Oldbury
1931-33	,,	J. Percival Britton
1933-35	,,	Arthur E. Terry
1935-37	,,	W. A. Perry
1937-38	,,	W. Bigwood
1938-40	,,	James J. Ogley
1940-42	,,	Walter Cobb
1942-43	,,	William Moss
1943-44	,,	W. E. Lawley
1944-45	,,	F. W. Terry
1945-46	,,	John W. Mayall

180

1946-47	„	Mrs. Kate M. Garrard
1947-49	„	C. H. Dainty
1949-50	„	Hubert Hothersall
1950-51	„	Rev. H. H. Keyse
1951-52	„	A. G. B. Owen, O.B.E.
1952-53	„	W. F. Taylor
1953-54	„	C. Stephens
1954-55	„	S. G. Brown
1955-56	„	H. H. Turner
1956-57	„	B. H. Hunt
1957-58	„	Mrs. K. E. Smith.
1958-59	„	Mrs. M. L. Grounds
1959-60	„	Arthur Gunby
1960-61	„	John J. Potter
1961-62	„	Douglas V. Smallwood
1962-63	„	F. Brassington
1963-64	„	Cecil H. Smith
1964-65	„	C. F. Beaumont-Edmonds, M.C.
1965-66	„	S. C. Rawlings
1966-67	„	H. Herringshaw
1967-68	„	F. E. Whitfield
1968-69	„	R. H. Phillips
1969-70	„	J. H. Hamilton
1970-71	Alderman	H. J. C. Musgrave
1971-72	„	Mrs. E. E. Dunnett
1972-73	Councillor	Mrs. M. E. Carpenter
1973-74	Alderman	D. W. Mills

BIBLIOGRAPHY

"*Itinerary.*" JOHN LELAND

"*The Antiquities of Warwickshire*" (1656). SIR WILLIAM DUGDALE

"*The History of Birmingham.*" WILLIAM HUTTON

"*The History of Sutton Coldfield*" (1762). "BY AN IMPARTIAL HAND"

"*History of the Forest and Chase of Sutton Coldfield*" (1860).
    MISS A. BRACKEN

"*History of Sutton Coldfield*" (1891). W. K. RILAND BEDFORD

"*Vesey Papers.*" W. K. RILAND BEDFORD

"*Three Hundred Years of a Family Living*" (1889).
    W. K. RILAND BEDFORD

"*Antiquities*" (1884). CHRISTOPHER CHATTOCK

"*A Short History of the Town and Chase of Sutton Coldfield*" (1904)
    W. MIDGLEY

"*Tales of Sutton Town and Chase with other Tales and Some
    Sketches*" (1904). Collected by "T.A.U."

"*The Bishop Vesey Houses and other Old Buildings in Sutton Cold-
    field.*" P. B. CHATWIN and E. G. HARCOURT

"*Men of Aldridge.*" JAMES T. GOULD

"*Tudor Cornwall.*"* A. L. ROWSE

"*The Ironmasters of Penns*" (1971). JOHN HORSFALL

*Transactions of the Birmingham and Warwickshire Archaeological
    Society.*

"*The Natural Resources of Sutton Park.*" DR. TOM PRITCHARD and
    J. A. THOMPSON (The Nature Conservancy).

"*History of Sutton Coldfield.*" Z. Twamley ⎱
                                              ⎰ in manuscript
"*Holbeche Diary.*"

"*Gleanings from Water Orton*" (1935). A. MORRIS

"*The Victoria County History of Warwickshire*" Vol. 4, Hemlingford
    Hundred (1947). (Edited by L. F. SALZMAN)

* Contains information on Vesey.

Supplement—As It Was

An additional selection of illustrations, depicting facets of Sutton's history

Winter scene, Sutton Parade, late nineteenth century

Turn-of-the-century view of Holland House, Sutton Coldfield

Penns Lane, (c. 1890) The cottages still survive

The Old Swan and Bishop Vesey's Grammar School

184

Sutton Coldfield stocks being 'tried for size' by a local worthy (1895)   Photograph: Sir Benjamin Stone

185   *Queen Victoria's Diamond Jubilee Celebrations,*
Victoria Road and Lower Parade (1897)

The Royal Agricultural Show, Four Oaks Park (1898)

Wyndley Pool Cottage (c. 1900)

White House, Maney, demolished 1935

Old Cottages, Birmingham Road, Wylde Green   opposite Penns Lane (c. 1963)
Photograph: Douglas V. Jones

*Sutton Coldfield Council House decorated and illuminated for
the Coronation of King George VI (1937)*

THIS STONE FROM THE WAR-DAMAGED
HOUSE OF COMMONS WAS PRESENTED BY
SIR JOHN S.P. MELLOR BART M.P. 1942.

*Stone from war-damaged House of Commons flanked by heads from the
Malt House in High Street, previously embodied in the Chapel of St. Blaize.
Now built into the wall at the top of Church Hill.*

Site of Bodington Gardens, Maney (c. 1946)

The Dispensary, Coleshill Street — Rectory Road junction (1955)

189

James Speight's shop and studio, Sutton Parade (c. 1910)

The White Lion, Hill Village (c. 1964)   *Photograph: Douglas V. Jones*

INDEX

Sutton Coldfield from the railway 1863—from a drawing by Miss A. Bracken

Other books by the same au

Sutton Coldfield 1974-1984, The

Memories of a 'Twenties Child

Duration Man 1939-46, My War
(An enthralling sequel to 'Memories of a 'Twenties Child')

Sutton Park, Its History and Wildlife

The Story of Erdington From sleepy hamlet to thriving
suburb